Lecture Notes in Business Information Processing 420

More information about this series at http://www.springer.com/series/7911

Danielle Costa Morais ·
Liping Fang · Masahide Horita (Eds.)

Contemporary Issues in Group Decision and Negotiation

21st International Conference
on Group Decision and Negotiation, GDN 2021
Toronto, ON, Canada, June 6–10, 2021
Proceedings

 Springer

Editors
Danielle Costa Morais ⓘ
Universidade Federal de Pernambuco
Recife, Brazil

Liping Fang ⓘ
Ryerson University
Toronto, ON, Canada

Masahide Horita ⓘ
University of Tokyo
Tokyo, Japan

ISSN 1865-1348   ISSN 1865-1356   (electronic)
Lecture Notes in Business Information Processing
ISBN 978-3-030-77207-9   ISBN 978-3-030-77208-6   (eBook)
https://doi.org/10.1007/978-3-030-77208-6

This Springer imprint is published by the registered company Springer Nature Switzerland AG
The registered company address is: Gewerbestrasse 11, 6330 Cham, Switzerland

Preface

The series of annual International Conferences on Group Decision and Negotiation (GDN) has provided a stimulating forum for disseminating, discussing, and critiquing the latest research on the theory and practice of group decision and negotiation. Conferences offer opportunities for participants to share and exchange ideas. The GDN conferences have taken place every year since 2000 with two exceptions (2000, Glasgow, UK; 2001, La Rochelle, France; 2002, Perth, Australia; 2003, Istanbul, Turkey; 2004, Banff, Canada; 2005, Vienna, Austria; 2006, Karlsruhe, Germany; 2007, Mont Tremblant, Canada; 2008, Coimbra, Portugal; 2009, Toronto, Canada; 2010, Delft, the Netherlands; 2011, cancelled; 2012, Recife, Brazil; 2013, Stockholm, Sweden; 2014, Toulouse, France; 2015, Warsaw, Poland; 2016, Bellingham, USA; 2017, Stuttgart, Germany; 2018, Nanjing, China; 2019, Loughborough, UK; and 2020, Toronto, Canada (conference cancelled due to the COVID-19 pandemic and proceedings published)).

The 21st International Conference on Group Decision and Negotiation (GDN 2021) was scheduled to be held on-site at Ryerson University, Toronto, Canada, during June 6–10, 2021. However, because of the ongoing COVID-19 pandemic, for the safety and wellbeing of our GDN community members, it was decided that GDN 2021 would be held virtually (online) in its entirety.

A total of 74 submissions were received, spanning six main streams related to GDN. After a thorough and careful review process involving a large number of reviewers, twelve papers from those submissions were chosen for publication in this volume entitled **Contemporary Issues in Group Decision and Negotiation**.

The twelve papers in this volume are organized into four sections, showing the wide spectrum of research presented at GDN 2021.

- The first section on "Pandemic Responses" contains two papers. Ekenberg et al. propose a model for policymaking in respect of hazardous events, bringing an important discussion regarding mitigating cognitive and behavioral biases during responses to pandemics. Eden et al. discuss improvisation within the frameworks of emergent strategizing and sensemaking and postulate that a group support system may be uniquely able to offer managers the possibility of encompassing improvisation into their strategic thinking. Their discussion is particularly relevant during the time of a worldwide pandemic and recovery thereafter.
- The second section of this volume contains five papers related to "Preference Modeling for Group Decision and Negotiation", focusing on supporting groups of decision-makers and negotiators in eliciting preferences. Paulsson and Larsson develop a survey-based approach towards simultaneous elicitation of criteria and weight rank orderings in a group decision analysis setting. Correia et al. present the utilization of the FITradeoff method to order improvement actions of a fish distribution company, taking into account the strategic planning of the organization. Suzuki and Horita study the ordinal social ranking problem of ascertaining the

ordinal ranking of individuals in terms of the ordinal rankings of their coalitions. Sabino et al. develop a group decision method for ranking sustainable cities by first building individual rankings supported by multicriteria analysis and then choosing a voting procedure to aggregate the individual priorities into a collective ranking. Roszkowska and Wachowicz present the results of an online survey, examining gender-specific expectations towards the support mechanisms offered in the decision support systems. They find that females are more likely to use rating and are more willing to declare their preferences using the non-numerical form.

- Two papers investigating strategic conflicts are included in the third section on "Conflict Resolution". Abraham and Ramachandran use a repeated game framework to study the conditions under which water can be shared efficiently and flood costs can be allocated according to the Sequential Upstream Proportional Allocation rule. Shahbaznezhadfard et al. propose the use of the Coupled Human and Natural System (CHANS) approach and its core concepts to deal with water and environmental conflicts that are both dynamic in nature and complex in essence.

- The last section on "Collaborative Decision-Making Processes" contains three studies of different collaborative and strategic decision processes. Chosokabe et al. develop a method to clarify the temporal transition of social issues by focusing on specific words in newspaper articles in the field of disaster prevention. Hogan et al. introduce Diplomat, a Python-based framework for implementing conversational agents to be deployed in group, goal-oriented discussion. Ferretti studies a collaborative multi-methodology intervention designed and deployed to support rural regeneration initiatives in a wicked problem context.

Organizing GDN 2021 and preparing this volume involved the efforts of many people. In particular, we would like to take this opportunity to express our appreciation to the Honorary Chair of GDN 2021, D. Marc Kilgour, and the General Chairs of GDN 2021, Keith W. Hipel, Adiel Teixeira de Almeida, and Rudolf Vetschera, for their contributions in organizing GDN 2021, and to the Group Decision and Negotiation (GDN) Section of the Institute for Operations Research and the Management Sciences (INFORMS), in general. We are also grateful to all the Stream Organizers: Liping Fang, Keith W. Hipel, and D. Marc Kilgour (Conflict Resolution); Tomasz Wachowicz and Danielle Costa Morais (Preference Modeling for Group Decision and Negotiation); Zhen Zhang, Yucheng Dong, Francisco Chiclana, and Enrique Herrera-Viedma (Intelligent Group Decision Making and Consensus Process); Pascale Zaraté (Collaborative Decision Making Processes); Haiyan Xu, Shawei He, and Shinan Zhao (Risk Evaluation and Negotiation Strategies); and Mareike Schoop, Philipp Melzer, and Rudolf Vestchera (Negotiation Support Systems and Studies (NS3)).

Special thanks go to the following reviewers for their informative and prompt reviews of papers: Sharafat Ali, Andrej Bregar, Ana Paula Costa, Ayşegül Engin, José Leão e Silva Filho, Michael Filzmoser, Eduarda Frej, Thalles Vitelli Garcez, Bingfeng Ge, Dmitry Gimon, Dorota Górecka, Aron Larsson, Kaveh Madani, Jerzy Michnik, Simone Philpot, Lucia Reis Roselli, Ewa Roszkowska, Maisa Silva, R. Sundarraj, Przemyslaw Szufel, Rudolf Vetschera, Tomasz Wachowicz, Yi Xiao, and Shinan Zhao.

We are also thankful to Ralf Gerstner and Christine Reiss at Springer for their excellent work.

April 2021

Danielle Costa Morais
Liping Fang
Masahide Horita

Organization

Honorary Chair

D. Marc Kilgour   Wilfrid Laurier University, Canada

General Chairs

Keith W. Hipel   University of Waterloo, Canada
Adiel Teixeira de Almeida   Federal University of Pernambuco, Brazil
Rudolf Vetschera   University of Vienna, Austria

Program Chairs

Liping Fang   Ryerson University, Canada
Danielle Costa Morais   Federal University of Pernambuco, Brazil
Masahide Horita   University of Tokyo, Japan

Program Committee

Melvin F. Shakun   New York University, USA
Adiel Teixeira de Almeida   Federal University of Pernambuco, Brazil
Amer Obeidi   University of Waterloo, Canada
Bilyana Martinovski   Stockholm University, Sweden
Bo Yu   Dalhousie University, Canada
Bogumił Kamiński   Warsaw School of Economics, Poland
Danielle Costa Morais   Federal University of Pernambuco, Brazil
Ewa Roszkowska   University of Białystok, Poland
Fran Ackermann   Curtin Business School, Australia
Fuad Aleskerov   National Research University HSE, Russia
Gert-Jan de Vreede   University of South Florida, USA
Ginger Ke   Memorial University of Newfoundland, Canada
Haiyan Xu   Nanjing University of Aeronautics and Astronautics,
                                      China
Hannu Nurmi   University of Turku, Finland
João Clímaco   University of Coimbra, Portugal
John Zeleznikow   Victoria University, Australia
José Maria Moreno-Jiménez   Zaragoza University, Spain
Keith W. Hipel   University of Waterloo, Canada
Kevin Li   University of Windsor, Canada
Liping Fang   Ryerson University, Canada
Love Ekenberg   Stockholm University, Sweden
Luis Dias   University of Coimbra, Portugal

Contents

Pandemic Responses

Mitigating Cognitive and Behavioural Biases During
Pandemics Responses 3
    Love Ekenberg, Adriana Mihai, Tobias Fasth, Nadejda Komendantova,
    Mats Danielson, and Ahmed Al-Salaymeh

Improvisation and Emergent Strategizing: The Role of Group
Support Systems 16
    Colin Eden, Fran Ackermann, and Vincenzo Vito

Preference Modeling for Group Decision and Negotiation

Survey-Based Multi-stakeholder Preference Elicitation with Relatively
Incomplete and Possibly Disjoint Rank Orderings 27
    Andreas Paulsson and Aron Larsson

Prioritizing Improvement Actions in a Fish Distribution Company:
Integrating Elicitation by Decomposition and Holistic Evaluation
with FITradeoff Method. 41
    Marina Carvalhedo Correia, Eduarda Asfora Frej,
    and Adiel Teixeira de Almeida

Social Ranking Problem Based on Rankings of Restricted Coalitions. 55
    Takahiro Suzuki and Masahide Horita

A Group Multicriteria Decision Model for Ranking Sustainable Cities 68
    Emerson Rodrigues Sabino, Gabriela Silva da Silva,
    Danielle Costa Morais, Adiel Teixeira de Almeida,
    and Leandro Chaves Rêgo

Does Gender Differentiate in Expectations Regarding the Representation
of Preferential Information in Decision Support Systems?. 82
    Ewa Roszkowska and Tomasz Wachowicz

Conflict Resolution

Stable Agreements with Fixed Payments on Transboundary Flood
Prone Rivers. 99
    Anand Abraham and Parthasarathy Ramachandran

Study of Water-Environmental Conflicts as a Dynamic
and Complex Human-Natural System: A New Perspective   113
  Mohsen Shahbaznezhadfard, Saied Yousefi, and Keith W. Hipel

Collaborative Decision Making Processes

Analysis on the Temporal Transition of Social Issues Related to Disaster
Prevention Using Text Data   131
  Madoka Chosokabe, Keishi Tanimoto, and Satoshi Tsuchiya

Diplomat: A Conversational Agent Framework for Goal-Oriented
Group Discussion   143
  Kevin Hogan, Annabelle Baer, and James Purtilo

Convergencies and Divergencies in Collaborative
Decision-Making Processes   155
  Valentina Ferretti

Author Index   171

Pandemic Responses

Mitigating Cognitive and Behavioural Biases During Pandemics Responses

Love Ekenberg[1,2(✉)], Adriana Mihai[3], Tobias Fasth[4,2], Nadejda Komendantova[1], Mats Danielson[2,1], and Ahmed Al-Salaymeh[5]

[1] International Institute for Applied Systems Analysis, IIASA, Schlossplatz 1, 2361 Laxenburg, Austria
ekenberg@iiasa.ac.at

[2] Department of Computer and Systems Sciences, Stockholm University, Postbox 7003, 164 07 Kista, Sweden

[3] Centre of Excellence for the Study of Cultural Identity, University of Bucharest, Pitar Moş, 7-13, 010451 Bucharest, Romania

[4] Department of Public Health Analysis and Data Management, Public Health Agency of Sweden, 171 82 Solna, Sweden

[5] Mechanical Engineering Department, School of Engineering, The University of Jordan, Amman 11942, Jordan

Abstract. Many countries seemed to a large extent to have been unprepared for the COVID-19 pandemic and national governments often acted uncoordinated resulting in many inconsistencies in the mitigation processes. The acknowledgement of the multiple factors at stake in handling the crisis has more often than not been omitted from public communication, where public officials' statements mostly framed the problem unilaterally, basing their narratives on warnings coming from the medical and public health scientific community. In this article, we propose a model for policymaking regarding hazardous events, such as a pandemic, to, in advance, forming better response strategies for future similar scenarios. We describe how an epidemic model can be integrated into a multi-stakeholder multi-criteria framework and how a more integrated analysis can be done, even under significant uncertainties.

Keywords: Pandemics · Multi-stakeholder · Multi-criteria decision analysis · Surrogate criteria weights

1 Introduction

The recent emergence of the COVID-19 pandemic situation has highlighted that many countries have, to a large extent, been unprepared for it [11], despite the known significant probability for such a scenario to unfold. The measures undertaken by bordering countries or regions within one country were many times inconsistent. For example, the decision to close or not to close children's primary care facilities was justified on very different grounds. Switzerland and Italy as countries share a border and the region Lombardy is bordering the Swiss Canton Ticino. On March 13, 2020, Switzerland decided not

© Springer Nature Switzerland AG 2021
D. C. Morais et al. (Eds.): GDN 2021, LNBIP 420, pp. 3–15, 2021.
https://doi.org/10.1007/978-3-030-77208-6_1

to close kindergartens to protect the most vulnerable groups of the population (namely the elderly/grandparents), who would have otherwise needed to take care of the children. Some kilometres away, in Northern Italy, the kindergartens were closed for the same basic reason. Austria and Switzerland also share borders and have a similar population size. On the 15th of March, 2020, Austria declared a state of emergency and decided for a domestic lockdown with 800 COVID-19 confirmed cases, whereas Switzerland had 2,300 COVID-19 confirmed cases and much lower levels of restrictions. In Albania, a lockdown was decided on the same day, with 40 COVID-19 confirmed cases. Romania closed schools on March 11th when there were 35 confirmed cases and no deaths at a national level, deciding for a lockdown on March 22nd when the first two deaths were reported. Decisions on whether or not to impose lockdowns were thus obviously not taken only based on the number of confirmed cases and the effects of these inconsistencies are to a large extent unforeseeable.

Independent of the narratives, particular biases and other preconditions that have been involved during the implementation of pandemic measures, many decisions on the risk reduction seem to have been influenced by cognitive and behavioural biases without proper consideration of impacts from disaster risk reduction measures. Measures need to be based on adequate risk estimations of a scenario, which include both epidemiologic modelling and integrated analyses of the costs of reducing the risk and also a more systematic analysis of the extent to which various measures can reduce it. Furthermore, individual perception and behaviours as factors influencing the said perceptions, including media reports, narratives, and framing, as well as the emotions stirred by representations and by the level of uncertainty, must be taken into consideration during the deliberation. And there must be a preparedness that should, as much as possible, be done in advance.

In this paper, we present a framework for decision analysis under ambiguity on how to contain the virus spread, which can serve pandemic mitigation policies. The framework makes way for a consideration of both epidemiologic estimations and socio-economic factors present in a complex, multi-faceted problem that needs to be managed. It also provides a starting point for designing future strategic communication in the public sphere which facilitates discussion towards informed policy, even in contexts of increased uncertainty. Our aim here is thus to suggest a framework for pandemic policy preparedness and have no ambitions to suggest a final policy or to provide an overview of the latest medical data regarding COVID-19. However, we assume that such a framework can provide a counter-balance to decisions that are made under uncertainty and which are influenced by cognitive and behavioural biases.

2   Measures Under Uncertainty

Currently, the existing estimations on epidemic evolution in essence use estimation-prediction methods such as spread models. Then time calibration is done using the observed number of case fatalities and estimates of the time between infection and death and the infection fatality risk. The assumptions which serve as a basis for predictions are that there is no change in behaviour and that preventive measures are put in place at one specific time-point. It is also assumed that the overall effect of preventive measures is known. The effects are estimated from the observed increased doubling time after preventive measures are put in place. The estimations are highly sensitive to the doubling times without and with mitigation measures, as well as to, for instance, the reproduction number, but less sensitive to the estimates used for time-calibration: observed number of fatalities, the typical time between infection and death, and the infection fatality risk [3]. The uncertainty of epidemiologic evidence led to general uncertainty about policy impact, which was shown to generate much higher socio-economic costs than the ones previously envisioned in simulated risk management scenarios for pandemics. Time pressure associated with the public health emergency also made the non-pharmaceutical mitigation measures be less a result of a deliberation taking various risks and stakeholders into consideration, and more the product of uncertain epidemiologic projections, which were translated in top-down policies and persuasively communicated to the public via strategic mobilizing narratives. These, however, inevitably leave many risks, preferences, and consequences unaddressed and unmodelled, a gap that can backfire and affect any mitigation strategy put in place to further contain the epidemic.

While a detailed analysis of all sectors is a tremendous work that goes beyond the scope of this article, we adopt a more high-level perspective and highlight some classes of measures, evaluating their effects upon several criteria. The baseline is that the response measures to the pandemic have to be analysed at specific local levels, to be seen relative to the demographic, social and economic conditions and practices, healthcare systems capacity, and stakeholders' needs, to make way for a variety of pandemic hazard scenarios which can be considered for development and revision of the national plans for pandemics in the future. Measures can be combined in various ways, depending on their estimated impact, both in terms of reducing the rate of transmissibility, and by looking at their different consequences upon other criteria. These can include indirect deaths in different groups, inhibited work capacity in the longer and short term, or social costs, such as human development, effects on democracy and human rights.

3 A Pandemic Decision Framework

Several studies are investigating specific performance aspects of interventions against pandemics, but they are typically using a single scenario and are rarely designed to explicitly acknowledge the inherent uncertainties in both simulation results and scenario likelihoods. The methodological components we suggest could, for instance, be divided into (i) a co-creative preference elicitation component, (ii) an epidemiological component, (iii) a socio-economical component, and (iv) an aggregation and analysis component. Relative to a set of possible mitigation measures, the main idea herein is basically to model the actual spread and its effects on the population concerning critical healthcare, taking demographic and regional conditions into account and estimate the impacts from other perspectives, predominantly various socio-economic effects.

The co-creative component refers to the involvement of stakeholders in decision-making processes and model development, an essential step for conforming to stakeholder requirements, but also for increasing transparency and the acceptability of the chosen set of measures. Not the least in public health emergencies, a distributed decision-making process could also contribute to a distributed responsibility for the result, thus lowering the political costs and gaining valuable input concerning the criteria relevant to the problem at hand. Several techniques may be employed here, relying on models from the decision-analytic field that aim to elicit users' values through studying their preferences and gathering preferential data. Adjusting the process to the available resources, the purpose is to elicit reasonable values from at least several stakeholders. Policymakers have the institutional legitimation and capacity to call for broader participation in the elicitation process and many of them have already had consultations with some of the stakeholders to, among other things, allocate financial stimuli packages to mitigate the socio-economic costs of lockdown. However, such consultations are unstructured, often non-transparent, lack negotiations between stakeholders, and can – intentionally or not – give a higher weight to preferences expressed by more dominant groups from the public sphere. From a decision analytic perspective, moreover, the preference assessments made by stakeholders during consultation meetings do not adequately feed into the decision problem and possible solutions without a framework that can aggregate them across a range of options and criteria.

There are already various guidelines to inform decision-makers on the acceptable norms which need to be taken into consideration when weighing the various policy solutions for managing the pandemic long-term, such as ensuring well-being, liberty, and justice [2], placing a high priority on the public health and economic costs caused by social distancing and unstructured reopening. This concern can further include ethics of care [14] to support vulnerable people, by which both groups affected directly by COVID-19 and groups affected by economic recession would need equal protection. It could be useful to furthermore define the problem using cultural norms [8, 19] which inform a criteria evaluation according to five cultural typologies - individualism (few imposed obligations), egalitarianism (to some extent regulate individual actions and promote reciprocity), hierarchism (a cast system), fatalism (leave individuals to their fates), and autonomy (more of a withdrawal from social interaction) - resonating in people's preferences on how to manage, for instance, a pandemic.

Such ethical and cultural norms can be identified in existing surveys and cultural analyses, but they can also be extracted from public texts produced by stakeholders and circulated in the local public spheres, once the problem becomes part of the public agenda. Since the most productive communication in emergencies is top-down, policymakers' and public officials' preferences can be elicited through various content, narrative, or discourse analyses. There is, however, unequal visibility of different voices in the public sphere, due to, among others, restricted access, media partisanship, echo chambers, or institutional and commercial dominance. There needs to be an awareness of the risk of reproducing the same inequalities in representation that are well-known in mainstream and social media when designing a participatory approach to multi-criteria decision analysis.

For our purposes herein concerning the epidemiologic estimations, we apply a regionalised demography-augmented SEIR model for the modelling of health effects of various risk mitigation measures. The model thus requires country-specific information including population size in country/region/city divided into age groups to model the effects of various measures in the desired area. The model we have used herein is deliberatively quite simple despite there being several candidates around. A general problem is that the more input parameters, the obscurity will raise due to the already enormous state space and models with higher complexity than the training and validation data should probably be used with great care. Future alternative models will hopefully take more parameters into account and produce better predictions. For instance, in order to model the effects of containment measures applied for a specific demographic, models such as [10] or the COVID-19 scenarios at the University of Basel [16], or another candidate in the abundance thereof, could also be considered depending on the circumstances and the available level of specificity for the data sets, social characteristics, and healthcare capacity. In any case, our main point here is the possibility to systematise the basis for policymaking. Each component herein can be substituted with better candidates and more accurate data when such becomes available.

For the particular evaluations in our suggested framework, we use a method for integrated multi-attribute evaluation under risk, subject to incomplete or imperfect information. The software originates from our earlier work on evaluating decision situations using imprecise utilities, probabilities, and weights, as well as qualitative estimates between these components derived from convex sets of weight, utility, and probability measures. To avoid some aggregation problems when handling set membership functions and similar, we introduced higher-order distributions for better discrimination between the possible outcomes [7]. For the decision structure, we use a common tree formalism but refrain from using precise numbers. To alleviate the problem of overlapping results, we suggest a new evaluation method based on the resulting belief mass over the output intervals, but without trying to introduce further complicating aspects into the decision situation. During the process, we consider the entire range of values as the alternatives presented across all criteria as well as how plausible it is that an alternative outranked the remaining ones, and thus provided a robustness measure. Because of the complexity in these calculations, we use the software tool Helision for the analysis, which allows for imprecision of the kinds that exist in this case. Stakeholder preference elicitation is used for building preference structures where potential conflicts can arise. Here so-called surrogate weights [5] have turned out to be useful, but this is only a part of the solution since the elicitation can still be uncertain and the surrogate weights might not be a fully adequate representation of the preferences involved. The P-SWING method, suggested in [6], is designed to overcome some of the typical problems associated with elicitation processes.

4   Modelling and Evaluation

The following is an example of how possible criteria can be systematically analysed in a larger setting. Needless to say, other data, such as business demographics data would be needed to produce an estimate of how many lives can be saved as well as what the direct short-term and long-term costs of different risk mitigation measures will be. For our purposes here, we will handle this on a significantly higher level of abstraction.

4.1   Criteria and Mitigation Measures

A fundamental component here is a set of criteria, under which the various options are considered. The options are valued under each criterion and the relative importance of the criteria themselves are usually represented by a set of weights that can be defined in several ways. For instance, a criteria set for the COVID-19 scenario could include:

a. Epidemiological & healthcare systems effects: (a1) direct fatalities, (a2) indirect fatalities;
b. Economic aspects: (b1) short term costs, (b2) unemployment, (b3) taxes, (b4) specific industries affected, (b5) growing industries;
c. Social and behavioural aspects: (c1) human rights, (c2) protection of vulnerable groups, (c3) criminality rates, (c3) mental health, (c4) education and training;
d. Environmental: (d1) climate change;
e. Political and governance: (e1) risk of short-term governmental abuses, (e2) citizen approval of measures, (e3) trust in government, (e4) resilience - improving preparedness for catastrophic events;

Typical mitigation measures are partitioned into sets with different subordinate restriction levels, reflecting some important aspects of possible mitigation strategies, such as [9] going from an unmitigated epidemic to a suppression strategy or [12] proposing a schedule for every industrial sector activity in a risk adjustment strategy. Another option is to devise a set of measures that combines these approaches and also reflects the most common public debates on this issue:

- Level 1: An unmitigated epidemic – a scenario in which no other action is taken except pharmaceutical measures and case isolation;
- Level 2: Mitigation adding to pharmaceutical measures and case isolation, public communication encouraging increased hygiene and personal protection, localized action (closing a school/workplace in case of several infection cases) - influenza epidemics protocol
- Level 3: Mitigation adding to pharmaceutical measures and case isolation, personal protective measures (stay home when sick, hand-washing, respiratory etiquette, clean frequently touched surfaces daily, wearing face masks), mild social distancing measures (large public gatherings banned, work from home where possible, social distancing recommended) - Sweden's measures;
- Level 4: Mitigation adding to pharmaceutical measures and case isolation, personal protective measures (stay home when sick, hand-washing, respiratory etiquette, clean frequently touched surfaces daily, wearing face masks), self-selected social distancing and comprehensive contact tracing, and publicly disclosed detailed location information of individuals that tested positive for COVID-19 - South Korea's measures;
- Level 5: Mitigation adding to pharmaceutical measures and case isolation, personal protective measures (stay home when sick, hand-washing, respiratory etiquette, clean frequently touched surfaces daily, wearing face masks), mild social distancing measures (large public gatherings banned, work from home where possible, social distancing recommended), the physical isolation of the elderly [15];
- Level 6: Suppression (partial lockdown) - pharmaceutical measures and case isolation, personal protective measures (stay home when sick, hand-washing, respiratory etiquette, clean frequently touched surfaces daily, wearing face masks), imposed social

distancing measures and restrictions on mobility: school closures, restaurants, and large shopping centres closed, people can go out only for their basic necessities and work - as implemented in Romania for 2 months.

A full-scale multi-criteria decision analysis should also include collected data following a criteria setup which is subject to refinement when gathering more available evidence, but in this demonstration setup, we use the following without sub-criteria:

- Number of cases (including critical, severe, and mild)
- Economic aspects
- Effects on education
- Human right violations

The estimates will be limited as such because we would have to include further information for a more complete picture. As more extensive data becomes available from these fields, the model can be continuously updated for every criterion.

4.2 Eliciting Stakeholder Preferences

To demonstrate a comparatively uncomplicated method for at least getting a template of how a larger-scale survey could look like, we designed a questionnaire by which to elicit some stakeholders' preferences and tested it in Romania on a very limited amount of stakeholders, addressing differences in risk perception and in assessing the severity of the risk. The participatory process was organized in a form of an in-depth web-based survey. We used an automatic web-questionnaire to elicit some stakeholder opinions for demonstration purposes, which was sent to 17 government officials, 16 healthcare experts, 11 representatives from the business sector, 9 non-governmental organizations and 11 experts from academia. 16 respondents filled in the questionnaire out of which three were medical doctors specialized in epidemiology, pulmonology, and public healthcare, working in hospitals in Bucharest, five were university researchers specialized in sociology, political sciences, and philosophy, one was a representative of a workers' federation in Romania and the rest were employees in the public sector and NGOs. In a full-scale setting, this should be quantitatively and qualitatively elaborated in a variety of respects, and augmented, e.g., via stakeholder discussion workshops.

The questions concerned what would be considered to be an unacceptably high mortality rate caused by COVID-19, how serious is the risk of high mortality rates caused by COVID-19, how likely it is for an unmitigated SARS-CoV-2 epidemic in Romania to have a high mortality rate, what other set of measures would be reasonable, as well as the most important political, educational and economic aspects to be addressed in a pandemic response action.

The most stringent problems brought along by the SARS-CoV-2 pandemic in Romania were, according to the responses, the following (in no particular order): premature deaths and threats to people's health; the economic impact, including social and economic depression, loss of jobs, small companies' bankruptcies; the increased social isolation of the elders and of those with fewer material means; overburdening the healthcare system, the lack of education for personal hygiene; the risks for mental health; the population's lack of trust long-term and disrespect towards rules, as well as the political calculations above medical and scientific interventions and the lack of evidence in decisions made. These suggested problems confirm the reliability of the proposed set of criteria for our integrated model of evaluation.

In evaluating the set of measures, respondents' preferences were expressed by ordering the given alternative measures, followed by ordering of the different criteria and sub-criteria, from the least important to the most important aspects for them. The results of their aggregated weights show that the measures preferred by respondents in mitigating the SAS-CoV-2 epidemic in Romania are the ones being applied during influenza epidemics (Level 2), followed closely in their order of preferences by the lockdown measures (Level 6), Sweden's approach (Level 3) and South Korea's approach (Level 4); these weighed significantly more than the remaining options - enhanced distancing for the elders (Level 5) and, lastly, not using any non-pharmaceutical measures to mitigate the epidemic (Level 1). In what concerns the criteria rankings relevant for our demonstration here, respondents considered that health and epidemiologic aspects are much more important than economic and social aspects and that the economic impact is more important than the social one. Concerning social and behavioural sub-criteria, the preservation of human rights was considered more important than ensuring access to education during the epidemic.

Furthermore, two-thirds of the respondents consider that the number of direct fatalities caused by COVID-19 is less important than children's and young learners' access to education than the preservation of human rights and the short-term risk of power abuses; however, they do believe that protecting vulnerable groups is more important than the risk of governmental abuses and the economic impact of the crisis on specific industries. As previously explained, more narrow definitions of vulnerable groups should further be employed, since there are various risks to which people are exposed during the pandemic, starting from the obvious health risk to the risk of becoming a victim of domestic abuse, social isolation, or poverty.

4.3 Input Data

The simulations of the measures' effects in containing the virus spread in Romania were made in AnyLogic 8, based on a still incomplete data set that should be adjusted and adapted to different regions. The model was calibrated according to the epidemiological evolution of the cases in Romania, obtaining a baseline from which the various strategies of mitigation can be simulated, starting with July 13th, 2020. The 14 d notification rate per 100,000 inhabitants was 31.2, an increased rate compared to the March-June period, notably either due to the increased testing or to milder social distancing measures (corresponding to Level 3 in our analysis).

As expected the effects of the different strategies show some significant differences. In particular, L4 and L6 show both more rapidly increasing behaviour before the second peak as well as a rapid decrease after it. Otherwise, the amount of cases from the different measures differs and the maximum such between the measures is around two million cases (L1 vs L5). Still, of course, keeping in mind that this demonstration is at country-level and not a regionalised simulation and that it is not taking into account the healthcare capacity in Romania and the fatalities that might result. If we would use the same model, in a more reasonable regionalised context, the result would be different.

Table 1. The value estimates for the respective measure under each criterion

Criterion/Measure	Cases (in 10 thousands)	Economy (GDP decline in %)	Human rights	Education[a]
Level 1	1415–1729	1–3	Better than L2	0
Level 2	1412–1725	1–4	Better than L3	1–5
Level 3	1334–1630	5–7	Better than L4	10–20
Level 4	1217–1487	5–10[b]	Better than L5	10–30
Level 5	1326–1621	8–15	Better than L6	20–30
Level 6	1293–1580	10–25		30–40

[a] A significant percentage of students having no access to online or any other schooling.
[b] Economic costs estimated to be 50% lower than a lockdown, cf. [1].

To roughly estimate the measures' impact upon the economy, education and human rights in Romania, we used macroeconomic estimates of government deficits made by the European Commission and by the OECD [17], reports on access to distance or online learning created by UNESCO [20], Save the Children Romania [18] and other national organizations, as well as media reports on human rights abuses and the Oxford COVID-19 Government Response Tracker [13]. It is important to note that impact assessments for every criterion depend on the available data, on the level of granularity aimed for and on how, for instance, epidemiologic and economic models can be adapted to changing conditions. Measures considered under the respective criteria are summarised in Table 1. For the epidemiological simulated data, we add ± 10% intervals around the values and round them to the nearest 10 thousands, compensating for the inherent uncertainties involved. Other values are tentatively estimated, but, needless to say, should in an extended analysis be refined due to economic models, empirical data, more well-deliberated qualified estimates, etc.

The (limited a priori) criteria ranking from the questionnaire results could basically be summarised as that health considerations are much more important than the economy, which is more important than human rights, which in turn is more important than education aspects. This is not a purely ordinal ranking and we have to use a different representation thereof. We need supplementary statements for the criteria to calibrate the different scales involved since they are very different and we simply assume that this representation means that:

- The maximum difference between L1 and L6 in Cases is much more important than the maximum difference between L1 and L6 in Economy.
- The maximum difference between L1 and L6 in Economy and training is more important than the maximum difference between L1 and L6 in Human rights.
- The maximum difference between L1 and L6 in Human rights is more important than the maximum difference between L2 and L4 in Education.

4.4 Aggregation and Evaluation

The multi-criteria decision problem is evaluated as a multi-linear problem against the (imprecise) background information. This means in this simple case, without sub-criteria, that we evaluate weighted averages of the figures involved, or, more precisely, equations of the format $E(M_j) = \Sigma w_i v_{ij}$, where w_i is the weight variable of criterion i and v_{ij} is the value variable of measure j under criterion i. We are thus taking a multi-attribute approach to the evaluation of the problem. The surrogate weights are generated from the method of [6] and an interval around them for facilitating the stability analyses. The value $E(M_j)$ is computed by solving successive optimisation problems using the program Helision, based on the algorithms in [7]. The result of our example is shown in Fig. 1.

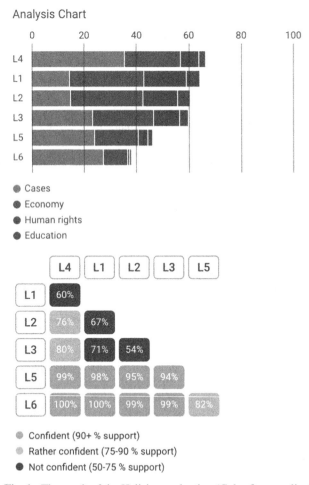

Fig. 1. The result of the Helision evaluation (Color figure online)

The bars also show how much each criterion contributes to the respective values, based on the possible ranges of the resulting weighted averages of the respective measures. The robustness of the opinions is colour-marked, based on the evaluation of the proportion of the resulting distribution over the differences between the weighted averages. A yellow box means that the mass, where this difference is positive, is between 75–90%. This means that the input values have to be changed significantly for the order to change. The meaning of a green square is that the corresponding mass is greater than 90%, i.e. that an even larger change must be done for a reversal. A black box signifies in the same way that there is no significant difference between the measures considering the weighted averages. The confidence measure is thus the proportion of the volume under the resulting distribution. A detailed explanation of the semantics regarding the bars and the colour-markings is provided in [7]. The difference between L1 and L4 is thus insignificant, but they seem to be the best options in this example. Furthermore, this result is comparatively robust. They are followed by L2 and L3, which are significantly better than L5 and L6.

5 Concluding Remarks

There is a wide range of social, political, and institutional factors that interact systemically and the multiple criteria at stake in crisis management has often been omitted from public communication. The current pandemic has primarily been considered a public health problem and a variety of measures with unclear effects have been imposed. Furthermore, the rationales behind the manifold of actions taken have often not been clearly communicated or motivated. Ethically justifiable use of narratives in science and evidence communication should, in principle, act for the common benefit and not "restrict an individual's autonomy to make decisions", cf. [4]. This means that a clear designation of roles (issue advocates or knowledge brokers) and purposes (to persuade or to facilitate comprehension) must be established. Independent of the probably benevolent purposes, the decisions and actions must be deliberated and motivated, while taking into account the uncertainties. The policy problem is broader than in most narratives and must be analysed in an integrated decision context and the top-down strategic narratives communicated to the public should make the deliberative process transparent, acknowledging the conditions of uncertainty and the different aspects which are weighed in adopting the proposed policy. There is a thus need for integrated methodologies and decision processes for how national strategies and action plans should be aligned with overall objectives and stakeholder perceptions and preferences. Deliberated strategies should be a prerequisite for policy formation and they should furthermore be developed together with the civil society in order to be better prepared for future crises.

Acknowledgements. This research was funded by the European Union's Horizon 2020 Programme call H2020-INFRAEOSC-05–2018-2019, Grant Agreement number 831644, via the EOSCsecretariat.eu.

References

1. Argente, D., Hsieh, C.T., Lee, M.: The cost of privacy: welfare effects of the disclosure of Covid-19 Cases. University of Chicago, Becker Friedman Institute for Economics Working Paper No. 2020–64, Available at SSRN: https://ssrn.com/abstract=3601143. (2020)
2. Bernstein, J., Hutler, B., Rieder, T., Han, H., Barnhill, A.: An Ethics Framework for the COVID-19 Reopening Process. John Hopkins University. Available: https://bioethics.jhu.edu/research-and-outreach/covid-19-bioethics-expert-insights/resources-for-addressing-key-ethical-areas/grappling-with-the-ethics-of-social-distancing/. (2020)
3. Britton, T.: Basic estimation-prediction techniques for Covid-19, and a prediction for Stockholm (2020). https://www.medrxiv.org/content/.10.1101/2020.04.15.20066050v1.full.pdf. Accessed 15 Apr 2020
4. Dahlstrom, M.F., Ho, S.S.: Ethical considerations of using narrative to communicate science. Sci. Commun. 34(5), 592–617 (2012). https://doi.org/10.1177/1075547012454597
5. Danielson, M., Ekenberg, L.: The CAR method for using preference strength in multi-criteria decision making. Group Decis. Negot. 25(4), 775–797 (2015). https://doi.org/10.1007/s10726-015-9460-8
6. Danielson, M., Ekenberg, L.: An improvement to swing techniques for elicitation in mcdm methods, knowledge-based systems (2019). https://doi.org/10.1016/j.knosys.2019.01.001
7. Danielson, M., Ekenberg, L., Larsson, A.: Evaluating multi-criteria decisions under strong uncertainty. In: de Almeida, A., Ekenberg, L., Scarf, P., Zio, E., Zuo, M.J. (eds.) Multicriteria Decision Models and Optimization for Risk, Reliability, and Maintenance Decision Analysis - Recent Advances. Springer (2021, to appear)
8. Douglas, M., Wildavsky, A.B.: Risk and Culture: An Essay on the Selection of Technical and Environmental Dangers. University of California Press, Berkeley (1982)
9. Ferguson, N., Laydon, D., Nedjati-Gilani, G., et al.: Impact of non-pharmaceutical interventions (NPIs) to reduce COVID-19 mortality and healthcare demand, 16 Mar 2020. Imperial College London (2020). https://doi.org/10.25561/77482
10. Flaxman, S., Mishra, S., Gandy, A., et al.: Estimating the effects of non-pharmaceutical interventions on COVID-19 in Europe. Nature (2020). https://doi.org/10.1038/s41586-020-2405-7
11. GHS. Global Health Security Index (GHS) (2020). https://www.ghsindex.org/ (2020)
12. Government of South Africa. Draft framework for consultation on COVID-19 risk adjusted strategy (2020). Available: https://sacoronavirus.co.za/covid-19-risk-adjusted-strategy/. Accessed 25 Apr 2020
13. Hale, T., Webster, S., Petherick, A., Phillips, T., Kira, B.: Oxford COVID-19 Government Response Tracker (2020). Blavatnik School of Government. https://covidtracker.bsg.ox.ac.uk/. (2020)
14. Held, V.: The Ethics of Care: Personal. Political and Global. Oxford University Press, Oxford (2006)
15. Institutul Naţional de Boli Infecţioase. "Prof.Dr. Matei Balş", "Pandemia SARS-COV-2/COVID-19: Programul 'Vacanţa Mare' de prevenire a îmbolnăvirilor cu SARS-CoV-2/COVID-19" February-March 2020. Available: https://www.scribd.com/document/457347309/Planul-lui-Streinu-Cercel?fbclid=IwAR2eMyxqqWtuWtI-XkSYMUw6l3GCxLKrRP68nD91rZoa9hbRSKMlDgcDmKY. (2020)
16. Noll, N., et al.: COVID-19 scenarios: an interactive tool to explore the spread and associated morbidity and mortality of SARS-CoV-2. https://doi.org/10.1101/2020.05.05.20091363. medRxiv 2020.05.05.20091363. (2020)
17. OECD. OECD updates G20 summit on outlook for global economy (2020). Available: https://www.oecd.org/newsroom/oecd-updates-g20-summit-on-outlook-for-global-economy.htm. Accessed 27 Mar 2020

18. Save the Children Romania. Impactul Covid-19 asupra copiilor din România (2020). https://www.salvaticopiii.ro/ce-facem/educatie/vreau-la-scoala/impactul-covid-19-asupra-educatiei. (2020)
19. Thompson, M., Ellis, R., Wildavsky, A.: Cultural Theory. Westview Press, Boulder Colo (1990)
20. UNESCO. Adverse consequences of school closures (2020). https://en.unesco.org/covid19/educationresponse/consequences. (2020)

Improvisation and Emergent Strategizing: The Role of Group Support Systems

Colin Eden[1(✉)] ⓘ, Fran Ackermann[2] ⓘ, and Vincenzo Vito[3]

[1] Strathclyde Business School, Glasgow G4 0QU, UK
colin.eden@strath.ac.uk
[2] Curtin Business School, Perth, Western Australia 6845, Australia
[3] Zurich, Switzerland

Abstract. This paper synthesises the conceptualisation of improvisation within the frameworks of emergent strategizing and sensemaking. In doing so, it explores how the arguments presented in the literature offer an important role for improvisation in strategy making, with particular attention to its significance in understanding emergent strategizing and sensemaking. Through a synthesis of the literature, we show that emergent strategizing, sensemaking and improvisation, working in harmony, provide a powerful combination, particularly when developing strategy following a pandemic. We postulate that a group support system may be able to uniquely offer management teams the possibility of encompassing improvisation into their strategic thinking. This is likely to be increasingly relevant as organisations move out of the uncertainties of a global pandemic.

Keywords: Improvisation · Sensemaking · Group support systems · Emergent strategising

1 Introduction

As the world of organizations and management moves out of a pandemic, management teams will need to rethink their strategy. Given the uncertainties around prospects for the future organisations are likely to need to improvise in ways never considered before. In this paper we review some of the key literature and concepts related to improvisation in organisations. We relate this literature to strategy making and, in particular, emergent strategizing. Our purpose is to set the scene for a debate about the role that most group support systems might play in helping organisations exploit improvisation in managerial strategizing in highly uncertain environments such as that following a pandemic.

Improvisation has been part of jazz and theatre for decades, however, in the last 20 years the nature of improvising in jazz and the theatre has influenced a discussion about improvisation in management, and particularly strategic management. This is for a range of reasons not limited to managers a) having to adapt to a fast paced and turbulent environment [1, 2], b) managing crises [3], c) building capability [4], and d) enabling strategic renewal [5].

© Springer Nature Switzerland AG 2021
D. C. Morais et al. (Eds.): GDN 2021, LNBIP 420, pp. 16–24, 2021.
https://doi.org/10.1007/978-3-030-77208-6_2

Recently, some have argued that improvisation is a vital consideration in strategy development [2] further blurring the lines of planning and execution [6] and arguing it can increase competitive advantage [7]. However, little attention has been paid to the significance of improvisation for a particular form of strategy development namely emergent strategizing and how improvisation along with sensemaking, might provide important benefits to strategy making in uncertain times. This is important because sensemaking and emergent strategy provide powerful means of supporting decision makers in times of turbulence and acknowledging and capitalising upon the contribution of improvisation within this realm could provide useful insights. This paper seeks to synthesise the conceptualisation of improvisation within the frameworks of emergent strategizing and sensemaking, and consider the role of group support systems as a platform for encouraging improvisation in strategy making.

The paper thus explores how the arguments offered in the literature present a role for improvisation in strategy making with particular attention to its significance in understanding emergent strategizing and sensemaking. We commence with a brief examination of the emergence of improvisation within the field of business and management, including an assessment of the several definitions that add value to the discussion. This examination touches on the genesis of the concept and its transfer to organizational science, as well as considering the research methods used to assess its role in management. This is followed by a consideration of the implications of improvisation in strategy, with a particular emphasis on emergent strategizing. The relevance of emergent strategizing leads on to a consideration of improvisation in sensemaking. We conclude by arguing that emergent strategizing, sensemaking and improvisation, working in harmony, can provide a powerful combination when developing strategy, particularly following a pandemic.

2   The Genesis of Improvisation

The concept of improvisation dates back as far as the 1920's, for example, Follett [8] talks about the creative interaction process experienced in groups. Until the 1950's very few research papers addressed the phenomenon, particularly within the context of organization studies.

Inevitably, researchers understand the concept of improvisation in different ways depending on their perspectives, epistemologies and field of work. Improvisation has been understood through a wide array of lenses including sociology, psychology, organizational learning [9–11], organizational creativity [12, 13], personal experience [14], memory [15], innovation [15–18], marketing [18], project management [19, 20], technology [21], structure [21, 22], and strategic management [23]. Others have sought to present an overview of the developing view of improvisation in the organizational field [24–26].

Whilst the above researchers suggest a wide range of fields interested in the role of improvisation, the following views of improvisation, taken from outside the organization and management literature, seem particularly useful in the context of this paper. Tyler and Tyler [27] suggest it is "the negation of foresight, of planned-for, of doing provided for by knowing, and of the control of the past over the present and future" (px). Whereas Powers sees improvisation as "the extent to which [meaning is] invented by the people immediately involved in a relationship" [28 p289]. Sharron's well quoted view is that improvisation, is an "immediate and spontaneous … process of creation" [29 p224], and Erickson [30] within a context of education saw it as a "… strategically adaptive action" (p161) "… making new kinds of sense together in adapting to the fortuitous circumstances of the moment" (p166). Reviewing these definitions highlights key phrases particularly when considering improvisation in the context of strategy namely improvisation as: the negation of foresight; decision making embedded in performance; and immediate, rapid, and spontaneous decisions and creative action.

During the period 1996–1998 the field rapidly developed. In 1996 Crossan, Lane, Kluss and White [31] published "The Improvising Organization: Where Planning Meets Opportunity" in which they looked at how theatre actors and jazz musicians improvised and what it means if transferred to organizations. This paper kicked-off the 'improvisational phenomenon' in management literature. Just one year later Eisenhardt [32] followed with her essay called "Strategic Decisions and All That Jazz". And, a year later Weick [33] wrote his influential essay "Improvisation as a Mindset for Organizational Analysis" in which he too uses the vehicle of jazz improvisation as a way to "improve on how we talk about organizational improvisation" (p543). Strategy making and improvisation were being seen as a potential powerful partnership.

Unfortunately, despite these articles, improvisation is still very often misunderstood, and thus the concept has little if any influence over organizational behaviour and surprisingly given the instability of markets, even less in terms of its role in influencing strategy. However, following the impact of a pandemic, we now have instabilities in society, commerce, globalisation as well as markets.

Managers predominantly understand strategy as a prescriptive, a priori, process that is bereft of improvisation. This view may possibly be because adopting an improvisation approach might indicate that things are not being properly managed. Without allowing for improvisation managers often forego real opportunities for their business because there is a strategic plan to adhere to and incentives coupled to it. The loss of such opportunities might be avoided by encouraging a more flexible technique - by improvising within an emergent strategizing environment. Where improvisation can enable strategy to meet the demands of a continually changing world in practice it can be powerful [32, 33].

Detecting improvisation and determining exactly how to adopt and measure it in an organizational context is not an easy task. The difficulties with measuring improvisation in organizations might be the reason why the concept has not become more widely researched, particularly by those focusing on quantitative methods in the social sciences. Many researchers have 'relied' on model developing, mostly using grounded research techniques. Inductive research, for example that undertaken by those looking at phenomenology, incorporates meaning and human interest [34] to a wider context which, in turn, might allow an understanding of the impact of improvisation on organizational strategy and yet this too is rare. Thus, the potential gained by adopting an improvisation approach is not fully explored, developed or realised.

3 Improvisation, Strategy, and Emergent Strategizing

Writers such as Weick [21, 35] or Mintzberg [36] have expressed their reservations concerning strategic planning and the danger of over reliance on analytical tools for the determination of the organizational future. Weick [22] argues that "a little strategy goes a long way. Too much can paralyse or splinter an organization" (p345). Both theorists belong to a school of researchers who emphasize the value and importance of experience, action and learning. This to a degree resonates with Cunha, Clegg and Kamoche [6] for whom "the idea of strategy as practice may be taken quite literally, given that there is no such a thing as improvisation in the absence of action" (p268). However, Weick is of the view that thought precedes action. Bridging this gap "between the utopia of the mind… and the realism of experience… falls squarely into strategy-as-practice research" [37 p537]. These authors also suggest "examining not only specific tools or actors, but also the rich interactions within which people and things are engaged in doing strategy work" (p537).

Thus, linking improvisation to organizational change and through that to strategy making, particularly the understanding and development of an emergent strategy [38], provides the opportunity to exploit organizational potential and manage uncertain and changing environments. But, it also links improvisation to sensemaking to reveal the factor of empowerment as a source of motivation and human interaction. Where organizational members are faced with different situations to those initially planned for, the act of sensemaking is necessary to determine how best to adapt the strategy to meet the new circumstances. The outcome is a proposition that segments the organization into elements of stability and elements of variety – continuity and change - in need for organizational attention to explain improvisation within its organizational context, but also to show that improvising can serve as a tool to exploit the organizational universe of existing variation and variety that nurtures best practice and competitive advantage.

Building on the research examining improvisation's contribution to organizational behaviour, strategic management researchers have begun to explicitly explore the contribution of improvisation to strategy. This has centred on "Organizational improvisation: what, when, how and why" [24] categorizing the conceptual evolution of improvisation into three stages or epochs. In the first stage "apart from fuelling interest in the topic, [was] the translating of jazz performance elements into the organizational arena" (p301) - companies were provided with lists of competencies and abilities to apply improvisation to an efficient degree. The second stage focuses on "using anecdotal and empirical evidence… emerging second-generation authors develop formal definitions and test, mostly using grounded theory, propositions that aim at surfacing triggers and elements of the phenomenon in organizational settings" (p301). This approach built a more solid ground for a positivist research approach. During that period a more general definition of the concept focusing on the temporal distance between conception and execution seemed to be shared by all the key writers. The third stage saw a comeback of the first stage, with authors criticizing the temporal definition of the phenomenon as being too limited, however they still failed to provide a more valid one [24].

Mintzberg introduced the concept of emergent strategy in 1972 [39] and later defined it as "a pattern in a stream of decisions" [38 p257]. Mintzberg and Waters did not focus on any process in their concept but 'emergent strategy' indicates an active process and thus "might be better named 'emergent strategizing'…" [40 p331]. Eden and Ackermann [41] state that "by emergent strategizing we refer to a process, a stream of actions that are not random but form a pattern… It is this detectable pattern in a stream of actions in the continuing cycle of sustaining relationships with those who have a stake in the organization, adapting and reacting to the environment, negotiating ways of doing this, and being opportunistic, that can be called emergent strategizing" (p21–22).

Emergent strategizing incorporates improvisational behaviour – sometimes referred to as being opportunistic. "The modifications that are implied by the organizing model are continuous, small-scale modifications that cumulate into a steady updating of the organization" [42 p247]. Lindblom [43] talks about 'muddling through' and Quinn [44] about 'logical incrementalism'. Being without an emergent strategy is impossible: i) all organizations have a 'way we do things around here', patterns of working, and an embedded culture, each of which determines a particular strategic future for the organization; ii) the environment is continuously changing so that "no operation extends with any certainty beyond the first encounter with the main body of the enemy" (attributed to Field Marshal Helmuth Von Moltke in the mid-nineteenth century). Improvisation is necessary for successful strategizing. If the strategy is implicit, if it is a result of patterns of action, the strategy is embedded in the culture, "the way we do things around here" and "in the head of managers as they take courses of action in relation to their 'world-taken-for-granted'" [41 p22]. Managers are seen as acting with an implicit perception of an appropriate direction for the organization and, because of that, problem solving finally resembles more 'firefighting' on a day to day basis.

4   Improvisation and Strategy Making

If we take seriously the discussion above, then all organizations will encompass some aspects of improvisation, which in turn will affect the future of the organization. If that is the case, then we need to understand the way in which improvisation affects the emergent strategy of the organization. Which in turn means we need to detect emergent strategizing in the unfamiliar environment of a 'retiring' pandemic. If we are not aware of the significance of the emergent strategizing on the future of the organization then we are unable to appreciate the blocks to strategically driven organizational change or the possibility of exploiting embedded improvising routines.

When seeking to understand improvisation it makes sense to employ some method to detect emergent strategizing. One proven approach is to conduct "an examination of structural properties of embedded routines, actual procedures and processes in use – 'the way we do things round here' – and how they relate to formal and informal reporting and decision-making structures of the organization; and capturing theories in use – the wisdom, belief systems, around and about the organization that are the basis for action" [41 p81]. The use of a Group Support System has been shown to be effective in uncovering emergent strategy [45, 46].

Attention to the significance of improvisation for strategy might imply that an organization is committed to a future that arises from deliberate emergent strategizing (in whole or part). Therefore, we conclude that there is a strong relationship between the concepts of an *improvising organization* and the concept of *emergent strategizing*.

Leybourne et al. [47] detect strong links "to current emerging managerial themes relating to the breakdown of traditional planning models, and the shift from [sustainable] competitive to 'transient' competitive advantage" (p354) (see also [47]). This is an insight Weick suggested some years earlier: "if improvisation is treated as a natural form of organizational life, then we become interested in a different form of strategy than we have seen before... This newer form I will call a just-in-time strategy" [22 p352].

Emergent strategizing, sensemaking, and improvisation working in harmony provide a powerful combination when developing strategy in fast moving uncertain times. Emergent strategizing and improvisation allow for creativity with the emergent strategizing aspect providing the structure through sensemaking and reflection. It allows for strategic renewal [48] and encourages a process of 'learning by doing'. Improvisation can be regarded as a legitimate strategy in the face of adversity [49]. For Weick [21 p36] improvisation is "about action" and enactment, "not about conceptual pictures". Thus, a strong cultural organizational foundation in favour of individual enactment counteracts institutionalization, organizational culture and thus power and politics matter. Improvisation might need to be actively encouraged, demanding different leadership styles away from control to more open approaches. It also suggests being able to be innovative and open to change, alongside being reflective and open to learning. This learning feature facilitates adaptability and flexibility allowing the organization to be more agile. Encouraging improvisation through planning is problematic, but understanding the role it can play, and is playing, in creating the strategic future of an organization means that the strategy needs to be malleable to unfolding creativity.

The above comments suggest a research agenda that focuses on the role of improvisation in the emergent strategizing of organizations, particularly when exploring the emergent strategy of organizations operating in a fast-changing environment. As Fisher and Barrett [14] note, improvisation in the performing arts is significantly different to that in organizations, and so it might help future research if it were to move away from the performing arts as the established reference point. They also make a strong case for adopting more "pragmatic views of knowledge and action, which de-emphasize plans and intentions" (p18) – a case supported by the position taken in this paper.

Given the current circumstances for organizations, as they come to terms with a significantly changed world after the Covid-19 pandemic, it seems likely that Group Support Systems could now be used as a basis for supporting improvisation in strategy making. We postulate that a group support system may be able uniquely to offer management teams the possibility of encompassing improvisation into their strategic thinking. In particular, improvisation in strategy making may be more likely in an environment where i) anonymity is possible, and ii) synergies can be exploited through the use of a transitional and boundary object. Each of these are key characteristics of group support systems. In addition, some group support systems, such as *Group Explorer* and *Strategyfinder* [50], that use causal mapping may be able to create improvisations through the synergy of connecting ideas from a variety of contributors participating in the group support system meeting. Group support systems allow for 'play', structuring conversations, supporting the creation of new options, and teasing out emergent embryonic opportunities. A group support system, additionally, might help at teasing out tacit knowledge [51], potentially revealing the culture and routines so that these can be strategically exploited.

This paper is presented as a conceptual and theoretical basis for beginning experiments with different group support systems facilitated in different ways - a research challenge for the GDN community.

References

1. Cunha, M.P., Cunha, J.V.: Towards a complexity theory of strategy. Manag. Decis. **44**, 839–850 (2006)
2. Hodgkinson, I.R., Hughes, P., Arshad, D.: Strategy development: driving improvisation in Malaysia. J. World Bus. **51**, 379–390 (2016)
3. Eriksson, K., McConnell, A.: Contingency planning for crisis management: recipe for success or political fantasy? Policy Soc. **30**, 89–99 (2011)
4. Pham, T., Jordan, E.: Improvisation as strategy: building an information technology capability. In: Donnellan, B., Larsen, T.J., Levine, L., DeGross, J.I. (eds.) TDIT 2006. IIFIP, vol. 206, pp. 139–156. Springer, Boston (2006). https://doi.org/10.1007/0-387-34410-1_10
5. Crossan, M.M.: Improvisation in Action. Organ. Sci. **9**, 593–599 (1998)
6. Cunha, M.P.e., Clegg, S.R., Kamoche, K.: Improvisation as "real time foresight". Futures. **44**, 265–272 (2012)
7. Perry, L.T.: Strategic improvising: how to formulate and implement competitive strategies in concert. Organ. Dyn. **19**, 51–64 (1991)
8. Follett, M.P.: Creative Experience. Longman Green and Co, New York (1924)
9. Crossan, M.M., Sorrenti, M.: Making sense of improvisation. In: Walsh, J.P., Huff, A.S. (eds.) Advances in Strategic Management, pp. 155–180. JAI Press, Greenwich (1997)
10. Miner, A.S., Bassoff, P., Moorman, C.: Organizational improvisation and learning: a field study. Adm. Sci. Q. **46**, 304–337 (2001)
11. Vendelo, M.T.: Improvisation and learning in organizations - an opportunity for future empirical research. Manag. Learn. **40**, 449–456 (2009)
12. Amabile, T.M., Pratt, M.G.: The dynamic componential model of creativity and innovation in organizations: making progress, making meaning. Res. Organ. Behav. **37**, 157–183 (2016)
13. Anderson, N., Ptocnik, K., Zho, J.: Innovation and creativity in organizations. J. Manag. **40**, 1297–1333 (2014)
14. Fisher, C.M., Barrett, F.J.: The experience of improvising in organizations: a creative process perspective. Acad. Manag. Perspect. **33**, 148–162 (2019)
15. Moorman, C., Miner, A.S.: Organizational improvisation and organizational memory. Acad. Manag. Rev. **23**, 698–723 (1998)
16. Kamoche, K., Cunha, M.P.: Minimal structures: from jazz improvisation to product innovation. Organ. Stud. **22**, 733–764 (2001)
17. Kyriakopoulos, K.: Improvisation in product innovation: the contingent role of market information sources and memory types. Organ. Stud. **32**, 1051–1078 (2011)
18. Slotegraaf, R.J., Dickson, P.R.: The paradox of market planning capability. J. Acad. Mark. Sci. **32**, 371–385 (2004)
19. Leybourne, S., Sadler-Smith, E.: The Role of institution and improvisation in project management. Int. J. Proj. Manag. **24**, 483–492 (2006)
20. Leybourne, S.A.: Improvisation and agile project management: a comparative consideration. Int. J. Managing Proj. Bus. **2**, 519–535 (2009)
21. Weick, K.E.: Sensemaking in Organizations. Sage, Thousand Oaks (1995)
22. Weick, K.E.: Making Sense of the Organization. Blackwell, Malden (2001)
23. Floyd, S.W., Woolridge, D.: Building Strategy From the Middle: Reconceptualizing the Strategy Process. Sage, Thousand Oaks (2000)

24. Cunha, M.P.e., Cunha, J. V., Kamoche, K.: organizational improvisation: what, when, how and why. Int. J. Manag. Rev. **1**, 299–341 (1999)
25. Cunha, M.P., Miner, A.S., Antonacopoulou, E.: Improvisation processes in organizations. In: Langley, A., Tsoukas, H. (eds.) SAGE Handbook of Process Organization Studies, pp. 559–573. Sage, London (2017)
26. Hadida, A.L., Tarvainen, W., Rose, J.: Organizational improvisation: a consolidating review and framework. Int. J. Manag. Rev. **17**, 437–459 (2015)
27. Russell, C.T., Angelopoulos, V.: Foreword. In: Russell, C., Angelopoulos, V. (eds.) The ARTEMIS Mission, pp. 1–2. Springer, New York (2012). https://doi.org/10.1007/978-1-4614-9554-3_1
28. Powers, C.: Role-imposition or role-improvisation: some theoretical principles. Econ. Soc. Rev. **12**, 287–299 (1981)
29. Sharron, A.: Time and space bias in group solidarity: action and process in musical improvisation. Int. Soc. Sci. Rev. **58**, 222–230 (1983)
30. Erickson, F.: Classroom discourse as improvisation: relationships between academic task structure and social participation structure in lessons. In: Wilkinson, L.C. (ed.) Communicating in the Classroom, pp. 153–181. Macmillan, New York (1982)
31. Crossan, M.M., Lane, H.W., Kluss, L., White, R.E.: The improvising organization: where planning meets opportunity. Organ. Dyn. **24**, 20–35 (1996)
32. Eisenhardt, K.M.: Strategic decisions and all that jazz. Bus. Strategy Rev. **8**, 1–3 (1997)
33. Weick, K.E.: Introductory essay: improvisation as a mindset for organizational analysis. Organ. Sci. **9**, 543–555 (1998)
34. Ramanathan, R.: The role of organizational change management in offshore outsourcing of information technology services. In: MOPAN Conference, Boston (2008)
35. Weick, K.E., Sutcliffe, K.M., Obstfeld, D.: Organizing and the process of sensemaking. Organ. Sci. **16**, 409–421 (2005)
36. Mintzberg, H.: The Fall and Rise of Strategic Planning. Harvard Bus. Rev. **Jan-Feb**, 107–114 (1994)
37. Jarzabkowski, P., Kaplan, S.: Strategy tools-in-use: a framework for understanding "technologies of rationality" in practice. Strateg. Manag. J. **36**, 537–558 (2015)
38. Mintzberg, H., Waters, J.A.: Of strategies, deliberate and emergent. Strateg. Manag. J. **6**, 257–272 (1985)
39. Mintzberg, H.: Research on strategy-making. In: Paper presented at the Academy of Management Conference, Minneapolis (1972)
40. Eden, C., van der Heijden, K.: Detecting emergent strategy. In: Thomas, H., O'Neal, D., Kelly, J. (eds.) Strategic Renaissance and Business Transformation, pp. 331–347. Wiley, New York (1995)
41. Eden, C., Ackermann, F.: Making Strategy: The Journey of Strategic Management. Sage, London (1998)
42. Weick, K.E.: The Social Psychology of Organizing. Addison-Wesley, Reading (1979)
43. Lindblom, C.E.: The science of muddling through. Public Adm. Rev. **19**, 79–88 (1959)
44. Quinn, J.B.: Strategies for Change: Logical Incrementalism. Irwin, Homewood (1980)
45. Eden, C., Ackermann, F.: Group decision and negotiation in strategy making. Group Decis. Negot. **10**, 119–140 (2001)
46. Ackermann, F., Eden, C.: Group support systems: concepts to practice. In: Kilgour, D.M., Eden, C. (eds.) Handbook of Group Decision and Negotiation. Springer, Dordrecht (2020). https://doi.org/10.1007/978-3-030-12051-1_59-1
47. Leybourne, S., Lynn, G., Vendelo, M.T.: Forms, metaphors, and themes: an introduction to the special issue on organizational improvisation. Creativity Innov. Manag. **23**, 353–358 (2014)
48. Morgan, G., Frost, P.J., Pondy, L.R.: Organizational symbolism. In: Pondy, L.R., Frost, P.J., Dandridge, T.C. (eds.) Organizational Symbolism, pp. 55–65. JAI Press, Greenwich (1983)

49. Best, S., Gooderham, P.: Improvisation: a legitimate strategy in the face of adversity. Small Enterp. Res. **22**, 49–68 (2015)
50. Ackermann, F.: Group support systems: past, present, and future. In: Kilgour, D.M., Eden, C. (eds.) Handbook of Group Decision and Negotiation, pp. 627–654. Springer, Dordrecht (2021)
51. Dorfler, V., Ackermann, F.: Understanding intuition: the case for two forms of intuition. Manag. Learn. **45**, 545–564 (2012)

Preference Modeling for Group Decision and Negotiation

Survey-Based Multi-stakeholder Preference Elicitation with Relatively Incomplete and Possibly Disjoint Rank Orderings

Andreas Paulsson[1](✉) and Aron Larsson[1,2]

[1] Department of Computer and Systems Sciences, Stockholm University,
16440 Kista, Sweden
{apaulsson,aron}@dsv.su.se
[2] Department of Information Systems and Technology, Mid Sweden University,
85170 Sundsvall, Sweden

Abstract. We present a survey-based approach towards simultaneous elicitation of criteria and weight rank orderings in a group decision analysis setting. Supporting such procedures is of interest for services facilitating online participatory decision analysis where citizens as stakeholders provide input in order to shape both a set of criteria and preferential statements over the set. However, in such a simultaneous approach, the stakeholders do not rank the same elements, as they propose them more or less independently, which leads to aggregation of relatively incomplete and possibly disjoint rank orderings. To address this, we present a useful conceptualization and subsequently identify techniques for aggregating such rank orderings. Furthermore, we propose a method for assessing the aggregation techniques' equitability by using data from a decision situation in a climate action case.

Keywords: Group decisions · Criteria elicitation · Weight elicitation · Incomplete rank orderings · Participatory approaches

1 Introduction

In the past few decades, facilitating group decision analysis through online surveys has received increased attention from the decision science community. One instance of this is the emergence of online services aimed at facilitating e-participation in public decision-making. There, stakeholders such as regular citizens may provide input on which decision elements a public decision-making body ought to consider as well as their preferences over those, see, e.g., Ref. [8].

Group decision analysis focuses on the aggregation of preferences from a set of group members typically called *stakeholders*, and on the processes that support the elicitation of their preferences. A traditional tenet in group decision analysis is that the sets of criteria are predefined and common to all stakeholders, and preference elicitation is carried out relative to those common criteria.

© Springer Nature Switzerland AG 2021
D. C. Morais et al. (Eds.): GDN 2021, LNBIP 420, pp. 27–40, 2021.
https://doi.org/10.1007/978-3-030-77208-6_3

Before the preference elicitation, a procedure for a group to generate the common criteria set might have been used, such as, e.g., a Delphi method involving all stakeholders, a limited subset of those, or other experts and members of the decision-making body, cf., [9,16]. These types of approaches have been reported in previous applications of "public decision analysis." In Ref. [7], a questionnaire composed by civil servants with predefined criteria and decision alternatives was sent by mail to the citizens living in their adherent municipality. A similar approach was taken in [13], with the difference that the criteria set was formed by politicians, and civil servants proposed reasonable alternatives for water quality management subject to preference elicitation by a wider audience. Other cases with shared criteria sets are covered in [1] and [10].

One prescriptive guideline advocated when promoting schemes for the elicitation of preferences is to aim for less cognitively demanding schemes and methods, cf., [15]. Methods to limit the cognitive burden put on the stakeholders from preference and weight elicitation have been proposed and discussed in the literature. Rank-based approaches, where a stakeholder provides ordinal rank orderings which are later interpreted in different methods, have emerged, e.g., rank sum, rank ordered centroid, and sum rank reciprocal weights [2,4,17]. These approaches allow stakeholders to partially rank the elements in a weak order, from the least important to the most important, when eliciting criteria weights.

However, as mentioned above, in the case of a large set of stakeholders, which is of concern within the domain of participatory practices, the methods used in practice consider a pre-defined set of criteria common to all stakeholders. In this paper, we address the situation where stakeholders submit both the decision elements to be ranked and their rank orderings, on condition that they find themselves in a situation that calls for a decision that would solve a problem or embrace an opportunity. In the literature, this view on stakeholders is similar to the one adopted in the multi-actor multi-criteria analysis (MAMCA) approach, where it is anticipated that different stakeholders do not share evaluation criteria, cf., e.g., [11].

The rationale behind supporting such a method lies primarily in not forcing a stakeholder to rank elements that he/she does not readily associate with the decision situation. All stakeholders combined will provide a set of elements that decision makers can use to shape a set of evaluation criteria, thereby enabling participation on an individual level. However, it is highly unlikely that the stakeholders will rank the same elements since they propose them more or less independently. That, in turn, leads to the need of aggregating what we herein call *relatively incomplete and possibly disjoint rank orderings*. This study aims to present and evaluate some methods of achieving that.

In this paper, we investigate how to develop a set of criteria from a flexible online survey—flexible in the sense that the stakeholders provide their own evaluation criteria and rank them with respect to their relative importance—and form an aggregate of the individual stakeholders' input. We start by presenting some concepts and techniques for aggregating relatively incomplete rank orderings, including a discussion of how such rank orderings can be modified for

aggregation purposes. After that, we propose a method for assessing the equitability of the aggregation techniques by using data from a decision situation
within a climate action case.

2 Conceptualization

In the setting described above, it is not clear how to shape a criteria set for a decision model from the stakeholders' combined answers. To distinguish between the
respondents' input at different stages of the process we conform to the following
conceptualization. We refer to the aspects directly suggested by respondents in
the survey as their *value drivers*, i.e., the aspects that, according to a respondent,
should be considered since they articulate value a decision alternative can provide given the decision context. Given that some, sufficiently large, proportion of
respondents have proposed the same value driver, a value-driver cluster will be
formed. A value-driver cluster can then be interpreted as a *criterion* equipped
with a weight resulting from an aggregation of the respondents value-driver rank
orderings.

More formally, let $i_q \equiv i_r$ mean that the value driver i_q proposed by respondent q is congruent to the value driver i_r proposed by respondent r. Then a
value-driver cluster V_i is a set of congruent value drivers $V_i = \{i_q, \ldots, i_r\}$ proposed by different stakeholders, among them q and r. Following this, we can
choose to promote the semantic meaning of V_i into a criterion c_i based upon,
e.g., the cardinality of V_i. A set of $C = \{c_1, \ldots, c_n\}$ can then be formed and kept
for decision analytical modeling.

Of importance is that when clustering value drivers, special care needs to be
taken to not generate any cycles in the responses once they are mapped to the
value-driver clusters. Let $\mathcal{V} = \{V_1, \ldots, V_n\}$ be the set of all value-driver clusters,
and let $i_q \succ j_q \succ k_q$ be a rank ordering of value drivers by respondent q with
$i_q, j_q, k_q \in I_q$. Then $\bigcup_q I_q$ is the universe of all proposed value drivers, and a
clustering $s : \bigcup_q I_q \to \mathcal{V}$ must result in $s(i_q) \neq s(j_q)$ whenever $i \neq j$.

Next, we introduce the decision model and techniques for weight elicitation
that form the basis for the aggregation method.

2.1 Decision Model

In this paper we conform to the multi-attribute value theory model of multi-
criteria decision analysis in which the value $V(a_k)$ of an alternative a_k is given
by

$$V(a_k) = \sum_{i=1}^{n} w_i v_i(a_k) \tag{1}$$

where w_i is the weight of the i:th criterion and $v_i(a_k)$ is the value function
over the i:th criterion. While acknowledging the relationship between the set of
alternatives $\{a_1, \ldots, a_k, \ldots, a_M\}$, which constitute the domain of each $v_i(a_k)$,
and the weights as scaling factors [20], the survey approach outlined in the case

presented in this paper will not (per se) meet the requirements for elicitation of weights with a scaling factor or SWING interpretation of the weights. A plausible interpretation of the criteria weights is analogous to that of "relative functional importance of criteria" [3], where the relative importance of the criterion c_i is related to the degree that the rank ordering of the alternatives under c_i, and the alternatives' overall rank-ordering, correspond. Refraining from further discussion on this matter but mentioning that the protocol of the survey could be designed otherwise to support more equitable weight interpretations for decision analysis purposes, we henceforth focus on rank based elicitation and subsequent aggregation of weights.

2.2   Criteria Rank Orders and Surrogate Weights

The difficulties involved in criteria weight elicitation have been pointed out by several authors (see, e.g., [2,5]). Precise number elicitations are unlikely to truly reflect the mind of a decision maker, and can impart an illusionary precision [6]. While less exact, ordinal weight elicitation is less cognitively demanding, and hence requires less effort from a decision maker or a respondent [14]. To increase the precision of an ordinal rank order, a notion of relative distance between the items can be included [6] to form a cardinal rank ordering. The ordinary $\succ$-relation would then be substituted by, e.g., $\succ_0, \ldots, \succ_3$ with the following suggested meanings:

$\succ_0$ "equally important"
$\succ_1$ "moderately more important"
$\succ_2$ "clearly more important"
$\succ_3$ "much more important"

Ordinal and cardinal rank orderings do, however, require a transformation from rank positions into real-numbered surrogate weights. For ordinal rank orderings, Ref. [17] proposed the rank sum (RS), and rank reciprocal (RR) functions to generate surrogate weights. The rank sum surrogate weight of the ith item in a rank ordering of N items is defined as

$$w_i^{\text{RS}} = \frac{N - i + 1}{\sum_{j=1}^{N} N - j + 1}. \tag{2}$$

Surrogate weights based on RS are linearly decreasing with the rank positions, and suits the assumption that a decision maker assigns weights with N degrees of freedom (i.e., analogous to direct rating). The RR weights, better suited to the assumption that decision makers are eliciting weights with $N - 1$ degrees of freedom (i.e., analogous to point allocation), are defined by

$$w_i^{\text{RR}} = \frac{1/i}{\sum_{j=1}^{N} 1/j}. \tag{3}$$

Due to the special properties of RS and RR, Ref. [5] proposed an additive combination of RS and RR referred to as SR and defined as:

$$w_i^{\text{SR}} = \frac{\frac{1}{i} + \frac{N+1-i}{N}}{\sum_{j=1}^{N} \frac{1}{j} + \frac{N+1-j}{N}}. \tag{4}$$

In an extensive simulation experiment, Ref. [4] evaluated the robustness of a number of ordinal surrogate weight functions with SR proving to be one of the most robust. The cardinal rank version of the SR weight method, CSR, requires a notion of relative rank positions. The total number of rank positions in a cardinal rank ordering with relations $\succ_0, \succ_1, \ldots, \succ_n$ is defined by $Q = \sum_{i=0}^{n} i |\succ_i|$. Let $p(i)$ be the absolute position of the ith ranked criteria, and let $p(1) = 1$ and $p(m) = Q$ in a cardinal rank ordering with m criteria. For any two criteria c_i and c_j, if $c_i \succ_k c_j$ then $p(c_j) = p(c_i) + k$. The CSR function is defined as follows (see [5]):

$$w_i^{\text{CSR}} = \frac{\frac{1}{p(i)} + \frac{Q+1-p(i)}{Q}}{\sum_{j=i}^{N} \frac{1}{p(j)} + \frac{Q+1-p(j)}{Q}}. \tag{5}$$

A mapping from a set of rank ordered criteria to a set of weights is a composite function

$$w_i \circ p \tag{6}$$

where w_i is a surrogate weight function such as w_i^{SR} and w_i^{CSR}, and $p(c_i)$ is the rank position of criteria c_i.

2.3 Criteria Rank Order Interpretations

Forming an aggregate from a set of respondent criteria rank orderings, based on value-driver rank orderings (see Sect. 2), can be done in several ways and is partly dependent on the assumptions made about the meaning of an individual's rank ordering. We make a number of such assumptions here. Firstly, we assume that a criteria rank-ordering can be transformed into a set of weights, based on surrogate numbers presented in [5]. Secondly, we interpret incomplete and possibly disjoint criteria rank orderings in four main ways. Note that a respondent is free to choose how many aspects he/she enters (up to a limit), and that it is very unlikely that all respondents would rank very similar aspects (i.e., the total number of aspects generated by the survey is very likely to be greater than the number of aspects entered by any respondent). In the exposition below we use the following notation for sets of criteria: C_q^{R} is the set of criteria in the criteria rank ordering proposed by respondent q, $C = \bigcup_q C_q^{\text{R}}$ is the set of universal criteria in a survey, C^{D} is a set of dummy criteria, and $C_q^{\text{E}} = C \setminus C_q^{\text{R}}$ is the set of universal criteria not in the rank-ordering provided by respondent q. Given the hitherto conceptualization, we can define four different ways of interpreting the respondents' criteria rank orderings outlined below.

I. Absence Is Irrelevance. Perhaps the most apparent perspective on an individual rank-ordering is that only the explicitly ranked criteria are important to the respondent and that any other criteria are completely irrelevant to him/her. As a consequence, all of the available weight would be allocated to the criteria in the rank-ordering, and only to those. In such a case we refer to the rank ordering as a *respondent criteria rank ordering*. To assign surrogate weights to the criteria in such a case, we consider the following. Let a respondent criteria rank ordering be a relational structure $\mathcal{R} = (C^{\mathrm{R}}, \succ)$ where C^{R} is a set of criteria ranked by a particular individual, and $\succ^{\mathrm{R}}$ is a strict weak order on C^{R}. For any criteria c_i and c_j in C^{R}, $c_i \succ_r c_j$ if and only if c_i is more important than c_j. Let w^{O} be a homomorphism from $\mathcal{R}$ and $\mathcal{D}$ into $(\mathbb{R}, >)$. If $\sum_{c' \in C'} w^{\mathrm{O}}(c') = 1$ for $C' \in \{C^{\mathrm{R}}, C^{\mathrm{D}}\}$, then w^{O} is a surrogate weight elicitation function of ordinally ranked criteria; one such function is $w^{\mathrm{SR}} \circ p$ defined in (4) and (6). Eliciting surrogate weights in this case is done by letting $(C_q^{\mathrm{R}}, \succ)$ be a particular respondent criteria rank ordering. Let $C_q^{\mathrm{R}} = \{c_1, \dots, c_m\}$ and $C = \bigcup_r C_r^{\mathrm{R}}$. Let p_q be a function that maps each criteria in a criteria rank ordering to its rank position. The *surrogate criteria weights* are in this case elicited by applying $w^{\mathrm{SR}} \circ p_q$ to each criteria in C_q^{R}.

II. Dummy Augmentation. Another way of interpreting an individual rank ordering in the context of this study is as follows. Assume that the individual is allowed to rank the importance of up to n criteria and that each rank position is equivalent to some number of points. Furthermore, the points allocated to any empty rank positions are void. It is only if a respondent places a criterion in all of the rank positions do all points get assigned. In this case, the weight of any empty rank positions would automatically be allocated to a number of dummy criteria to reflect such an interpretation. We call this relational structure $\mathcal{D} = (C^{\mathrm{D}} \cup C^{\mathrm{R}}, \succ^{\mathrm{D}})$ a *dummy-augmented criteria rank ordering* with C^{R} as above, and C^{D} representing a set of dummy criteria such that $C^{\mathrm{D}} \cap C^{\mathrm{R}} = \varnothing$. The relation $\succ^{\mathrm{D}}$ is a strict weak order on $C^{\mathrm{R}} \cup C^{\mathrm{D}}$ such that $c_i \succ^{\mathrm{D}} c_j$ if and only if c_i is more important than c_j for any criteria c_i and c_j in $C^{\mathrm{R}} \cup C^{\mathrm{D}}$. It has the special property that $c \succ^{\mathrm{D}} d$ for all $c \in C^{\mathrm{R}}$ and $c^{\mathrm{D}} \in C^{\mathrm{D}}$. Let w^{O} be a homomorphism from $\mathcal{R}$ and $\mathcal{D}$ into $(\mathbb{R}, >)$. If $\sum_{c' \in C'} w^{\mathrm{O}}(c') = 1$ for $C' \in \{C^{\mathrm{R}}, C^{\mathrm{D}}\}$, then w^{O} is a surrogate weight elicitation function of ordinally ranked criteria; one such function, $w^{\mathrm{SR}} \circ p$, is defined in (4) and (6). To elicit surrogate weights to criteria in a dummy-augmented criteria rank ordering, we append a rank ordering of dummy criteria $d_1 \succ \dots \succ d_n$, where $n = N - m$ and N is the maximum number of allowed entries in a rank ordering of value drivers, to a respondent criteria rank ordering $c_1 \succ^{\mathrm{D}} \cdots \succ^{\mathrm{D}} c_m$ with $c_1, \dots, c_m \in C_q^{\mathrm{R}}$, to obtain $c_1 \succ^{\mathrm{D}} \cdots \succ^{\mathrm{D}} c_m \succ^{\mathrm{D}} d_1 \succ^{\mathrm{D}} \cdots \succ^{\mathrm{D}} d_n$. Then, $w^{\mathrm{SR}} \circ p_q$ is applied to the dummy-augmented criteria rank ordering, and the surrogate weights of the dummy-criteria are discarded before the subsequent aggregation.

III. Dummy Extension. A third way would be to consider the meaning of the criteria rank orderings only after the total number of unique criteria specific to the given survey is known. Here, a given criteria rank-ordering would be extended by one additional rank position. The explicitly ranked criteria would receive weights according to their positions, similar to the first interpretation above. The rest of the criteria in the survey would share the weight of the additional position. In other words, the explicitly ranked criteria would maintain their order, and the least important criteria would be more important than the rest of the criteria, which would be considered to be of equal importance. In this way, the collective idea about which criteria are important (i.e., the universe of criteria in the context particular to the inquiry) would be shared among all the respondents. An *extended criteria rank ordering* is a relational structure $\mathcal{E} = (C^E \cup C^R, \succ^E, \sim^E)$ with C^E and C^R being disjoint sets of criteria. For any two criteria $c_i, c_j \in C^E \cup C^R$, $c_i \succ^E c_j$ if and only if c_i is more important than c_j, and for any criteria $c_i \in C^R, c_k \in C^E$, $c_i \succ^E c_k$. The relation $\sim^E$ is a quasi order on C^E such that $\sim^E = C^E \times C^E$. For any criteria $(c_i, c_j) \in \sim^E$, $c_i \sim^E c_j$ if and only if c_i and c_j are equally important. Similar to above, a homomorphism w^E from $\mathcal{E}$ into $(\mathbb{R}, >, =)$ is a surrogate weight function of the criteria in $\mathcal{E}$ if $\sum_{c_i \in C^E \cup C^R} w^E(c_i) = 1$. We let $(w^{SR} \circ p)/l$ be such a homomorphism, where $l_i = |\{c_k : p(c_k) = i\}|$ denotes the number of criteria at the ith rank position. Surrogate weights for an extended criteria rank ordering are elicited by extending the criteria rank ordering $c_1 \succ^E \cdots \succ^E c_m$, $c_1, \ldots, c_m \in C^R_q$, with the criteria $c'_1, \ldots, c'_n$ in $C \setminus C^R_q$ such that $c_1 \succ^E \cdots \succ^E c_m \succ^E c'_1 \sim^E \cdots \sim^E c'_n$, and then applying $(w^{SR} \circ p)/l$ to the criteria in that extended criteria rank ordering.

IV. Dummy Extension with Cardinality Steps.

A fourth approach is similar to the previous one, but with a cardinal step denoting the level of difference in importance between the criteria (see Sect. 2.2). Here, we consider possibly different step sizes between the explicitly ranked criteria, and between the least important criterion in the response set and the criteria that make up the extension of the rank ordering. The step sizes would stand for "moderately more important," "clearly more important," and "much more important." A *cardinally extended criteria rank ordering* is a relational structure $\mathcal{C} = (C^E \cup C^R, \succ^C_1, \ldots, \succ^C_q, \sim^C)$ with C^E and C^R being disjoint sets of criteria. The union of the relations $\succ^C_1, \ldots, \succ^C_q$ is a strict weak order on $C^E \cup C^R$. For any criteria $c_i, c_j, c_k, c_l \in C^E \cup C^R$ and any two relations $\succ^C_o$ and $\succ^C_p$ with $o > p$, the following holds: $c_i \succ^C_o c_j$ and $c_k \succ^C_p c_l$ if and only if c_i is more important than c_j to a greater extent than c_k is more important than c_l. For any $c_i \in C^R, c_j \in C^E$ we have $c_i \succ_k c_j$, $k = 1, \ldots, q$. The relation $\sim^C$ is a quasi order on C^E such that $\sim^C = C^E \times C^E$.[1] For all criteria in $c_i, c_j \in C^E$, $c_i \sim_r c_j$ holds if and only if c_i and c_j are equally important. Let $(\mathbb{R}, >_1, \ldots, >_q, =)$ be a relational structure with $x_i >_o x_j$ and $x_k >_p x_l$, for $o > p$, if and only if $x_i - x_j > x_k - x_l$, for any $x_i, x_j, x_k, x_l \in \mathbb{R}$. Analogously to the extended criteria rank ordering, the union of $>_1, \ldots, >_q$ is a strict weak order on $\mathbb{R}$. If w^C is a homomorphism from $\mathcal{E}$ into $(\mathbb{R}, >_1, \ldots, >_q, =)$, and $\sum_{c \in C^E \cup C^R} w^C(c) = 1$, then w^C is a surrogate

---

[1] In Sect. 2.2 the relation $\sim$ was denoted by $\succ_0$.

weight elicitation function of cardinally ranked criteria. The function w^{CSR} in (5) is such a function. Cardinally extended surrogate criteria weights are elicited by extending the criteria rank ordering $c_1 \succ \ldots \succ c_m$, $c_1, \ldots, c_m \in C_q^{\mathrm{R}}$, with the criteria $c_1', \ldots, c_n'$ in $C \setminus C_q^{\mathrm{R}}$ such that $c_1 \succ_i^{\mathrm{E}} \cdots \succ_i^{\mathrm{E}} c_m \succ_j^{\mathrm{E}} c_1' \sim^{\mathrm{E}} \cdots \sim^{\mathrm{E}} c_n'$, where $i, j = 1, 2, 3$. The function $w^{\mathrm{CSR}} \circ p_q$ is applied to the resulting rank ordering to generate the surrogate weights.

2.4   Aggregation Techniques

An *aggregate* $\mathcal{A}$ of a set of respondent criteria rank orderings, is a set whose elements are triples $(c_j, w_j^{\min}, w_j^{\max})$ where c_j is a criteria in $C = \bigcup_q C_q^{\mathrm{R}}$, with $w_j^{\min}$ and $w_j^{\max}$ being the minimum and maximum of the uniform weight distribution of c_j. For any two triples $(c_j, w_j^{\min}, w_j^{\max})$ and $(c_k, w_k^{\min}, w_k^{\max})$, $c_j \neq c_k$. The mean weight of a criteria c_j in an aggregate is denoted by $\overline{w}_j = (w_j^{\max} - w_j^{\min})/2$. Note that the sets of criteria in any two respondent criteria rank orderings may be disjoint.

We consider two ways of aggregating the surrogate weights once elicited: (1) take the *average* of the surrogate weights assigned to a given criterion, and (2) take the *sum* of those same surrogate weights. These techniques are, as far as we can see, reasonable and not least comprehensible. The latter technique would also account for the number of responses containing a specific criterion. It has the same effect, for every respondent, as assigning zero weight to all criteria in C that are not in that respondent's criteria rank-ordering. Thereby the mean and the sum differ only for the respondent's original rank orderings, and the dummy augmented rank orderings. Alternatives, such as the geometric mean and the median, would be too sensitive to small weights and not sensitive enough to the spread, respectively.

In both cases, the results are normalized to sum to one, and the standard deviations of the weight distributions would serve as bases for the intervals $[w_i^{\min}, w_i^{\max}]$. When normalizing the averages (or sums), let $f(x_i) = bx_i$ to be the normalization function where $x_1, \ldots, x_n$ are the averages (or sums) of the criteria weights, and $b = \frac{1}{\sum x_j}$ is the normalization factor of f. Then, apply f to all of the criteria weights to obtain normalized weight distributions, based on either the averages or the sums of the criteria weights. We let the standard deviations of those form the bases of the uncertainty intervals surrounding each of the criteria; the result is the same as applying f to the standard deviation of the original distributions.

3   Method

Many techniques for assessing the similarity between rank orderings either require the rank orderings to be conjoint or one has to perform the similarity assessment based only on a prefix of the orderings [19]. In this study, we evaluated each of the aggregation method's robustness relative to the individual criteria rank orderings in two ways: (1) by calculating the Kendall's τ distance between each individual rank ordering and a sample rank ordering generated from the aggregate weight distributions by stochastic simulation, and (2) by calculating the average of the sums of the absolute differences between a sample, generated from the aggregate weight distribution, and each criteria rank-ordering interpreted in the different manners as outlined in Sect. 2.4. Surrogate weights for each of the criteria were sampled from the aggregate distribution based on the algorithm in [18] described below. For the evaluation based on Kendall's τ distance, the weighted criteria were converted into a strict weak order.

Given an aggregate $\mathcal{A} = \{(c_1, w_1^{\min}, w_1^{\max}), \ldots, (c_n, w_n^{\min}, w_n^{\max})\}$, let $C = \sum w_i^{\min}$. Generate a random sample $U_1, \ldots, U_{n-1}$ from $U(0, 1 - C)$ and sort them to obtain $u_1, \ldots, u_{n-1}$ where $i < j$ if and only if $u_i < u_j$.[2] Set $u_0 = 0$ and $u_n = 1 - C$ and let the weights in a sample weighted criteria rank ordering $s_i = \{(w_1^{s_i}, c_1), \ldots, (w_n^{s_i}, c_n)\}$ be defined by $w_j^{s_i} = u_j - u_{j-1} + w_j^{\min}$.

We calculate the Kendall's τ distance based on [12], but incur a penalty in cases where a pair of elements exist in one rank ordering but only one of the elements in that pair is part of the other rank ordering and the element existing only in the first rank ordering has a higher rank than the element existing in both rank orderings. Let the Kendall's τ distance $K(r_a, r_b)$, between two rank orderings r_a and r_b be defined as

$$K(r_a, r_b) = \sum_{(c_i, c_j) \in r_a \cup r_b} \chi_a(c_i > c_j) \chi_b(c_j > c_i) \tag{7}$$

where χ is a characteristic function such that $\chi_a(c_i > c_j) = 1$ if and only if $p_a(c_i) < p_a(c_j)$ for any criteria c_i and c_j in a criteria rank ordering r_a. The normalized version, which incurs a penalty as described above, is

$$K_N(r_a, r_b) = K(r_a^{\text{ext}}, r_b^{\text{ext}}) \Big/ \frac{n(n-1)}{2} \tag{8}$$

where n is the number of elements both in r_a and r_b. The rank orderings r_a^{ext} and r_b^{ext} are extensions of r_a and r_b such that

$$r_a^{\text{ext}} = r_a \cup \{(a, b) \in \succ \mid a \in r_a \text{ and } b \in r_b \setminus r_a\} \tag{9}$$

and r_b^{ext} is defined similarly.

The sum of absolute differences Δ is defined as follows. Let $C_a \subseteq C$ and $C_b \subseteq C$ be two sets of weighted criteria. Either $C_a = C$ or $C_b = C$. Let w_i^a be the weight of criteria c_i in C_a and let w_j^b be the weight of criteria c_j in C_b. We then have

$$\Delta(C_a, C_b) = \sum_{c_i \in C} \begin{cases} w_i^a, & \text{if } c_i \in C_a \text{ and } c_i \notin C_b \\ w_i^b, & \text{if } c_i \notin C_a \text{ and } c_i \in C_b \\ |w_i^a - w_i^b|, & \text{if } c_i \in C_a \text{ and } c_i \in C_b \\ 0, & \text{otherwise} \end{cases} \tag{10}$$

In contexts similar to this, the last case will never occur since the sample of the aggregate always will contain all criteria in C.

---

[2] If any two random numbers in the sample $U_1, \ldots, U_{n-1}$ would be exactly equal then it should be replaced with another sample.

4   Case and Data Preparation

We provide an example using data collected from European climate policy experts using an online survey tool. The main question of the survey was "Which factors do you think will be decisive for reaching net-zero emissions by 2045–what should be on the agenda?" Each respondent was asked to provide a maximum of seven aspects and subsequently rank them in order of importance for reaching the climate goal mentioned in the question. In total, 155 respondents from academia, agencies, and industry provided their views on the matter. A clustering of the aspects in those responses, as outlined in Sect. 2, resulted in twenty-two criteria used for evaluating the aggregation methods in this paper.

The result of the survey could potentially have included 1085 value drivers, and we needed to find a way of reducing the responses into a set of functional criteria for subsequent use in a multi-criteria model for evaluating various future climate strategies as well as support a value-focused development of such strategies. The smallest value-driver cluster was obtained from seven different responses.

5   Results and Discussion

The aggregation and evaluation methods were implemented as a computer program. For each interpretation $\mathcal{I}_i$ of the criteria rank orderings (see Sect. 2.3), and for each aggregation technique, an aggregate $\mathcal{A}_i$ of the 155 respondents criteria rank orderings was computed according to the definitions in Sect. 2.4, with ± 3.0 standard deviations serving as the uncertainty interval. Then 10,000 samples were drawn from $\mathcal{A}_i$. Each sample was evaluated against each of the respondents' criteria rank orderings under I_i, based on the Kendall's τ distance and the sum of absolute differences (see Sect. 3). The means and standard deviations of the evaluations are presented in Table 1.

Note that the Kendall's τ distance is relatively high for the aggregation methods based on the average weights of the respondents' original rank orderings as well as their dummy-augmented counterpart. Similarly, there is a notable difference in the sum of absolute differences between the CAR-based aggregations and the other aggregation methods.

The flexible survey-based approach proposed herein requires a method for aggregating so-called relatively incomplete and possibly disjoint rank orderings. In this paper, we provide a number of solutions for aggregating such input for the purposes of decision analysis. The informed reasoning in Sect. 2.3 led to four different main approaches of interpreting the stakeholder input in terms of their individual (relatively incomplete and possibly disjoint) rank orderings for aggregation purposes; cardinal extensions (in nine selected sub-approaches), dummy-augmented, regular extension, and respondents' original rank orderings. Subsequently, two different approaches to aggregate weights were identified, leading to 24 instances of aggregation techniques—of which 10 pairs essentially are the same (see Sect. 2.4)—subject to an evaluation using data from a climate action case.

Table 1. The results of 10,000 simulations with an evaluation based on sums of absolute differences and the Kendall's τ distance. The cardinally extended criteria rank orderings (CAR) are denoted by a pair, $(\succ_i, \succ_j)$, where $\succ_i$ holds between the criteria in the respondents' rank orderings while $\succ_j$ holds between the former and the rank ordering extensions.

Aggregation method	Mean SAD	SD SAD	Mean τ	SD τ
Sum of weights (CAR, $\succ_1$, $\succ_1$)	0.423	0.003	0.1092	0.0023
Average weight (CAR, $\succ_1$,$\succ_1$)	0.423	0.003	0.1093	0.0023
Sum of weights (CAR, $\succ_2$,$\succ_1$)	0.430	0.005	0.1102	0.0026
Average weight (CAR, $\succ_2$,$\succ_1$)	0.430	0.004	0.1102	0.0026
Sum of weights (CAR, $\succ_3$,$\succ_1$)	0.445	0.008	0.1107	0.0028
Average weight (CAR, $\succ_3$,$\succ_1$)	0.445	0.008	0.1107	0.0028
Sum of weights (CAR, $\succ_1$,$\succ_2$)	0.503	0.004	0.1086	0.0020
Average weight (CAR, $\succ_1$,$\succ_2$)	0.503	0.004	0.1086	0.0020
Sum of weights (CAR, $\succ_2$,$\succ_2$)	0.504	0.005	0.1096	0.0024
Average weight (CAR, $\succ_2$,$\succ_2$)	0.504	0.005	0.1096	0.0024
Sum of weights (CAR, $\succ_3$,$\succ_2$)	0.511	0.006	0.1101	0.0026
Average weight (CAR, $\succ_3$,$\succ_2$)	0.511	0.006	0.1101	0.0026
Sum of weights (CAR, $\succ_2$,$\succ_3$)	0.571	0.005	0.1091	0.0022
Average weight (CAR, $\succ_2$,$\succ_3$)	0.571	0.005	0.1092	0.0022
Sum of weights (CAR, $\succ_3$,$\succ_3$)	0.573	0.006	0.1098	0.0025
Average weight (CAR, $\succ_3$,$\succ_3$)	0.573	0.006	0.1097	0.0024
Sum of weights (CAR, $\succ_1$,$\succ_3$)	0.574	0.005	0.1084	0.0019
Average weight (CAR, $\succ_1$,$\succ_3$)	0.574	0.005	0.1084	0.0019
Sum of weights (dummy augmented)	1.222	0.006	0.1036	0.0005
Average weight (extended)	1.382	0.006	0.1093	0.0023
Sum of weights (extended)	1.383	0.006	0.1093	0.0023
Average weight (dummy augmented)	1.385	0.007	0.1415	0.0093
Sum of weights (respondents' rank orderings)	1.425	0.009	0.1050	0.0010
Average weights (respondents' rank orderings)	1.580	0.011	0.1418	0.0098

The 24 techniques were assessed by first calculating the Kendall's τ distance between each respondent's rank ordering and a sample rank ordering that was generated from the aggregate weight distribution. That resulted in a mean statistic equal to or less than 0.15 for all 24 techniques, but none below 0.1036, indicating a quite satisfying average distance between the aggregate and the stakeholders' rank orderings. Thus, allowing for relatively incomplete and possibly disjoint rank orderings does not seem to be an issue for the proposed rank aggregation techniques. There is, however, a relatively large difference between the aggregation techniques based on the average and the sum of weights for the non-extended variants. The weight distributions based on the average are comparatively flat, i.e., the criteria' mean weights are close to one another.

The distributions based on the sum present a much greater diversity. Therefore, it is easier to generate rank orderings from the former, opposite the respondents' rank orderings.

The second approach to evaluating the aggregation methods was by calculating the mean of the sums of absolute differences. Here, there was a notable jump between the aggregation methods based on a cardinal extension to the other techniques. Using an aggregation method based only on the actual responses is evidently producing the largest sums of absolute differences relative to this paper's case data. However, an aggregation method based on a cardinal extension, with a single step between the least important element that is explicitly ranked by a stakeholder and the extension, marginally outperforms the harsher treatment of elements in the extension when the number of steps increases. A likely explanation is that the aggregation methods based on CAR-extended rank orderings distribute the weights more evenly relative to the other aggregation methods while maintaining the relative order of the means.

6   Concluding Remarks

When it comes to applications of multi-stakeholder multi-criteria decision analysis, it is a balancing act between the formalism of the model and the feasibility of retrieving views and preferences of a large number of diverse stakeholders to be included in the model. This is especially true when there is an aspiration to reach out to a wide spectrum of public stakeholders during a limited time frame and with limited resources. When the structure of the protocol for interacting with stakeholders is largely predefined and, in turn, less flexible from the stakeholders' perspective, the level of involvement in the problem formulation is reduced.

Based upon the results of this study, we believe that certain applications of participatory decision analysis can benefit from adopting survey-based elicitation practices where stakeholders simultaneously provide their views regarding the bases on which alternatives should be evaluated and their relative importance. In particular, for applications of MAMCA where stakeholder groups are asked explicitly for input to a common decision model and where constraints on resources or cognitive efforts limit the use of more elaborate elicitation approaches. Given the case data, we found that the normalized sum approach is advantageous compared to the approach based on the normalized mean when aggregating the criteria rank-order weights. Furthermore, cardinally extended criteria rank orderings fare much better in terms of the sum of absolute differences while only slightly worse, in some cases, when considering the Kendall's τ distance. Future research will include applying the proposed techniques to develop generic criteria sets and weight rank orderings for decision analysis of municipal climate action strategies.

References

1. Bana, E., Costa, C.A.: The use of multi-criteria decision analysis to support the search for less conflicting policy options in a multi-actor context: case study. J. Multi-Criteria Decis. Anal. **10**(2), 145–162 (2001)
2. Barron, F.H., Barrett, B.E.: Decision quality using ranked attribute weights. Manage. Sci. **42**(11), 1501–1625 (1996)
3. Choo, E.U., Schoner, B., Wedley, W.C.: Interpretation of criteria weights in multicriteria decision making. Comput. Ind. Eng. **37**(3), 527–541 (1999)
4. Danielson, M., Ekenberg, L.: Rank ordering methods for multi-criteria decisions. In: Zaraté, P., Kersten, G.E., Hernández, J.E. (eds.) GDN 2014. LNBIP, vol. 180, pp. 128–135. Springer, Cham (2014). https://doi.org/10.1007/978-3-319-07179-4_14
5. Danielson, M., Ekenberg, L.: Using surrogate weights for handling preference strength in multi-criteria decisions. In: Kamiński, B., Kersten, G.E., Szapiro, T. (eds.) GDN 2015. LNBIP, vol. 218, pp. 107–118. Springer, Cham (2015). https://doi.org/10.1007/978-3-319-19515-5_9
6. Danielson, M., Ekenberg, L.: A robustness study of state-of-the-art surrogate weights for mcdm. Group Decis. Negot. **26**(4), 677–691 (2017)
7. Fasth, T., Larsson, A., Ekenberg, L., Danielson, M.: Measuring conflicts using cardinal ranking: An application to decision analytic conflict evaluations. Adv. Decis. Sci. **2018**, 1–14 (2018)
8. French, S., Ríos Insua, D., Ruggeri, F.: e-participation and decision analysis. Decis. Anal. **4**(4), 173–273 (2007)
9. Kilgour, D.M., Chen, Y., Hipel, K.W.: Multiple criteria approaches to group decision and negotiation. In: Ehrgott, M., Figueira, J.R., Greco, S. (eds.) Trends in Multiple Criteria Decision Analysis, pp. 317–338. Springer, Boston (2010) https://doi.org/10.1007/978-1-4419-5904-1_11
10. Lotov, A.V.: Internet tools for supporting of lay stakeholders in the framework of the democratic paradigm of environmental decision making. J. Multi-Criteria Decis. Anal. **12**(2–3), 145–162 (2003)
11. Macharis, C., Turcksin, L., Lebeau, K.: Multi actor multi criteria analysis (mamca) as a tool to support sustainable decisions: state of use. Decis. Support Syst. **54**(1), 610–620 (2012)
12. Pihur, V., Datta, S., Datta, S.: Rankaggreg, an r package for weighted rank aggregation. BMC Bioinform. **10**(1), 62 (2009)
13. Riabacke, M., Åström, J., Grönlund, Å.: Eparticipation galore? - extending multicriteria decision analysis to the public. Int. J. Public Inf. Syst. **7**(2), 79–99 (2011)
14. Riabacke, M., Danielson, M., Ekenberg, L., Larsson, A.: A prescriptive approach for eliciting imprecise weight statements in an MCDA process. In: Rossi, F., Tsoukias, A. (eds.) ADT 2009. LNCS (LNAI), vol. 5783, pp. 168–179. Springer, Heidelberg (2009). https://doi.org/10.1007/978-3-642-04428-1_15
15. Riabacke, M., Ekenberg, L., Danielson, M.: State-of-the-art prescriptive criteria weight elicitation. Adv. Decis. Sci. **2012**, 1–24 (2012)
16. Salo, A., Hämäläinen, R.P.: Multicriteria decision analysis in group decision processes. In: Kilgour, D.M., Eden, C. (eds.) Handbook of Group Decision and Negotiation, pp. 269–283. Springer, Dordrecht (2010) https://doi.org/10.1007/978-90-481-9097-3_16
17. Stillwell, W.G., Seaver, D.A., Edwards, W.: A comparison of weight approximation techniques in multiattribute utility decision making. Organ. Behav. Hum. Perform. **28**(1), 62–77 (1981)

18. Tervonen, T., Lahdelma, R.: Implementing stochastic multicriteria acceptability analysis. Eur. J. Oper. Res. **178**(2), 500–513 (2007)
19. Webber, W., Moffat, A., Zobel, J.: A similarity measure for indefinite rankings. ACM Trans. Inf. Syst. (TOIS) **28**(4), 1–38 (2010)
20. Weber, M., Borcherding, K.: Behavioral influences on weight judgments in multi-attribute decision making. Eur. J. Oper. Res. **28**, 1–12 (1993)

Prioritizing Improvement Actions in a Fish Distribution Company: Integrating Elicitation by Decomposition and Holistic Evaluation with FITradeoff Method

Marina Carvalhedo Correia, Eduarda Asfora Frej$^{(\boxtimes)}$,
and Adiel Teixeira de Almeida

Universidade Federal de Pernambuco – UFPE, CDSID - Center for Decision Systems and
Information Development, Av. Acadêmico Hélio Ramos, s/n – Cidade Universitária,
Recife, PE 50.740-530, Brazil
eafrej@cdsid.org.br

Abstract. In this paper, a prioritization problem of strategic improvement actions of a Fresh Fish Distribution Company (FFDC) is approached. Improvement actions to be prioritized are defined based on critical success factors derived from the SWOT analysis of the company, conducted by multiple stakeholders of the organization. Four criteria were defined to evaluate these actions, and then the FITradeoff (Flexible and Interactive Tradeoff) multicriteria method is applied to aid the decision process and preferences assessment. This method works based on partial information of the DMs to elicit criteria scaling constants in additive models, considering structured elicitation process based on tradeoffs. Throughout an interactive Decision Support System (DSS), this work illustrates how the decision process can be carried out with FITradeoff based on an integration of two paradigms in preference modeling: elicitation by decomposition and holistic evaluations.

Keywords: Strategic planning · Multicriteria decision making/aiding (MCDM/A) · Preference modeling · FITradeoff method

1 Introduction

The use of multiple criteria decision making/aiding (MCDM/A) methods to conduct strategic planning in organizations is extremely useful due to the multiple factors that are inherently involved and conflicting with each other. This work focuses on the strategic planning of a Fresh Fish Distribution Company (FFDC), situated in Brazil, which has the need to prioritize improvement actions in a systematic way, so that costs with minor actions that could result in waste of time or cause an insignificant impact on its profit margin, are avoided.

This work is conducted based on two main phases. In the first phase, the strategic planning of the company is conducted based on an interaction of multiple stakeholders of FFDC. This is carried out throughout a SWOT analysis that resulted in the listing

© Springer Nature Switzerland AG 2021
D. C. Morais et al. (Eds.): GDN 2021, LNBIP 420, pp. 41–54, 2021.
https://doi.org/10.1007/978-3-030-77208-6_4

of critical success factors that allowed the verification of the external and internal environment. A situational diagnosis is then defined and improvement actions are derived from those success factors. These actions express multifaceted objectives that conflict with each other and compose most of the decision problems faced by organizations. Therefore, after that, the second phase of this work consists of the prioritization of such improvement actions derived from the strategic analysis, throughout a multicriteria decision approach, in order to provide a structured methodology to support managers of FFDC in their decisions.

Using multicriteria decision tools for aiding strategic planning is a quite common in the literature [1–3]. In order to conduct the multicriteria analysis for prioritization of actions in FFDC, the FITradeoff method for the ranking problematic was applied [4, 5]. This method works based on partial information of the DMs, saving time and cognitive effort during the elicitation process. The FITradeoff method was extensively applied in the literature, and has shown to be a useful tool to solve practical problems such as supplier selection problems [6]; selection of strategic information systems [7]; scheduling problems [8]; selection of agricultural technology packages [9]; problems in the energy sector [10, 11]; portfolio selection problems [12], among others.

In this paper, a particular feature of the FITradeoff method is illustrated. The possibility of integrating elicitation by decomposition and holistic evaluation during the process is explored [13], as a way of shortening the decision process and providing insightful information for DMs through graphical visualization given by the Decision Support System (DSS) based on which the method is operated.

This work is structured as follows. Section 2 first presents the description of the context in which FFDC in emerged, and the construction of the SWOT matrix as part of the strategic planning of the company; then, the improvement actions derived from this step are described as multicriteria decision alternatives. Section 3 describes the application of the FITradeoff method to construct a ranking of the alternatives, illustrating how the integration of holistic evaluation and elicitation by decomposition can be made to facilitate the decision process. Finally, Section 4 presents the final remarks of this paper.

2   Structuring the Problem

2.1   FFDC Diagnosis and Context

The Fresh Fish Distribution Company treated in this paper operates in two different activities within the same industrial sector, one is the physical distribution of fish and shrimp, and the other, the production of fish (Tilapia) and shrimp in two different farms, activities that fit in the cultivation of aquatic organisms under controlled conditions, called Aquaculture. The Company is a family business that has a production director at the top of its organization chart, responsible for the farms where the final product is grown, and at the same level, a commercial director, responsible for the Logistics Warehouse, which is defined by the place for landing, processing and storage of fish, before taken to final customers.

The organization has two points of production or product industry which are located in different Brazilian states, one in Guadalupi in the state of Piauí, Boa Esperança farm (Tilapia fish) and the other in the state of Ceará, Lagoa Grande farm (shrimp), in Alto Santo. This latter state also houses the Logistics Warehouse, located in the municipality of Aquiraz. This work focuses on the activities of handling, storage and order processing of final products, which [14] defines by "Physical Distribution", carried out from the Logistics Warehouse until their arrival to customers, which are composed by supermarkets, restaurants, market stalls, wholesalers and industrial kitchens.

Throughout its existence, the company under study has faced at least three major crises. The first, characterized by the drought in the northeastern states of Brazil, which lasted from 2012 until 2017, forced the Production Director to transfer the cultivation of Tilapia from the Castanhão dam in the state of Ceará to the Guadalupe dam in the state of Piauí. The decrease in water levels in dams affects its quality and makes it difficult to grow fish. This attitude, essential for maintaining the business, resulted in high extra costs not accounted in the company's strategic planning. Still for reasons related to the drought of that period, there was a limitation in the water grants granted by the State of Ceará, also harming the cultivation of shrimp, since the activities of the industry were paralyzed until the concession of water.

The economic crisis that started in 2014, with a slight recovery in 2018, culminated in the truckers' strike that same year, greatly affecting the company's logistics, causing it to lose loads of its fished. In addition, the last and not least crisis, was the arrival of the "white spot" in the state of Ceará in the middle of 2017. This is the disease of captive shrimp, caused by a virus that manifests itself in the initial stages of its growth, causing its death and entire productions to be lost even before reaching the final consumer. This latest crisis forced the company to change its production techniques by building equipment that prevents contamination of the product allowing its healthy growth for commercialization.

Some evidence about this business justifies the practical application of management philosophies. In 2019, the fish distribution company, defined in the initial presentation of this text as the Logistics Warehouse and which, as mentioned, will be the object of study of this work, found itself in a situation of recurring loss of customers due to lack of certifications required by them. In that same year, there was a 4.9% growth in the production of Tilapia in Brazil, taking it to the position of fourth largest producer in the world. For this reason, the species started to represent 57% of the national fish production, going beyond the production of native fish.

Another important evidence was the increase in exports of fish farming by 26% in 2019. The recurring loss of customers and the promising indexes of the sector combined with the benefits in food security, arouse in the directors, who own the company, the immediate need to formalize its procedures and seek management techniques that allow it to mature in a sustainable manner, seeking continuous improvement of its processes. This will facilitate the conquest of new customers in the domestic and foreign markets, which can occur through quality certifications and implementation of sustainable management philosophies.

According to Slack et al. [15], companies that wish to expand and become competitive, seek management and quality management techniques that promote relevant productivity indicators, by reducing waste that can provide cheaper operations throughout the entire production chain. Thus, it is easy to conclude that these operations will have their costs reduced through the implementation of methods, tools, philosophies or management systems that best suit the needs and reality of the organization. Therefore, these management techniques need to undergo a previous study in order to be implemented in an assertive manner, without generating unnecessary costs or wasting time.

2.2 SWOT Analysis and MCDM Modeling

Given the context in which FFDC is emerged, it is necessary to, first of all, prepare a diagnosis of the company, to later prioritize the actions to be implemented. For this, the strategic planning accomplished in the year 2020 by multiple stakeholders of the company, resulted in the elaboration of the SWOT analysis and consequently in the organization's SWOT matrix.

The SWOT analysis is a tool that allows checking the internal and external environment of the company, analyzing scenarios and defining a situational diagnosis. This technique allows its strategic positioning through the identification of the strengths, weaknesses, opportunities and threats and results in the listing of its critical success factors. The elaboration of the SWOT matrix of FFDC was conducted during the strategic planning of the company, in which three internal stakeholders of the managerial level were reunited in a meeting to discuss such aspects. The strategic planning is annually conducted by the stakeholders of the company; time consumption in such exercise is already considered in their schedule. A brainstorming approach was followed in order to derive the success factors and subsequent improvement actions, that were considered as alternatives to prioritize. The evaluation criteria were also considered from a group-view perspective based on this brainstorming. The SWOT matrix is illustrated in Fig. 1.

Strengths	Synergy between business	Weaknesses	Absence of well-defined processes
	Mechanization of production processes		New team in training
	Adequate infrastructure		Lack of logistical leadership
	Consumer loyalty		Tilapia survival problems
	Credibility in the freshed fish market		Boxes Restriction
	Distribution regularity		High production cost
	Customer portfolio		High logistical cost
	Reliable larvae supplier (shrimp)		High financial cost
	Technical knowledge (tilapia)		High indebtedness level
Oportunities	Concern about healthy eating	Threats	Low water availability due to drought
	Demand in the foreign market		Government's restrictive position on water use
	Interest of laboratories in developing vaccines (tilapia)		WS and nin diseases (shrimp)
	Growth of the frozen fish market		Market opening (Import)
	Low verticalization of enterprises located in the Northeast region		Local public insecurity (theft)
	Access to fish suppliers to expand the product mix		Rapid development of the production chain
			Low number of fry suppliers
			Increased inspection of fished with SIF requirement
			High competition
			Informal trade
			Economic crisis

Fig. 1. SWOT analysis of FFDC

After performing the SWOT analysis, improvement actions that could be derived from the success factors that appeared in the SWOT analysis were defined as the alternatives to be prioritized. As a result of this process, 21 actions were defined, as illustrated in Table 1.

Table 1. Improvement actions derived from the SWOT analysis

SWOT analysis	Critical success factors	Alternatives	
Strengths	Consumer loyalty	A1	Create process for measuring customer satisfaction
	Customer portfolio	A2	Implement top manager to increase productivity, thus enabling the increase of this portfolio
		A3	Investment in sales training for employees to play a commercial role, increasing the customer portfolio
	Credibility in the fresh fish market	A4	Implement ISO 9001 QMS to monitor the main processes for quality control, thus maintaining this credibility
Weaknesses	Lack of logistical leadership/High logistical cost	A5	Hire consultancy with logistics expertise to suggest new models of logistics approach
	Tilapia survival problems	A6	Development of new fry suppliers
		A7	Continued development with the most efficient vaccines against type 3 streptococci
	Restriction of fish storage boxes	A8	Develop box return control method
	High production cost	A9	Implementation of new animal feeding methodologies, using automatic feeders, minimizing labor for feeding
		A10	Development of new feed suppliers
Threats	Tilapia Diseases	A11	Evaluate results of the effectiveness of vaccines performed in Tilapia
		A12	Decrease production costs- Double the capacity of the pumping system to exchange and supply water to the nurseries, allowing these actions to be carried out at dawn with lower electricity rates
	Local public insecurity (theft)	A13	Increase number of reflectors
		A14	Extend video monitoring system by cameras

(*continued*)

Table 1. (*continued*)

SWOT analysis	Critical success factors	Alternatives	
	Increased inspection of fish	A15	Hire Food Engineering Consultancy, Fisheries Engineer, professional specialized in preparing projects for the implantation of a refrigerator and obtaining the SIF issued by MAPA, as this seal ensures the quality of edible products of animal origin, destined for the internal and external market
		A16	Implement refrigerator design
Opportunities	Concern with Healthy Eating	A17	Reinforce Marketing actions with healthy dishes options using the company's products
	Demand in the foreign market	A18	Hire consultancy in the area of foreign trade to conduct market research thus identifying potential buyers and their requirements, in addition to an economic/financial feasibility study for the expansion
		A19	BAP certification (Best Aquaculture Practices)
	Access to fish suppliers to expand the product mix	A20	Prospect producers by identifying production levels for each one to make commercial arrangements and get the fish to process
		A21	Prospect certified slaughterhouses to process this fish and carry out an economic/financial feasibility study for expanding the product mix

It is worth mentioning that the improvements actions that can be taken by the company can be interconnected, in the sense that implementing a package of several actions can bring more benefits than the implementation of individual actions. However, the proposed approach considers actions as independent from each other, as well as their individual benefits. The main goal here is to build a ranking of the actions in order to have an idea of which of them should be prioritized, according to the company's objectives.

In order to establish the criteria based on which these actions could be evaluated, maximizing the company's profit margin was consider as the main objective. To achieve this larger and general objective, specific objectives such as reducing the cost of buying fish feed, reducing the costs of creation of the animal in the production farms, minimization of the costs involved for freight and consolidation of the brand in the market, were considered giving rise to the establishment of four criteria for this problem:

C1 - *Cost of implementation:* it is the amount paid in local currency to implement an improvement action, considered fundamental since the company's resources are limited and since low cost actions can often represent high financial returns.

C2 - *Time of implementation:* it is the time necessary to implement an action, also considered fundamental, since the company identifies an erosion of its customers to its competitors as urgent in improving processes.

C3 - *Difficulty of implementation:* some of the actions described may require specific technical knowledge not known to the organization or run into government bureaucracy.

C4 - *Benefits and relevance for the company:* this criterion is fundamental for evaluating the prioritization of actions, since all related actions are important for the organization's growth, but not all are considered urgent.

Table 2. Consequences matrix

Alternatives	Cost of implementation (C1)	Time of implementation (C2)	Implementation difficulty (C3)	Benefits and relevance for the company (C4)
A1	5	5	5	4
A2	2	1	2	5
A3	3	3	4	5
A4	3	3	3	4
A5	2	4	4	4
A6	4	3	3	5
A7	1	1	1	5
A8	3	3	3	3
A9	2	2	2	5
A10	5	5	4	5
A11	5	4	3	4
A12	2	2	3	5
A13	4	3	5	3
A14	4	3	3	4
A15	3	1	2	5
A16	1	2	2	5
A17	3	3	4	5
A18	3	2	4	4
A19	1	2	2	5
A20	4	2	3	4
A21	3	3	3	4

All criteria were defined a 5-point Likert scale, according to which the alternatives were evaluated. The consequences matrix illustrated in Table 2 shows the evaluation of the alternatives in each criterion.

3 Prioritizing Improvement Actions with FITradeoff

3.1 FITradeoff Method

The FITradeoff (Flexible and Interactive Tradeoff) multicriteria method was developed with the aim of facilitating the decision-making process by requiring partial information about the decision makers' preferences, throughout a structured elicitation process based on tradeoffs [4, 5].

This method was built upon the axiomatic structure of the classical tradeoff procedure [16], but improves its applicability for DMs with easier elicitation questions. In the classical tradeoff, to determine criteria scale constants, the DM needs to specify the exact point of indifference between two consequences, which makes this a high cognitive demanding. Therefore, although this procedure has a robust axiomatic structure [17], it presents high rates of inconsistency when applied, due to the high level of cognitive effort required. This issue motivated the development of the FITradeoff method, which works based on comparison of consequences considering strict preference statements, rather than indifference, which facilitates the process. Moreover, FITradeoff allows intracriteria value functions to be non-linear, different from other partial information methods in the literature.

The FITradeoff method is operated by means of a Decision Support System (DSS). Throughout an interactive process with the decision maker, the DSS puts questions for the DM so that he/she has to compare consequences by considering tradeoffs amongst criteria, following the traditional elicitation by decomposition protocol. The statements given by the DM when answering such questions allow the achievement of a weights space that is reduced as more questions of strict preference are answered [4]. Based on the information provided, FITradeoff uses linear programming (LP) models in order to compute a recommendation to the DM. Depending on the problematic being treated, the LP model formulation may change. For the choice problematic, the LP model searches for potentially optimal alternatives at each interaction [4]. For the ranking problematic, the LP model searches for dominance relations between alternatives in order to build a ranking of them [5]. The FITradeoff DSS also provides graphical visualization of partial results during the process, which allows DMs to perform holistic assessments in order to fasten the decision process.

3.2 Decision Process: Integrating Elicitation by Decomposition and Holistic Evaluation

The FITradeoff method for the ranking problematic was applied to rank the actions defined by the stakeholders to FFDC to be prioritized. The preferences of the owner of FFDC were elicited, and the whole process was guided by an analyst with well background on MCDM and on FITradeoff method. The first information given by the DM is the ranking of criteria scaling constants, which should be performed by considering the ranges of consequences. The ranking was defined as follows.

$$k_{C1} > k_{C2} > k_{C3} > k_{C4} \tag{1}$$

Then, the DSS starts asking the DM questions, asking him to compare different consequences, considering tradeoffs amongst criteria. The first question put for the DM was a comparison between a consequence with an intermediate outcome of criterion C1 (C1 = 3) and the worst outcome in all other criteria, and another consequence with the best outcome of criterion C4 (C4 = 5) and the worst outcome in all other criteria; the DM chose preference for the latter. In the second question, the DM was asked to choose between a consequence with an intermediate outcome of criterion C1 (C1 = 4) and the worst outcome in all other criteria, and another consequence with the best outcome of criterion C2 (C2 = 5) and the worst outcome in all other criteria; the DM also chose preference for the latter.

Figure 2 illustrates the third elicitation question put by the DSS, as part of the elicitation by decomposition process. In this figure, the DM is asked to compare two consequences: consequence A, with an intermediate outcome of criterion C2 (Time of implementation) and the worst outcome for all other criteria; and consequence B, with the best outcome for criterion C3 (Difficulty of implementation) and the worst outcome in all other criteria.

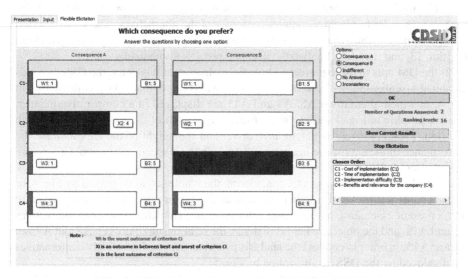

Fig. 2. Elicitation by decomposition in FITradeoff DSS

In the right side of the screen in Fig. 2 it is possible to see that this is the third question put for the DM (two other questions have been answered already), and sixteen ranking levels were obtained at this point. By clicking on the button "show current results", the DM has the possibility to analyze the partial ranking obtained until that point. Figure 3 illustrates these partial results throughout a Hasse diagram of the alternatives, which is displayed by FITradeoff DSS. This diagram allows the dominance relations found by the LP models to be visualized by the DM. Directed arrows indicate a dominance relation; nondirected lines (such as the ones in Position 5 and Position 10 of the ranking) indicate indifference relations between alternatives. The absence of an arrow in alternatives that belong to the same position in the ranking indicates that, for the current level of information obtained until that point, those alternatives are still incomparable (i.e., none of them dominates the other). This can be illustrated by the alternatives that belong to Position 13, in which A8 is incomparable to A15 and to A9.

By analyzing the Hasse diagram in Fig. 3, it can be seen that, in order to obtain a complete preorder of the alternatives, the incomparabilities in Position 13 should be solved. Alternatives A8 and A15 are still incomparable to each other; and A8 and A9 are also incomparable to each other. Therefore, it is not possible to define whether of these three situations would be more appropriate: situation 1 with A8 in position 13, A15 in position 14 and A9 in position 15; situation 2 with A15 in position 13, A9 in position 14 and A8 in position 15 or situation 3 with A15 in position 13, A8 in position 14 and A9 in position 15. This is why these three alternatives remain in the same position of the ranking.

At this point, the flexilibility of the FITradeoff DSS allows the DM to deal with this issue in two different possible manners [13]. The first one is to continue answering questions similar to that of Fig. 2, until the information provided by the DM is suffient to define dominance relations through the LP models and complete the ranking. In this way, it is not possible to predict how many aditional judgments from the DM would be necessary in order to obtain a complete preorder of the alternatives. The second option is to perform a hoslitic evaluation between those alternatives that are incomparable in Position 13, and therefore finalize the decision process immediately.

If the DM opts to try to perform a holistic evaluation at this point, the DSS provides graphical visualization with the alternatives he wants to compare. This is illustrated in Fig. 4, in which alternatives A8, A9 and A15 are displayed in a comparative manner. The bar graphic in Fig. 4 shows the performance of each of these alternatives in each criterion. Each color represents an alternative, and the height of the bars indicate the performance of the alternative in a ratio 0–1 scale in the respective criterion. Criteria are ordered from left to right.

The DM can make the analysis considering the whole set, as displayed by Fig. 4, or he can choose a subset of these alternatives to analyze, pairwise. This makes more sense in the present case, since a dominance relation is already defined between alternatives A9 and A15, and the objective here is to define the relationships between A8 and A9 and A8 and A15. In order to conduct the analysis pairwise, bar graphics with two alternatives are displayed by the DSS, as illustrated by Fig. 5.

The graphic on the right side of Fig. 5 shows a comparison between A8 and A15, while the graphic on the left side shows a comparison between A8 and A9. By comparing A8 and A15, it is possible to see that these alternatives are tied in the first-ranked criterion, but A8 has a significant advantage in the second and third-ranked criteria, while A15 beats A8 only on the last-ranked criterion. In this sense, the DM could define preference for A8 over A15, such that a dominance relation would be holistically defined. A similar

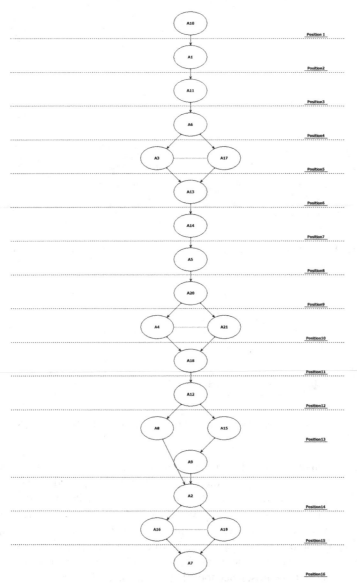

Fig. 3. Partial ranking displayed by FITradeoff DSS

analysis could be conducted for the comparison between A8 and A9, in which A8 has advantage in three out of four criteria.

By defining those dominance relations through holistic evaluation, a complete pre-order of the alternatives would be obtained at this point, since the incomparability relations that appeared in position 13 would be solved. In this sense, the elicitation process would be completed, with only two elicitation questions answered by the DM, besides these holistic judgments.

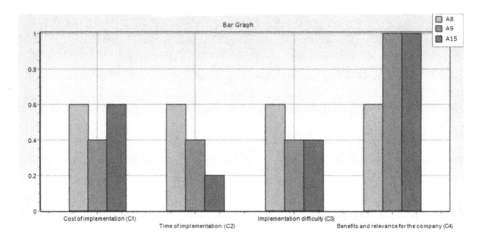

Fig. 4. Bar graphic to compare alternatives in Position 13 (FITradeoff DSS)

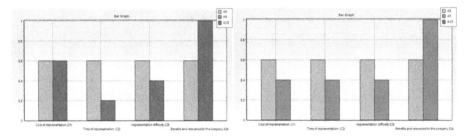

Fig. 5. Bar graphics to compare alternatives pairwise (FITradeoff DSS)

It should be highlighted that, even though the holistic evaluation may feasten the decision process, the key feature of the FITradeoff DSS is to provide flexibility for the DM, so that he can choose which way to follow: continue the elicitation by decomposition or to perform holistic assessments. However, if the DM did not feel confident to perform such analysis, he could continue the elicitation by decomposition, and answer questions until those incomparabilities were solved. The role of an analyst in this process to guide the DM and advise him on whether to perform a hoslitic evaluation or not is crucial, and behavioral studies with neuroscience tools have concentrated efforts on this theme [18].

4   Final Remarks

This paper presented an application of the FITradeoff method to order improvement actions of a fish distribution company, considering the strategic planning of the organization to model the MCDM problem. Decision alternatives were derived from critical success factors stablished on the SWOT analysis performed by multiple stakeholders of the organization. Then, preferences of the owner of the company were elicited following the decision protocol of the FITradeoff method. The FITradeoff decision support system was used a support tool for the elicitation process. Using a structured methodology to aid the prioritization of actions in FFDC was truly valuable for the owners, according to their feedback and perception after the application of the method. Regarding the implementation of the improvement actions that were analyzed in this problem, it will now depend on resources availability of the company considering its particular aspects.

The application presented in this paper illustrated how the FITradeoff method combines two paradigms of preference modeling on its structure: elicitation by decomposition and holistic evaluation. The flexibility of the FITradeoff DSS allows the DM to follow different ways during the decision process. Graphical visualization is provided in order to aid users in their decisions. For the problem addressed in this paper, a complete preorder of the alternatives was achieved after two elicitation questions answered, and a final holistic assessment to conclude the decision process. It should be highlighted that holistic assessments can be used not only to finalize the decision process, but in the middle of the process as well, in order to supply the mathematical model with additional information and reduce the space of weights even more, fastening the elicitation process [13]. The FITradeoff system can be downloaded for free at www.fitradeoff.org.

As deeply discussed by [13], the integration of those two types of preference modeling is an innovative aspect present in the FITradeoff, since other methods usually adopt one of those two types to follow. These two paradigms of preference modeling can jointly bring improvements to the decision-making process, including the possibility of shortening it, saving time and effort from DMs.

Acknowledgments. The authors are most grateful for CNPq and CAPES, for the financial support provided.

References

1. Parreiras, R.O., Ekel, P.Y., Morais, D.C.: Fuzzy set based consensus schemes for multicriteria group decision making applied to strategic planning. Group Decis. Negot. **21**(2), 153–183 (2012). https://doi.org/10.1007/s10726-011-9231-0
2. Tsyganok, V., Kadenko, S., Andriychuk, O., Roik, P.: Usage of multicriteria decision-making support arsenal for strategic planning in environmental protection sphere. J. Multi-Criteria Decis. Anal. **24**(5–6), 227–238 (2017)
3. Stewart, T.J., French, S., Rios, J.: Integrating multicriteria decision analysis and scenario planning—review and extension. Omega **41**(4), 679–688 (2013)
4. de Almeida, A.T., de Almeida, J.A., Costa, A.P.C.S., de Almeida-Filho, A.T.: A new method for elicitation of criteria weights in additive models: flexible and interactive tradeoff. Eur. J. Oper. Res. **250**, 179–191 (2016). https://doi.org/10.1016/j.ejor.2015.08.058
5. Frej, E., de Almeida, A., Costa, A.: Using data visualization for ranking alternatives with partial information and interactive tradeoff elicitation. Oper. Res. **19**(4), 909–931 (2019). https://doi.org/10.1007/s12351-018-00444-2
6. Frej, E.A., Roselli, L.R.P., de Almeida, J.A., de Almeida, A.T.: A multicriteria decision model for supplier selection in a food industry based on FITradeoff method. Math. Prob. Eng. **2017**, 1–9 (2017)
7. Gusmao, A.P.H., Pereira Medeiros, C.: A model for selecting a strategic information system using the FITradeoff. Math. Prob. Eng. **2016**, 1–7 (2016)

8. Pergher, I., Frej, E.A., Roselli, L.R.P., de Almeida, A.T.: Integrating simulation and FITradeoff method for scheduling rules selection in job-shop production systems. Int. J. Prod. Econ. **227**, 107669 (2020). https://doi.org/10.1016/j.ijpe.2020.107669

9. Carrillo, P.A.A., Roselli, L.R.P., Frej, E.A., de Almeida, A.T.: Selecting an agricultural technology package based on the flexible and interactive tradeoff method. Ann. Oper. Res. (2018). https://doi.org/10.1007/s10479-018-3020-y

10. Kang, T.H.A., Soares, A.M.C., Jr., De Almeida, A.T.: Evaluating electric power generation technologies: A multicriteria analysis based on the FITradeoff method. Energy **165**, 10–20 (2018)

11. Fossile, D.K., Frej, E.A., da Costa, S.E.G., de Lima, E.P., de Almeida, A.T.: Selecting the most viable renewable energy source for Brazilian ports using the FITradeoff method. J. Clean. Prod. **260**, 121107 (2020). https://doi.org/10.1016/j.jclepro.2020.121107

12. Frej, E.A., Ekel, P., de Almeida, A.T.: A benefit-to-cost ratio based approach for portfolio selection under multiple criteria with incomplete preference information. Inf. Sci. **545**, 487–498 (2021)

13. de Almeida, A., Frej, E., Roselli, L.: Combining holistic and decomposition paradigms in preference modeling with the flexibility of FITradeoff. CEJOR **29**(1), 7–47 (2021). https://doi.org/10.1007/s10100-020-00728-z

14. Ballou, R.H.: The evolution and future of logistics and supply chain management. Eur. Bus. Rev. **19**(4), 332–348 (2007)

15. Slack, N., Chambers, S., Johnston, R.: Operations Management. Pearson, Harlow (2010)

16. Keeney, R.L., Raiffa, H.: Decision Analysis with Multiple Conflicting Objectives. Wiley, New York (1976)

17. Weber, M., Borcherding, K.: Behavioural influences on weight judgments in multiattribute decision making. Eur. J. Oper. Res. **67**(1), 1–12 (1993)

18. Roselli, L., de Almeida, A., Frej, E.: Decision neuroscience for improving data visualization of decision support in the FITradeoff method. Oper. Res. **19**(4), 933–953 (2019). https://doi.org/10.1007/s12351-018-00445-1

Social Ranking Problem Based on Rankings of Restricted Coalitions

Takahiro Suzuki[1]([⊠]) and Masahide Horita[2]

[1] Department of Civil Engineering, The University of Tokyo, 7-3-1, Hongo,
Bunkyo-ku, Tokyo, Japan
`suzuki-tkenmgt@g.ecc.u-tokyo.ac.jp`
[2] Department of International Studies, Graduate School of Frontier Sciences,
The University of Tokyo. 5-1-5, Kashiwanoha, Kashiwashi, Chiba, Japan
`horita@g.ecc.u-tokyo.ac.jp`

Abstract. Evaluations of individuals; such as workers, researchers, team-sports athletes, etc.; are often based on the performance of their coalitions. The present paper will study the so-called ordinal social ranking problem; i.e., to determine the ordinal ranking of individuals according to the ordinal rankings of their coalitions. To be more specific, we study the problem with restricted domain of coalitions. It has earlier been proven that dominance (DOM) (if an alternative wins another alternative in every ceteris paribus comparison, social ranking must judge them in that way) and independence of irrelevant coalitions (IIC) will generate a dictatorship of coalition sizes. We will first prove that a similar dictatorship is generated as a result of weak DOM and IIC, under any domain of coalitions, as long as any two individuals can be compared ceterris paribus. Finally, we will study an extended problem for the ranking of the whole coalitions, e.g., determining the best coalitions for some award, and will prove that such a dictator must also be generated within this extended framework.

Keywords: Social ranking problem · Preference over coalitions · Arrow's impossibility theorem · Procedural choice

1 Introduction

In many practical situations, individuals are often judged based on the performances of coalitions. Researchers are often judged by their papers, which are often made in cooperation with other researchers; athletes in team sports are often judged by the team's records; the quality of group decisions might reflect the competence of a facilitator. While the numerical analysis in these contexts is a classic topic in cooperative game theory; say, the Banzhaf index [2], or the Shapley value [3]; it is only recently that its ordinal counterpart has developed. Moretti & Öztürk (2017) were the first to study the ordinal *social ranking problem*, i.e., to determine the appropriate function called the Social Ranking Solution (SRS), which maps each power relation (weak order over the power set) to a weak order over the base set. A benefit of such an ordinal counterpart is clear when it is difficult to determine the cardinal score of each coalition. Let us illustrate this by an example:

© Springer Nature Switzerland AG 2021
D. C. Morais et al. (Eds.): GDN 2021, LNBIP 420, pp. 55–67, 2021.
https://doi.org/10.1007/978-3-030-77208-6_5

Example 1 (ordinal social ranking problem). Let $X = \{1, 2, 3\}$ be the set of workers. When there is only *ordinal* ranking of each coalition $A \subseteq X$, say $23 \succ 31 \succ 12 \succ 1 \succ 2 \succ 3 \succ 123$, what is the appropriate social ranking of X, i.e., the ranking of individuals in X?

Moretti & Öztürk [1] introduces three properties:

- Dominance (DOM): if candidate i is at least as good as j in every ceteris paribus comparison, then i is socially at least as good as j.
- Symmetry (SYM): the social ranking between i and j should coincide with that of p and q whenever they are ranked in the same way, and
- Independence of Irrelevant Coalitions (IIC): the social ranking between i, j must be determined solely by their impacts when added to the same coalitions.

Several impossibilities concerning these conditions are demonstrated. One of them states that the combination of DOM and IIC leads to the existence of "dictatorial" size. A growing number of subsequent studies look into the design of normative SRSs, including

Table 1 Related literatures on SRS[a]

		Domain	Codomain	Results
General	Moretti & Öztürk [1]	$\mathcal{C}(2^X)$	$\mathcal{T}(X)$	DOM and IIC⇒size dictatorial, etc.
	Allouche et al. [8]	$\mathcal{T}(\mathcal{P})$ on $\mathcal{P} \subseteq 2^X$	$\mathcal{T}(X)$	LES is not manipulable, manipulation of OBI is NP-hard, etc.
CP-majority	Fayard & Ozturk [4]	$\mathcal{B}(2^X)$	$\mathcal{T}(X)$	Determine the prob of Condorcet-like cycle under CP-majority, etc.
	Haret et al. [5]	$\mathcal{B}(2^X)$	$\mathcal{T}(A)$	Characterize CP-majority with EC, N, and PR, etc.
LES	Bernardi et al. [6]	$\mathcal{T}(2^X)$	$\mathcal{T}(X)$	Characterize LES with N, CA, M, and IWS, etc.
Banzhaf	Khani et al. [7]	$\mathcal{L}(2^X)$	$\mathcal{T}(A)$	Characterize OBI with CA, N, and M, etc.

[a]In this table, we denote by $\mathcal{T}(\cdot)$ and $\mathcal{B}(\cdot)$ the set of all weak orders or binary relations over the base set, respectively. The domain of Moretti & Öztürk [1]'s SRS is on $\mathcal{C}(2^X) \subseteq \mathcal{T}(2^X)$.

Other abbreviations are as follows: EC (Equality of Coalitions), N (Neutrality), PR (Positive Responsiveness), CA (Coalitional Anonymity), M (Monotonicity), IWS (Independence from the Worst Set).

CP-majority [4, 5], lexicographic excellence solution (LES) [6], ordinal Banzhaf index (OBI) [7], etc. (Table 1).

The purpose of this paper is to develop the social ranking problem when the set of feasible coalitions is restricted and when there are multiple potential indicators (i.e., when more than one ordinal rankings of coalitions are given, because of some different standpoints. For instance, when there are several rankings of coalitions, $\succ_1, \succ_2, \ldots, \succ_n$ over the set of coalitions in Example 1). Our main contribution is that the counterpart of Arrow's impossibility theorem [9] in the context of social ranking problem, which is implied by Moretti & Öztürk [1], holds robustly even under such restricted domain of coalitions with multiple indicators.

Finally, we note that another interesting application of SRS is found in procedural choice. Nurmi [10] argues the procedural choice based on preferences over criteria. In one of such methods, Nurmi proposes to first determine the ranking $\succsim$ of criteria and then to take the intersection of criteria from top-ranked to the bottom-ranked in order to determine the best procedures. For instance, suppose Pareto $\succ$ IIA $\succ$ Condorcet Winner Criterion $\succ \cdots$. If there is a unique procedure satisfying Pareto, that is chosen. Otherwise, if there is a unique procedure satisfying Pareto and IIA, that is chosen, and so on. Let us formulate this procedure. Let X be the set of feasible decision procedures and $\mathcal{C} = \{\{x \in X \mid x \text{ satsifies } C\} : C \text{ is a criterion}\}$. Then, the second step of Nurmi's method can be regarded as a function from a ranking of $\mathcal{C} \subseteq 2^X$ to an element of X. From a social ranking problematic point of view, it is nothing but an SRS with restricted domain of coalitions. Furthermore, if the first step is taken into account, it can be interpreted as a function that maps each voter's preference profile over criteria, i.e., $\succ_1, \succ_2, \ldots, \succ_n$ over $\mathcal{C}$, to a ranking/the best element of X (see [11] for an axiomatic study of this whole process under dichotomous preferences over criteria). Therefore, to consider restricted domain of coalitions $\mathcal{C}$ and multiple indicators $1, 2, \ldots, n$ in social ranking problem has importance in the application of procedural choice.

This paper is organized as follows: Sect. 2 introduces the basic model. Sect. 3 shows several results on how the "dictator" is generated under such extended environments. As an extended model, Sect. 4 shows the corresponding impossibility when the ranking of the whole coalitions is required. Sect. 5 is for concluding remarks.

2 Basic Model

Let $X = \{1, 2, \ldots, m\}$ be the set of workers, where $3 \leq m < +\infty$ and $\mathcal{C} \subseteq 2^X$ be the nonempty set of all feasible coalitions. We also call $\mathcal{C}$ as the domain of coalitions. Let $N = \{1, 2, \ldots, n\}$ ($n \in \mathbb{N}$) represent the set of indicators. The set of all weak orders[1] over a set A is denoted by $\mathcal{T}^A$. Each indicator $i \in N$ is supposed to have a ranking $\succsim_i \in \mathcal{T}^{\mathcal{C}}$. The combination of n indicators' rankings $\succsim = (\succsim_1, \ldots, \succsim_n) \in (\mathcal{T}^{\mathcal{C}})^N$ is

---

[1] As usual, a binary relation R is called a *weak order* if it is reflexive (aRa for all $a \in A$), complete (for all distinct $a, b \in R$, either aRb or bRa), and transitive (for all $a, b, c \in A$, if aRb and bRc, then aRc).

called a profile.[2] Our purpose is to determine the social ranking $R \in \mathcal{T}^X$ for each profile $\succsim$ in a rational way.[3]

Definition 1 (Social Ranking Solution). A *collective social ranking solution* (CSRS) is a function $f : \left(\mathcal{T}^C\right)^N \to \mathcal{T}^X$. When $n = 1$, it is called as *social ranking solution* (SRS). In that case, it is simply written as $f : \mathcal{T}^C \to \mathcal{T}^X$.

Remark 1 ($C = C_1$). The possibility of designing CSRSs varies by the structure of C. For instance, suppose $C_1 = \{\{x\}|x \in X\}$ (i.e., a trivial case where no one makes coalitions with others). In this case, C can be identified with X. So, there is no essential difference between a CSRS $f : \left(\mathcal{T}^C\right)^N \to \mathcal{T}^X$ and a social welfare function $f : \left(\mathcal{T}^X\right)^N \to \mathcal{T}^X$.

Example 2 (the domain of coalitions).

- $C_X := 2^X$ (every subset of X is supposed to be a coalition),
- $C_k := \{S \subseteq X \mid \#S = k\}$ (only size-k subset is supposed to be a coalition), and
- $C_{M,M'} := C_M \cup C_{M'}$ for some partition $\left(M, M'\right)$ of X.

The first two, C_X and C_k, are easy to understand. Note that most of the related literatures of social ranking problem considers C_X (Table 1). Suppose, for instance, there are two departments in a school: the Department of Engineering (Eng.) and the Department of International Studies (Int.), and that coalitions are made only within the same department. As such, the set of feasible coalitions should be a subset of $C_{Eng.,Int.}$. Specifically, we say that C satisfies *pairwise discernibility* (PD) if $\Sigma_{xy}(C) \neq \phi$ for all $x, y \in X$. Note that all of C_X, C_k, and $C_{M,M'}$ satisfy PD.[4]

For the ease of argumentation, we will introduce some notations. For two sets, S and T, their union $S \cup T$ is denoted by $S + T$ if they are disjoint, i.e., $S \cap T = \phi$. With a slight abuse of notation, if T is a singleton, we write as $S + x$ instead of $S + \{x\}$. Let

$$\Sigma_{xy}(C) := \{S \subseteq X \mid x, y \notin S, S + x, S + y \in C\},$$
$$\Sigma_{xy}^{+x}(C) := \left\{S + x \mid S \in \Sigma_{xy}(C)\right\}, \Sigma_{xy}^{+y}(C) := \left\{S + y \mid S \in \Sigma_{xy}(C)\right\},$$
$$\Sigma_{xy}^{+}(C) := \Sigma_{xy}^{+x}(C) \cup \Sigma_{xy}^{+y}(C)$$
$$\Sigma_{xy}^{\mu}(C) := \left\{S \in \Sigma_{xy} \mid \#S = \mu\right\}.$$

When C is obvious, we simply write them as $\Sigma_{xy}, \Sigma_{xy}^{+x}, \cdots$.

Example 3 (SRSs).

1. Suppose $C_1 \subseteq C$. Then, *primitive* SRS f is defined as follows: for all $x, y \in X$ and $\succsim \in \mathcal{T}^C$: $xf\left(\succsim\right)y \Leftrightarrow \{x\} \succsim \{y\}$.

---

[2] As usual, $\left(\mathcal{T}^C\right)^N := \mathcal{T}^C \times \cdots \times \mathcal{T}^C$ ($|N| = n$ times). It is worth noting that we implicitly assume "universal domain", i.e., we assume any weak order over C is admissible.

[3] In principle, we use symbols $\succsim, \succsim', \succsim_i, \ldots$ for rankings on C and $R, R', \ldots$ for rankings on X.

[4] For $C_{M,M'}$, we have that $\Sigma_{xy} = \{\phi\}$ for all $x, y \in X$.

2. For $x, y \in X$ and $\succsim \in \mathcal{T}^C$, let $d_{xy}(\succsim) := \#\{S \in \Sigma_{xy} \mid S + x \succsim S + y\}$. Then, ceteris paribus majority (CP majority) f returns a binary relation $f(\succsim)$ for each $\succsim \in \mathcal{T}^C$ in such a way that $x f(\succsim) y \Leftrightarrow d_{xy}(\succsim) \geq d_{yx}(\succsim)$. Note that $f(\succsim)$ is not necessarily transitive [5], so, generally speaking, it is not an SRS.

3. For $x \in X$, $\succsim \in \mathcal{T}^C$, and $C \in \mathcal{C}$, let $b(\succsim : C) := \#\{D \in C \mid C \succ D\}$ and

$$s_x(\succsim) := \sum_{C \ni x} b(\succsim : C).$$

Define $f_B(\succsim)$ as $x f_B(\succsim) y \Leftrightarrow s_x(\succsim) \geq s_y(\succsim)$.

4. SRS f is called *unanimous* if for all $\succsim \in \mathcal{T}^C$, $x f(\succsim) y$ for all $x, y \in X$.

Finally, we introduce two types of axioms, dominance (as well as weak dominance), and independence of irrelevant coalitions.

For $x, y \in X$ and $\succsim \in \mathcal{T}^C$, we say that

- x *dominates* y (denoted as x dom y) if $S + x \succsim_i S + y$ for all $S \in \Sigma_{xy}$ and $i \in N$.
- x *strongly dominates* y (denoted as x s-dom y) if x dominates y and $S + x \succ_i S + y$ holds for some $S \in \Sigma_{xy}$ and $i \in N$.
- x *entirely dominates* y (denoted as x edom y) if $S + x \succ_i S + y$ for all $S \in \Sigma_{xy}$ and for all $i \in N$, and if such S and i exist.

For the ease of arguments, we write as $x\ edom_i^\mu\ y$ if $S + x \succ_i S + y$ holds for all $S \in \Sigma_{xy}^{\mu-1}$. Also, we write as $x\ edom_i\ y$ if $x\ edom_i^\mu\ y$ for all size μ.

Definition 2 (Dominance). A CSRS $f : (\mathcal{T}^C)^N \to \mathcal{T}^X$ is said to satisfy.

- *Dominance* (DOM) if for all $x, y \in X$ and for all $\succsim \in (\mathcal{T}^C)^N$, x dom y implies $x f(\succsim) y$ and x s-dom y implies $x P(f(\succsim)) y$.
- *Weak dominance* (WDOM) if for all $x, y \in X$ and for all $\succsim \in (\mathcal{T}^C)^N$, $x\ edom\ y$ implies $x P(f(\succsim)) y$.

Definition 3 (Independence of irrelevant coalitions). A CSRS $f : (\mathcal{T}^C)^N \to \mathcal{T}^X$ is said to satisfy *independence of irrelevant coalitions* (IIC) if for all $x, y \in X$ and for all $\succsim, \succsim' \in (\mathcal{T}^C)^N$: if

$$S + x \succsim_i S + y \Leftrightarrow S + x \succsim_i' S + y \quad \forall i \in N \text{ and } \forall S \in \Sigma_{xy},$$

then $x f(\succsim) y \Leftrightarrow x f(\succsim') y$.

Remark 2. When $n = 1$ and $\mathcal{C} = \mathcal{C}_X$, our definition of DOM and IIC coincides with those stated in [1]. Recall that the design of SRS is equivalent to that of the social welfare function $f : (\mathcal{T}^X)^N \to \mathcal{T}^X$ when $\mathcal{C} = \mathcal{C}_1$ (Remark 1). Under such circumstances, it is worth noting that WDOM and IIC is equivalent to weak Pareto and independence of irrelevant alternatives.

3   CSRS Satisfying WDOM and IIC

A relation $\succsim \in \mathcal{T}^C$ is called ps-sdom if for all $x, y \in X$ and $\mu = 1, 2, \ldots, m - 1$, either $x \ edom^\mu \ y$ or $y \ edom^\mu \ x$. Let $\mathcal{S}^C$ be the set of all such relations. Moretti & Öztürk [1] prove that the "dictatorship of the coalition's size" is generated by DOM and IIC:

Moretti & Öztürk [1]'s Theorem 2 (p.178)

If an SRS $f : \mathcal{S}^{C_X} \to \mathcal{T}^X$ satisfies DOM and IIC, there is $t^* \in \{1, 2, \ldots, m - 1\}$ such that for all $x, y \in X$, $\left[xf(\succsim)y \Leftrightarrow x \ edom^{t^*} \ y \right]$.

The size t^* in this theorem behaves like a dictator, because such a CSRS judge workers x and y based solely on their performances in size-t^* coalitions. In this section, we show that the dictatorship in a slightly weak sense must be demanded by WDOM and IIC whenever $\mathcal{C}$ satisfies PD.

We say that $G \subseteq N \times \{1, 2, \ldots, m - 1\}$ is *decisive* over (x, y) if for all $(i, \mu) \in G$, $\succsim \in (\mathcal{T}^C)^N$ and $x, y \in X$, if $S + x \succ_i S + y$ for all $S \in \Sigma_{xy}^{\mu-1}$, then xPy. Also, G is called *(universally) decisive* if it is decisive over all pairs. A pair (i, μ) is called a *dictator* if $\{(i, \mu)\}$ is decisive and a CSRS is called *dictatorial* if there is a dictator. Note that this "dictator" is not a certain person, but a pair of indicator $i \in N$ and size μ. The reason that we call such a pair as a "dictator" will be clear in the proof of Theorem 1. In fact, the pair (i, μ) behaves just as the dictator in Arrow's (1951) impossibility theorem.

Theorem 1. Suppose that the domain of coalitions $\mathcal{C}$ satisfies PD.

If a CSRS $f : (\mathcal{T}^C)^N \to \mathcal{T}^X$ satisfies WDOM and IIC, then it is dictatorial.

This theorem states that the combination of WDOM and IIC yields a dictator, as long as $\mathcal{C}$ satisfies PD (i.e., when ceteris paribus comparison is possible for each pair of workers (PD), we cannot design CSRS satisfying WDOM and IIC without giving certain (i, μ) such a dictatorial power).

We say that a pair $(x, y) \in X \times X$ is *free*[5] under certain conditions if there is no restriction on $\succsim \in (\mathcal{T}^C)^N$ for the ranking between $S + x$ and $S + y$ for each $S \in \Sigma_{xy}$.

---

[5] Although bothersome, a formal definition is as follows: For $x, y \in X$, let $\Sigma_{xy} = \{S_1, S_2, \ldots, S_t\}$ and $\sigma_{xy}(i, \succsim) = \in \{0, 1\}^t$ such that the j-th term is 1 if $S + x \succ_i S + y$, 0 if $S + x \sim_i S + y$, and -1 if $S + y \succ_i S + x$. A pair (x, y) is called free under conditions $P, Q, \ldots$ when for all $a_1, \ldots, a_n \in \{0, 1\}^t$, there is a profile $\succsim \in (\mathcal{T}^C)^N$ satisfying $P, Q, \ldots$ such that $a_i = \sigma_{xy}(i, \succsim)$ for all $i \in N$.

The proof of Theorem 1 is made via two lemmas, field expansion (Lemma 1), and group contraction (Lemma 2). As seen in [12], p. 287, these lemmas are originally invented for proving Arrow's impossibility theorem. Our proof shows that the dictator of CSRS is derived through almost the same reasoning, except that the existence of certain profiles is not so apparent in our context (for instance, whether (x, z) is free or not given that $x\ edom_i\ y$ is not so apparent, because $x\ edom_i\ y$ is determined by the ranking between Σ_{xy}^{+x} and Σ_{xy}^{+y}; but it is possible that Σ_{xy}^{+x} and Σ_{yz}^{+y} has common elements).

Lemma 1 (field expansion for social ranking problem). For any $G \subseteq N \times \{1, 2, \ldots, m - 1\}$, if G is decisive over (x, y), then G is decisive.

Proof of Lemma 1: Assume that $G \subseteq N \times \{1, 2, \ldots, m - 1\}$ is decisive over (x, y). Take distinct $a, b \in X \backslash \{x, y\}$. For $U \subseteq X$, let $[U]^\mu = \{C \in C \mid C \cap \{x, y, a, b\} = U$ and $|C| = \mu\}$. With a little abuse of notation, we often write the content U without $\{\}$, e.g., $[a, b]$ instead of $[\{a, b\}]$. Note that $[U]^\mu \cap [U']^\nu = \phi$ whenever $U \neq U'$ or $\nu \neq \nu'$.

For all $(i, \mu) \in G$, let[6]

$$\begin{cases} [a]^\mu \succ_i [x]^\mu \succ_i [y]^\mu \succ_i [b]^\mu, \\ [ax]^\mu \succ_i [ay]^\mu \succ_i [xy]^\mu \sim_i [ab]^\mu \succ_i [bx]^\mu \succ_i [by]^\mu, \text{ and} \\ [axy]^\mu \succ_i [abx]^\mu \succ_i [ayb]^\mu \succ_i [bxy]^\mu. \end{cases} \quad (1)$$

Then, we have that $a\ edom_i^\mu\ x$, $x\ edom_i^\mu\ y$, and $y\ edom_i^\mu\ b$. To see this, take any $S \in \Sigma_{ax}$. Since $a \in S + a$ and $x \notin S + a$, we have that $S + a$ is either in $[a]^\mu$, $[ay]^\mu$, $[ab]^\mu$, $[aby]^\mu$. In each case, $S + x$ is in $[x]^\mu$, $[xy]^\mu$, $[xb]^\mu$, $[bxy]^\mu$, respectively. Therefore, Eq. (1) implies that $S + a \succ_i S + x$ for all $S \in \Sigma_{ax}^{\mu-1}$. In other words, $a\ SDOM_i^\mu\ x$. Similarly, $x\ edom_i^\mu\ y$, and $y\ edom_i^\mu\ b$ can be verified.

Next, for $(j, \nu) \notin G$, let

$$\begin{cases} [a]^\nu \succ_j [x]^\nu \text{ and } [y]^\nu \succ_j [b]^\nu, \\ [ay]^\nu \succ_j [ab]^\nu \succ_j [bx]^\nu, \\ [ay]^\nu \succ_j [xy]^\nu \succ_j [bx]^\nu, \\ [aby]^\nu \succ_j [bxy]^\nu \text{ and } [axy]^\nu \succ_j [abx]^\nu. \end{cases} \quad (2)$$

In this case, we also have that $a\ edom_j^\nu\ x$ and $y\ edom_j^\nu\ b$. Also, (a, b) is free under Eq. (2). To see this, for any $S \in \Sigma_{xy}$, if $S \in \Sigma_{xy}^{\mu-1}$, then $S + x$ is either in $[x]^\nu$, $[ax]^\nu$, $[bx]^\nu$, $[abx]^\nu$ and $S + y$ is either in $[y]^\nu$, $[ay]^\nu$, $[by]^\nu$, $[aby]^\nu$, respectively. Since there is no condition on the ranking between $[a]^\nu$ and $[b]^\nu$, that between $[ax]^\nu$ and $[bx]^\nu$, that between $[ay]^\nu$ and $[by]^\nu$, and that between $[axy]^\nu$ and $[bxy]^\nu$, (a, b) turns out to be free.

Now, PD guarantees that $a\ edom\ x$ and $y\ edom\ b$. By WDOM, we have $aP(f(\succsim))x$ and $yP(f(\succsim))b$. Since G is assumed to be decisive over (x, y) and $x\ SDOM_i^\mu\ y$, we have

---

[6] Technically speaking, $[a]^\mu$, $[x]^\mu$, ... are sets. The first equation of (1) is an abbreviation of the following: for all $C \in [a]^\mu$, $D \in [x^\mu]$, $E \in [y]^\mu$, $F \in [b]^\mu$, assume $C \succ_i D \succ_i E \succ_i F$. With a slight abuse of notation, we use this abbreviation in the subsequent argument.

that $xP(f(\succsim))y$. By transitivity of $f(\succsim)$, it follows that $aP(f(\succsim))b$. Recall that (a, b) is free for all $(j, v) \in \overline{G}^7$. So, by IIC, we can conclude that G is decisive over (a, b), as well.

Like in Sen [12]'s proof on Arrow's impossibility theorem, the reasoning is exactly similar when two of them are the same alternative (for instance, when $a = x$, omit $[a] \succ_i [x]$, $[ab] \succ_i [bx]$, $[ay] \succ_i [xy]$, and $[aby] \succ_i [bxy]$ in (1), and (2). Similarly, it follows that G is decisive over (x, b)). ■

Lemma 2 (Group Contraction for social ranking problem). If $G \subseteq N \times \{1, 2, \ldots, m - 1\}$ is decisive and $|G| \geq 2$, then a proper subset of G is also decisive as well.

Proof of Lemma 2. Suppose G is decisive. Let $G_1, G_2 \subseteq G$ be a partition with $G_1 \cup G_2 = G$, $G_1 \cap G_2 = \phi$, and $G_1, G_2 \neq \phi$. Let $x, y, z \in X$ be distinct and $[U]^\mu = \{C \in \mathcal{C} \mid C \cap \{x, y, z\} = U \text{ and } |C| = \mu\}$.

For $(i, \mu) \in G_1$, let

$$[x]^\mu \succ_i [y]^\mu, [x]^\mu \succ_i [z]^\mu$$
$$[xz]^\mu \succ_i [yz]^\mu, [xy]^\mu \succ_i [yz]^\mu. \tag{3}$$

As in the proof of Lemma 1, it easily turns out that $x\ edom_i^\mu\ y$, $x\ edom_i^\mu\ z$, and (y, z) is free under Eq. (3).

For $(j, v) \in G_2$, let

$$[x]^v \succ_j [y]^v, [xz]^v \succ_j [yz]^v$$
$$[z]^v \succ_j [y]^v, [xz]^v \succ_j [xy]^v. \tag{4}$$

It follows that $x\ edom_j^v\ y$ and $z\ edom_j^v\ y$, and (x, z) is free under (4).

Finally, we impose no condition on $(k, \xi) \in G_3 := \overline{G_1 \cup G_2}$. Note that $\Sigma_{zx}^{+z} \subseteq [z] \cup [yz]$, $\Sigma_{zx}^{+x} \subseteq [x] \cup [xy]$, $\Sigma_{yz}^{+y} \subseteq [y] \cup [xy]$, and $\Sigma_{yz}^{+z} \subseteq [z] \cup [xz]$. So, (y, z) is free under any specified ranking between Σ_{zx}^{+z} and Σ_{zx}^{+x}.

Since $x\ edom_i^\mu\ y$, $x\ edom_j^v\ y$, and $G = G_1 \cup G_2$ is decisive, we have $xP(f(\succsim))y$. If $zf(\succsim)x$ holds under certain configuration of the ranking between Σ_{zx}^{+z} and Σ_{zx}^{+x} in G_2 and G_3, transitivity of f demands that $zP(f(\succsim))y$. But recall that (z, y) is free both in G_2 and G_3. So, G_2 must be decisive over (z, y). By Lemma 1, G_2 must be universally decisive. Otherwise, i.e., $xP(f(\succsim))z$ for all configurations of the ranking between Σ_{zx}^{+z} and Σ_{zx}^{+x} in G_1 and G_3 (when $x\ edom_i^\mu\ z$ for $(i, \mu) \in G_1$), G_1 must be decisive over (x, z). By Lemma 1, G_1 is decisive. In either case, we find a proper decisive subset. ■

Proof of Theorem 1: Because of PD and WDOM, $N \times \{1, 2, \ldots, m - 1\}$ is decisive. By repeating Lemma 2, we can finally find a singleton decisive set, which is nothing but a dictator. ■

---

[7] Complement set of A is denoted by $\overline{A}$.

Remark 3 (Dropping WDOM, IIA, and transitivity). By dropping one of WDOM, IIA, and transitivity of $f(\cdot)$, there are some counterexamples (for certain C), i.e., non-dictatorial procedures that satisfy the other conditions in Theorem 1. Unanimous SRS satisfies IIA, transitivity but not WDOM. CP-majority satisfies WDOM and IIA, but not necessarily transitive. For $C = C_k$ ($k = 1, 2, \ldots, m - 1$) or $C = C_X$, f_B satisfies WP and transitivity but not IIA.

Remark 4 (Dropping PD). Let $n = 1$, $X = \{1, 2, 3\}$ and $C = \{\{1\}, \{1, 2\}, \{1, 2, 3\}\}$. Literally speaking, each 1, 2, 3 dominates each other under any $\succsim \in T^C$, because $\Sigma_{12} = \Sigma_{23} = \Sigma_{31} = \phi$. So, an SRS satisfies DOM if and only if it is unanimous. Similarly, any SRS satisfies WDOM, because no element of X can, entirely dominates others. This example implies that if there is no chance of a ceteris paribus comparison (i.e., $\Sigma_{xy} = \phi$), it is useless to consider DOM or WDOM. In this sense, PD is a natural condition, so the impact of Theorem 1 is essential in a ceteris paribus comparison.

Remark 5 (Relevance with Arrow's impossibility theorem). Since we prove Theorem 1 (via Lemma 1 and Lemma 2) in the same way as Arrow's impossibility theorem, one might wonder if there is some difference between SWF and SRS. The difference looks clearer once we introduce "dominance" in a different manner. Define, for instance, $x \ \overline{edom} \ y$ as

$$x \ \overline{edom} \ y \Leftrightarrow S + x \succ_i T + y \text{ for all } S, T \in \Sigma_{xy} \text{ and } i \in N, \text{ with } \Sigma_{xy} \neq \phi.$$

And QWDOM (quasi-weak dominance) as $x \ \overline{edom} \ y \Rightarrow xPy$. Clearly, QWDOM is logically weaker than WDOM. But once we weaken the axiom to this extent under $C = C_X$, we can no longer consider a ranking such that $x \ \overline{edom} \ y$ and $y \ \overline{edom} \ z$, i.e., linearly-ordered triples. This is because Σ_{xy}^+, Σ_{yz}^+, Σ_{zx}^+ have common elements in general. Therefore, $\Sigma_{xy}^{+x} \succ \Sigma_{xy}^{+y}$ can interfere with $\Sigma_{yz}^{+y} \succ \Sigma_{yz}^{+z}$. Indeed, the following SRS satisfies QWDOM and IIC without being dictatorial: if there exists $x, y \in X$ such that $x \ \overline{edom} \ y$, $xP(\succsim)(X \setminus \{z\})$, and otherwise, unanimous SRS.

Remark 6 (Dictatorship does not necessarily make an SRS). Note that Theorem 1 does not claim that dictatorial aggregation always makes an SRS satisfying WDOM and IIC. It depends on the structure of C. For instance, suppose $X = \{1, 2, 3, 4, 5\}$ and $C = \{13, 23, 24, 34, 35, 15\}$. Let $13 \succ_i 23 \succ 24 \succ_i 34 \succ_i 35 \succ_i 15$ for all $i \in N$. In this case, we have that 1 $edom_i$ 2, 2 $edom_i$ 3, and 3 $edom_i$ 1. Therefore, WDOM demands that $1P(f(\succsim))2$, $2P(f(\succsim))3$, and $3P(f(\succsim))1$. So, there is no SRS satisfying even triple-acyclicity, which is weaker than transitivity, under this C.

4   Social Ranking Between Coalitions

In some circumstances, the social ranking of subgroups, rather than each worker, is required. For instance, when giving an award for the best coalitions/teams, when determining which subgroup or connection between workers are working well, etc. The present section defines an *extended CSRS* as a function $f : \left(T_X^C\right)^N \to T_X^C$, and see if similar result as Theorem 1 also holds or not under this extended framework.[8] To explore technical arguments, let us revise related concepts.

For $S, T \subseteq X$, let

$$\Sigma_{S,T} := \{U \subseteq (X \setminus (S \cup T)) \mid U + S, U + T \in \mathcal{C}\}.$$

Also, $\Sigma_{S,T}^{+S}, \Sigma_{S,T}^{+T}, \Sigma_{S,T}^{+}$ are defined in a similar way. When there is little risk of confusion, we simply write $\Sigma_{S,T}$ as Σ_{ST} (without a comma), and $\Sigma_{\{x\},T}$ as Σ_{xT}. We write as $S \; edom_i \; T$ if $S + U \succ_i T + U$ for all $U \in \Sigma_{ST}$ and as $S \; edom \; T$ if $S \; edom_i \; T$ for all $i \in N$ (note that $\Sigma_{ST} \neq \phi$ holds for $\mathcal{C} = \mathcal{C}_X$). An extended CSRS f satisfies WDOM if $SP(f(\succsim))T$ holds whenever $S \; edom \; T$. Also, IIC demands that $Sf(\succsim)T \Leftrightarrow Sf(\underset{\sim}{\succ'})T$ holds whenever $S + U \succsim_i T + U \Leftrightarrow S + U \underset{\sim i}{\succ'} T + U$ for all $i \in N$ and $U \in \Sigma_{ST}$. An indicator $i \in N$ is *decisive* over (S, T) if $S \; edom_i \; T$ implies $SP(f(\succsim))T$. It is called a *dictator* if it is decisive over any pair $(S, T) \in \mathcal{C}_X \times \mathcal{C}_X$. Also, f is called *dictatorial* if there is a dictator. As a corollary of Theorem 1, the following holds:

Corollary 1. If an extended CSRS $f : (\mathcal{T}^{\mathcal{C}_X})^N \to \mathcal{T}^{\mathcal{C}_X}$ satisfies WDOM and IIC, there is an indicator which is decisive over (S, T) for any distinct $S, T \in \mathcal{C}_1$.

Our result says that the dictator's influence covers the whole $\mathcal{C}$.

Theorem 2. If an extended CSRS $f : (\mathcal{T}^{\mathcal{C}_X})^N \to \mathcal{T}^{\mathcal{C}_X}$ satisfies WDOM and IIC, there is a dictator.

This theorem says that the combination of WDOM and IIC indicates a dictator, a certain indicator, in this extended framework, too. The proof of Theorem 2 is made by showing that if i is decisive over $\mathcal{C}_1$, i's influence expands to any pair (A, B). Specifically, Lemma 3 proves this expansion when $A \setminus B \neq \phi$ and Lemma 4 proves it when $A \subseteq B$.

Lemma 3 (expansion from $\mathcal{C}_1$ to (A, B) with A $\setminus$ B $\neq \phi$). Let $f : (\mathcal{T}^{\mathcal{C}_X})^N \to \mathcal{T}^{\mathcal{C}_X}$ be an extended SRS satisfying WDOM and IIC. Let $A, B \in \mathcal{C}_X$ and $A \setminus B \neq \phi$. If $i \in N$ is decisive over $\mathcal{C}_1$, then he/she is decisive over (A, B), as well.

Proof of Lemma 3. Let $a \in A \setminus B$. The statement is trivial when $|A| = |B| = 1$. So, we consider two cases,[9] (1) $|A| = 1$ and $|B| \geq 2$ and (2) $|A| \geq 2$.

---

[8] As an anonymous reviewer points it out, an extended CSRS is, from purely formal point of view, nothing but a SWF with $\mathcal{C}_X$ as the set of alternatives. But the subsequent argument is different from Arrow's because WDOM or IIC sees the internal structure of each "alternative" (i.e., coalition). For WDOM to judge S above T, it is not sufficient that every indicator i ranks S above T; $S \; edom_i \; T$ demands that $S + U \succ_i T + U$ for all $U \in \Sigma_{ST}$.

[9] The cases of $B = \phi$ (in Lemma 3) and $A = \phi$ (in Lemma 4) can be also shown in a similar way. If $B = \phi$ and $|A| \geq 2$, assume $A \succ_i a \succ_i \phi$ and $a \succ_j \phi$ for $j \neq i$. By decisiveness for nonempty case, $AP(f(\succsim))a$. By WDOM, $aP(f(\succsim))\phi$. Similarly, transitivity demands $aP(f(\succsim))\phi$ and IIC declares that i is decisive over $(A, B) = (A, \phi)$. The other cases ($B = \phi$ and $|A| = 1$ and $A = \phi \neq B$) are similar.

(1) Suppose $|A| = 1$, i.e., $A = \{a\}$, $b \in B$, and $|B| \geq 2$. For i, let

$$C \succsim_i D \Leftrightarrow \#(D \cap B) \geq \#(C \cap B). \tag{5}$$

For $j \neq i$, let

$$\{C \in \mathcal{C} \mid \#(B \cap C) = 1\} \succ_j \{C \in \mathcal{C} \mid B \subseteq C\}. \tag{6}$$

Then, we can verify that

(1-1). $a \; edom_i \; b$, $b \; edom_i \; B$, and $a \; edom_i \; B$[11]. $\because$ Take any $S \in \Sigma_{ab}$. Since $S + a$ and $S + b$ differ only in $a \notin B$ and $b \in B$, we have $S + a \succ_i S + b$. So, $a \; edom_i \; b$. Take any $S \in \Sigma_{bB}$. Since $|B| \geq 2$, it follows that $\#(S + b) \cap B < \#(S + B) \cap B$. So, $S + b \succ_i S + B$, which shows $b \; edom_i \; B$. Finally, for $S \in \Sigma_{aB}$, $\#(S + a) \cap B < \#(S + B) \cap B$ also follows. So, $a \; edom_i \; B$.

(1-2). $b \; edom_j \; B$. $\because$ For $S \in \Sigma_{bB}$, we have that $B \cap (S + b) = \{b\}$ and $B \subseteq (S + B)$. So, we have $S + b \succ_j S + B$, which implies that $b \; edom_j \; B$.

(1-3). (A, B) is free for j under Eq. (6). $\because$ There is no condition on the ranking between $\{C \in \mathcal{C} \mid B \cap C = \phi\} \supseteq \Sigma_{aB}^{+a}$ and $\{C \in \mathcal{C} \mid B \subseteq C\} \supseteq \Sigma_{aB}^{+B}$.

By (1–1), (1–2) and WDOM, we have $bP(f(\succsim))B$. Since $a \; edom_i \; b$ and i is assumed to be decisive over (a, b), we have that $aP(f(\succsim))b$. Transitivity of f demands that $aP(f(\succsim))B$. Because of (1–3) and IIC, i must be decisive over $(a, B) = (A, B)$.

(2) Suppose that $|A| \geq 2$.

For i: for all $C, D \in \mathcal{C}$, if $\#(C \cap (A \backslash B)) > \#(D \cap (A \backslash B))$, then $C \succ_i D$. If $\#(C \cap (A \backslash B)) = \#(D \cap (A \backslash B))$, then $\#(C \cap A) \geq \#(D \cap A) \Leftrightarrow C \succsim_i D$.

For all $j \neq i$: for all $C, D \in \{C \in \mathcal{C} \mid a \in C\}$, let

$$C \succsim_j D \Leftrightarrow \#(C \cap A) \geq \#(D \cap A). \tag{6}$$

In the same way as (1), one can verify the followings.

(2-1) $A \; edom_i \; a$, $a \; edom_i \; B$, and $A \; edom_i \; B$.

(2-2) $A \; edom_j \; a$

(2-3) (A, B) is free for $j \neq i$ under (7).

Now, (2–1), (2–2), and WDOM implies that $AP(f(\succsim))a$. With case (1), i is decisive over (a, B). So, (2–1) implies $aP(f(\succsim))B$. By transitivity of f, we have $AP(f(\succsim))B$. With (2–1), (2–3), and IIC, we can conclude that i is decisive over (A, B), too. ∎

Lemma 4 (expansion from $\mathcal{C}_1$ to (A, B) with $A \subseteq B$). Let $f : (T^{\mathcal{C}_X})^N \to T^{\mathcal{C}_X}$ be an extended SRS satisfying WDOM and IIC. Let $A, B \in \mathcal{C}_X$ and $A \subseteq B$. If $i \in N$ is decisive over $\mathcal{C}_1$, then he/she is decisive over (A, B), too.

Proof of Lemma 4. Let $b \in B \backslash A$. For i: let

$$\{C \in \mathcal{C} \mid b \notin C\} \succ \{C \in \mathcal{C} \mid b \in C\}, \text{ and} \tag{7}$$

$$\left[C \succsim_i D \Leftrightarrow \#(C \cap B) \leq \#(D \cap B)\right] \forall C, D \ni b. \tag{8}$$

For $j \neq i$: let

$$\left[C \succsim_j D \Leftrightarrow \#(C \cap B) \leq \#(D \cap B)\right] \forall C, D \ni b. \tag{9}$$

Then, it is straightforward to verify the following: (1–1) A $edom_i$ b, b $edom_i$ B, and A $edom_i$ B, (1–2) b $edom_j$ B for $j \neq i$, and (1–3) (A, B) is free for $j \neq i$ under (10).

With Lemma 3 and $b \notin A$, we have that i is decisive over (A, b). So, (1–1) demands that $AP(f(\succsim))b$. With (1–1), (1–2), and WDOM, we have that $bP(f(\succsim))B$. By transitivity of f, we have $AP(f(\succsim))B$. Because of (1–1), (1–3), and IIC, i must be decisive over (A, B), too. ∎

5   Concluding Remarks

This paper studies social ranking problem with restricted domain of coalitions (Sect. 3) and extend the model to determine the ranking of the whole coalitions (Sect. 4). In both cases, we prove that a certain dictator is generated by WDOM and IIC.

From a theoretical point of view, Theorem 1 shows that the Arrovian impossibility shown in Moretti & Öztürk [1]'s Theorem 2 (p.178) is quite robust against the restriction of feasible coalitions and increasing the number of indicators$n$; it holds whenever there exists a chance of ceteris paribus comparison for each pair of candidates. Theorem 2 verifies a similar impossibility still holds when the output of the CSRS is turned into a ranking over the whole coalitions. From a practical point of view, our model expands the scope of social ranking problem. In many practical situations, e.g., the evaluation of team-sports athletes or researchers, evaluation of each agent is made based on the performances of existing groups, rather than of the whole logically possible groups. Theorem 1 tells us the impossibility for such contexts. It is also worth noting that a subgroup, not necessarily an agent, often has a key role in the group's performances (say, a couple of workers plays a critical role together). Extended CSRS determines the relative competence between subgroups.

For Theorem 1, we gave several escape routes from this impossibility by dropping a particular condition (Remarks 3 and 4), it is worth noting that both WDOM and IIC are based on the ceteris paribus comparison (IIC is based on that also, because it sees the individual rankings between Σ_{xy}^{+x} and Σ_{xy}^{+y}). On the other hand, there are other social ranking methods and/or ideas that are not based on the ceteris paribus comparison, such as LES [6], QWDOM (Remark 5), etc. To develop these under restricted domain of coalitions would be an interesting open question.

References

1. Moretti, S., Öztürk, M.: Some Axiomatic and Algorithmic Perspectives on the Social Ranking Problem. Lecture Notes in Computer Science (Including Subseries Lecture Notes in Artificial Intelligence and Lecture Notes in Bioinformatics). LNAI, vol. 10576, pp. 166–181 (2017)
2. Banzhaf, J.F., III.: Weighted voting doesn't work: a mathematical analysis. Rutgers L. Rev. **19**, 317–344 (1964)
3. Shapley, L.S.: A value for n-person games. Contrib. to Theory Games **2**(28), 307–317 (1953)
4. Fayard, N., Ozturk, M.E.: Ordinal Social ranking : simulation for CP-majority rule. DA2PL'2018 (From Multiple Criteria Decision Aid to Preference Learning), November 2018, Poznan, Poland (2018)
5. Haret, A., Khani, H., Moretti, S., Ozturk, M.: Ceteris Paribus Majority for social ranking. In: 27th International Joint Conference on Artificial Intelligence (IJCAI-ECAI-18), Jul 2018, Stockholm, Sweden, pp. 303–309 (2019)
6. Bernardi, G., Lucchetti, R., Moretti, S.: Ranking objects from a preference relation over their subsets. Soc. Choice Welfare **52**(4), 589–606 (2019)
7. Khani, H., Moretti, S., Ozturk, M.: An ordinal banzhaf index for social ranking. In: 28th International Joint Conference on Artificial Intelligence (IJCAI 2019), Aug 2019, Macao, China, pp. 378–384 (2019)
8. Allouche, T., Escoffier, B., Moretti, S., Öztürk, M.: Social ranking manipulability for the cp-majority, banzhaf and lexicographic excellence solutions. In: Twenty-Ninth International Joint Conference on Artificial Intelligence and Seventeenth Pacific Rim International Conference on Artificial Intelligence {IJCAI-PRICAI-20}, p.17–23 (2020)
9. Arrow, K.: Social choice and individual values. Wiley (1951)
10. Nurmi, H.: The choice of voting rules based on preferences over criteria. In: Kamiński, B., Kersten, G., Szapiro, T. (eds.) GDN 2015. LNBIP, vol. 218. Springer, Cham (2015). https://doi.org/10.1007/978-3-319-19515-5_19
11. Suzuki, T., Horita, M.: A characterization for procedural choice based on dichotomous preferences over criteria. In: Morais, D., Fang, L., Horita, M. (eds.) Group Decision and Negotiation: A Multidisciplinary Perspective. GDN 2020. LNBIP, vol. 388. Springer, Cham (2020). https://doi.org/10.1007/978-3-030-48641-9_7
12. Sen, A.: Collective Choice and Social Welfare: An Expanded Edition. Penguin UK (2017)

A Group Multicriteria Decision Model for Ranking Sustainable Cities

Emerson Rodrigues Sabino[1]([⊠]) [ID], Gabriela Silva da Silva[1] [ID],
Danielle Costa Morais[1] [ID], Adiel Teixeira de Almeida[1] [ID],
and Leandro Chaves Rêgo[1,2] [ID]

[1] PostGraduate Program in Management Engineering, Universidade Federal de Pernambuco
– UFPE, Avenida da Arquitetura – Cidade Universitária, Recife, PE 50740-550, Brazil
[2] Statistics and Applied Math Department, Universidade Federal do Ceará, Fortaleza, CE, Brazil

Abstract. The evaluation of cities regarding environmental and sustainable development practices should be made by a set of criteria expressing their economic, social, and environmental objectives. A ranking of sustainable cities aims to encourage the continuity of actions that contribute to the reduction of environmental problems and help cities develop sustainably. This paper proposes a group decision model for ranking sustainable cities. It is based on a multi-criteria method to support decision-makers to build individual rankings, and on a framework for choosing a voting procedure to aggregate the individual priorities into a collective ranking of sustainable cities. The applicability of the model is illustrated with a real environmental problem in a hydrographic basin in Brazil.

Keyword: Group decision making · Multicriteria method · Voting procedure · Sustainable city

1 Introduction

Many studies are discussing the problems faced to manage water resources in river basins in different regions [1–5]. These studies show that the growth of urbanization and the demand for water, pollution intensification, and worsening climate change are highlighted as factors that aggravate environmental problems [2, 3].

On that perspective, concerns about economic growth impacts and environmental protection strategies have been motivating studies on sustainable development [6]. The sustainable development goal is to promote the development of a region in balance with economic, social and environmental issues [7]. Sustainable indicators are the main resources used to measure the effectiveness of the implemented sustainable actions and it is an important activity to environmental protection [8, 9].

The analysis of sustainable development practice performance is a classical complex group decision-making problem [10], which involves different decision-makers (DMs) and the analyst to support the process in a collaborative environment [11]. The difficulty to maintain communication between different DMs' and their different objectives are some ingredients to give more complexity to this group decision process [12].

© Springer Nature Switzerland AG 2021
D. C. Morais et al. (Eds.): GDN 2021, LNBIP 420, pp. 68–81, 2021.
https://doi.org/10.1007/978-3-030-77208-6_6

One way to reach a solution in this kind of group decision process is by applying a Voting Procedure (VP) [13, 14]. There are several group decision problems that can be easily solved using an appropriate VP. However, the main issue is to choose a suitable VP for the problem. To deal with this difficulty, a framework proposed by [14] guides how to choose an appropriate VP to apply in the decision process using a multi-criteria approach.

In this context, the current study proposes a group decision model to analyze the performance of cities related to sustainable development, with a focus on environmental issues, to ranking cities with a better sustainable profile. This model is based on a multi-criteria method to support decision-makers to build individual rankings, and on the framework for choosing a VP to aggregate the individual preferences into a collective ranking of sustainable cities. It becomes an important tool to manage environmental practices indicating which cities most contribute to environmental protection.

To illustrate the proposed model, an application was made to evaluate the municipalities in the Salgado basin, a region of Ceará state, Brazil, with a focus to avoid worsening this problem and its consequence on the water supply system on the state. The Salgado basin is an important affluent of the Jaguaribe River [15], which supplies Castanhão reservoir to attain water demands in the metropolitan region of Fortaleza, Ceará state capital. The Salgado basin already shows signs of environmental impacts and research can contribute to finding a better way to deal with this situation [16].

This paper is organized as follows. Section 2 provides a basic description of group decisions making, the multi-criteria decision approach, and the techniques to reach a collective choice (the voting procedures). Sect. 3, the group decision model is proposed to assess the sustainable profile of the municipalities in the development environment context. Section 4 presents the application of the proposed model and Sect. 5 concludes the research.

2 Framework for Choosing a Voting Procedure

Group decision-making is present in a wide variety of situations such as water management [4, 5], supplier selection [17], sustainable development [7, 10], and others. In each situation, DMs can share the same objectives or different and conflicting ones [14]. According to [12] poorly structured issues, dynamics of the environment, and different goals of individuals with their own value systems are some aspects that increase the complexity to the group decision problem.

Two types of procedures for aggregating preferences are discussed in the literature [14]. Procedure 1 aggregates the initial preferences of DMs and Procedure 2 aggregates the results and choices of DMs. In the first case, the aggregation happens from the initial information of preference of each DM until the consensus is reached. For this reason, each DM acts in favor to reach the group's goals and their individual priorities are renounced. In the second case, the aggregation of preference occurs from the individual rankings of the DMs, and it means that each DM is independent and has his/her own value system. The focus of this aggregation process is on the alternatives prioritized by the DMs.

Voting procedures (VPs) are common tools used in Procedure 2 to aggregate individual rankings into a collective ranking [13, 14]. There is a wide variety of VP available in the literature, some examples are Amendment, Copeland, Dodgson, Maxmin, Kemeny, Plurality, Borda, Approval Voting, Black, Plurality runoff, Nan-son, and Hare [14, 18]. A specific concern then is how to choose an appropriate VP for a specific decision.

The properties of VPs are relevant and must be correctly considered when choosing a VP for a decision problem [14]. These properties are mainly related to simple and conditional paradoxes [18] and their evaluation is reflected by the level of democratization of the decisions reached by VP [19, 20]. A framework proposed by [14] can be used to guide the process for choosing a VP.

The framework applies a multicriteria decision-making/aid (MCDM/A) method for choosing a VP, following a sequence of steps that involve the DMs and the analyst to support structuring and modeling the problem [14].

The first stage of the framework is the selection of the appropriate VP for the decision process. The VPs incompatible with the decision context should not be considered. The VP will be the alternatives of the decision-making model.

The second step is the evaluation of VP properties and paradoxes, which will be considered as criteria in the decision model. The choice of these criteria to select the VP should seek to maximize the use of the natural characteristics of each VP (properties and paradoxes) that have a relevant impact on the business. Also, it should be considered the maximization of the best form of interaction between the data input and how DMs provide this information to the VP.

The performance of VP properties can be classified into two types: discrete binary outcome and continuous outcome. The discrete binary outcome indicates whether a VP satisfies a property or not. The consequence matrix for this case is represented in Table 1. A number 1 means that the VP satisfies the property, and a number 0 means that the VP does not satisfy the property. The continuous outcome indicates the frequency of occurrence in which a VP satisfies a specific property in a range of values between 0 – 1. So, the value 0 indicates that the property was not violated, and any values between $0 > v_{ij} \geq 1$ indicate that the property was violated in a v_{ij} score. More details about the continuous case can be found in [14].

Following the framework steps, a MCDM/A needs to be chosen. Issues related to the DMs' compensatory or non-compensatory rationality and the appropriate DMs' preference structure must be considered. The parameter of the scale constants (if a compensatory) or relative importance (if a non-compensatory), and the DM's preference functions are required when parameterizing the model.

Finally, the MCDM/A method is applied to choose the VP and then, the VP chosen is applied to the decision organizational problem. All the details presented about this framework can be found in greater detail in [14].

Table 1. Consequence matrix for discrete binary outcome.

Voting systems	Criteria								
	Condorcet Winner	Condorcet Loser	Strong Condorcet	Monotonicity	Pareto	Consistency	Chernoff	Independence of IA	Invulnerability to the no-show Paradox
Amendment	1	1	1	1	0	0	0	0	0
Copeland	1	1	1	1	1	0	0	0	0
Dodgson	1	0	1	0	1	0	0	0	0
Maxmin	1	0	1	1	1	0	0	0	0
Kemeny	1	1	1	1	1	0	0	0	0
Plurality	0	0	1	1	1	1	0	0	1
Borda	0	1	0	1	1	1	0	0	1
Approval	0	0	0	1	0	1	1	0	1
Black	1	1	1	1	1	0	0	0	0
Pl. runoff	0	1	1	0	1	0	0	0	0
Nanson	1	1	1	0	1	0	0	0	0
Hare	0	1	1	0	1	0	0	0	0

Source: De Almeida et al. (2019) [14]

3 The Proposed Group Decision Model for Ranking Sustainable Cities

In this section, we describe the group decision model to build the ranking of cities with the best sustainability profile and concern for environmental issues. The model is divided into four phases: (1) intelligence, (2) individual analysis, (3) choosing a voting procedure, and (4) group aggregation. Figure 1 shows the model proposed in this study.

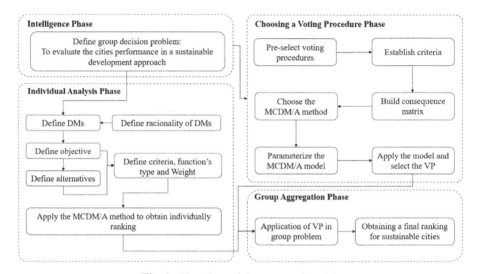

Fig. 1. Flowchart of the proposed model.

The objective of the intelligence phase is to investigate the municipalities in the Salgado basin to be considered for the ranking of sustainable cities. The problem identification requires an exploration of the environment to characterize in detail the decision problem.

In the individual analysis phase, is necessary to define the Decision-Makers (DMs) involved in the process and their rationality in order to apply an MCDM/A method suitable to their rationality and preference structure to find the individual priority ranking. The objectives of the problem were identified according to the DMs' interests. Next, the set of criteria were defined, as well as all the parameters required by the MCDM/A method.

Based on the intelligence and individual analysis, it can be found the rankings made by each DM, and so, the framework for choosing a VP is applied. This phase finds an appropriate VP to aggregate the individuals' rankings into a collective group ranking. The set of VPs for aggregation of the individual rankings of cities was pre-selected. Next, the criteria representing the properties and paradoxes used to analyze the performance of the VPs were established. The literature mentions several characteristics of the VPs [13, 14], and the analyst is responsible for defining which properties are important for the specific situation [14]. Following, the consequence matrix was constructed by considering a discrete binary outcome (if the VP violates a property, it gets "0" in the consequence matrix, and if the VP does not violate a property, it gets "1", therefore, the result "1" is preferable to the result "0") [14]. After, the model was parameterized mainly on the specification of the weights according to the rationality of the decision problem. The application of the MCDM/A method to choose the most appropriate VP concludes this phase.

Finally, the aggregation phase objectives to apply the VP chosen to aggregate individual rankings and obtain a global ranking for the group.

4   Application of the Model

The proposed model was applied to evaluate the performance of the municipalities in the Salgado basin considering the performance in the economic, social, and environmental indicators defined for this study. The execution of each phase of the model is detailed in the following subsections.

4.1   Intelligence Phase

The Salgado basin is formed by 23 municipalities and concentrates a population of almost 900 thousand people [21]. The urbanization growth is worsening the problems of urban density and water pollution, and adding to the drought problem, which is already commonly faced by the region [22], has drawn the attention of public authorities, research, and civil society to the consequences of these impacts on the environment [16].

This situation concerns the environmental management authorities in the sense of the Salgado basin's importance for the water resources system in the Ceará state. This region is inserted in an important hydrographic system that discharges water into Castanhão reservoir to supplying water demands of Ceará capital [15].

Based on the previous context, a group decision problem can be characterized. Several actors are involved, and they represent the public institutions, as the main part responsible for developing policies and defending the environment and society interests, universities, who produce scientific knowledge, and civil society. The goal of this problem is to encourage municipalities to develop practices to protect the environment and develop sustainability to prevent degradation in the Salgado basin.

4.2   Individual Analysis Phase

This group decision problem is composed by three decision-makers. DM 1 is the Secretariat for the Environment (SEMA), representing the government; DM 2 is the representative of universities and scientific research society; and, DM 3 is the representative of civil society, outlining the main users of the Salgado basin. It is assumed that DMs' rationalities are non-compensatory, since the idea of compensation between criteria with a low performance by criteria with high performance, is inappropriate for this study. According to [23] in a sustainable development problem, there is no clear reason to consider tradeoffs in inter-criteria analysis.

Then a non-compensatory approach was considered appropriate to this study and the Promethee-ROC method [24] applied to support building the individual rankings. This method has the advantage of promoting preference elicitation over criteria, using surrogate weights to facilitate establishing weights by DMs and combining it within the Promethee method [25]. In PROMETHEE-ROC [24, 25], the process of elicitation of preferences consists of asking the DMs the importance of criteria by requiring them only ordinal information. The Rank Order Centroid (ROC) [25] turns the order of priorities into weights for each criterion.

The Salgado basin municipalities represent the alternatives of this model. The region owns 23 municipalities but 10 were excluded since do not have a reservoir for water retention (dams). The 13 alternatives considered to this study are described as follows: Aurora (A1), Baixio (A2), Barro (A3), Brejo Santo (A4), Caririaçu (A5), Cedro (A6), Crato (A7), Granjeiro (A8), Icó (A9), Juazeiro do Norte (A10), Lavras da Mangabeira (A11), Mauriti (A12) and Várzea Alegre (A13).

Table 2. Description of criteria.

Code	Criteria	Description	Max/Min
CR1	GDP per capita (R$)	Assess the income of the inhabitants of the cities under study	Max
CR2	Electricity consumption (mwh)	Assess energy consumption in each of the municipalities	Min
CR3	Vehicle fleet (unit)	Quantify the number of cars that are currently part of the vehicle fleet	Min
CR4	Adequate sanitary sewage (%)	Measures the percentage of the population living in a household that has adequate sanitation	Max
CR5	Number of garbage collectors (person)	Measure how many garbage collectors each city has to collect household waste	Max
CR6	Available water in reservoirs (%)	Assesses the percentage of water available to meet the population's consumption needs	Max
CR7	Reservoir capacity of municipalities (million m^3)	Quantify the volume of water that can be stored in the reservoirs	Max
CR8	Number of health units (unit)	Indicates the number of health units for the population of the municipalities	Max
CR9	Education quality index (%)	Assess the quality of the basic education system offered to the population	Max

For this study, nine criteria were defined to verify the performance of the cities in environmental, economic, and social aspects [2]. Table 2 shows the set of criteria and their principal characteristics.

The consequence matrix of the problem is presented in Table 3. The consequences values were obtained from different websites sources as follows: in the Brazilian Institute of Geography and Statistics [21] (criteria 1 and 4), in the Institute of Research and Economic Strategy of Ceará [26] (criteria 2, 7 and 8), in the National Traffic Department [27] (criteria 3), in the IBGE Automatic Recovery System [28] (criteria 5), in the National Water Agency [29] (criteria 6), and in the Ministry of Education [30] (criteria 9).

Table 3. The consequence matrix for the decision problem.

Alternatives	CR1	CR2	CR3	CR4	CR5	CR6	CR7	CR8	CR9
A1	7951	14737	6086	0,122	4	0,454	34330	42	4,9
A2	7333	3911	1618	0,015	0	0,254	41400	8	3,9
A3	8005	14466	5293	0,103	3	0,550	32500	32	4,9
A4	12106	47169	21318	0,597	36	0,174	72552	88	4,1
A5	7427	15667	8239	0,160	3	0,373	2250	36	4,5
A6	7493	16574	8926	0,087	15	0,827	31800	52	4,4
A7	11773	135383	55098	0,422	44	0,398	28780	136	4,4
A8	8727	2602	576	0,253	0	0,414	2030	14	4,6
A9	8289	52513	25215	0,348	32	0,151	69100	80	4,2
A10	16375	342775	127329	0,472	264	0,082	37180	266	4,4
A11	7951	20337	7261	0,277	11	0,906	47220	30	4,5
A12	7972	34069	12931	0,181	3	0,249	34170	74	4,5
A13	8593	29835	16109	0,176	12	0,469	19000	36	4,1

The preference functions of the DMs were defined according to each criterion. The usual function was assigned for criteria 4, 6, and 9. This implies that any difference in the performance of two alternatives will reflect a strict preference for the alternative with higher performance for DMs. A V-Shape function was assigned for criteria 1, 2, 3, 5, 7, and 8. It means that the preference intensity of one alternative over another increases linearly with the difference in performance between the alternatives until that difference reaches the threshold of preference "p", where after that value the preference is strict. The same preference functions were considered for all DMs, however, preference thresholds were specified according to each DM. Table 4 contains information about the preference functions, preference thresholds, and the order of criteria used to obtain the DMs' alternatives ranking. And Table 5 presents the individual rankings after apply Promethee-ROC.

Table 4. Parameters used to obtain individuals rankings.

DM 1	Criteria								
	CR1	CR2	CR3	CR4	CR5	CR6	CR7	CR8	CR9
Preference function	V-Shape	V-Shape	V-Shape	Usual	V-Shape	Usual	V-Shape	V-Shape	Usual
Order	6	2	3	5	9	1	7	8	4
p	900	100	500	–	12	–	7000	5	–
DM 2	Criteria								
	CR1	CR2	CR3	CR4	CR5	CR6	CR7	CR8	CR9
Preference function	V-Shape	V-Shape	V-Shape	Usual	V-Shape	Usual	V-Shape	V-Shape	Usual
Order	9	6	5	3	2	4	8	7	1
p	600	300	700	–	10	–	7000	4	–
DM 3	Criteria								
	CR1	CR2	CR3	CR4	CR5	CR6	CR7	CR8	CR9
Preference function	V-Shape	V-Shape	V-Shape	Usual	V-Shape	Usual	V-Shape	V-Shape	Usual
Order	6	9	8	1	4	7	2	5	3
p	700	300	1000	–	8	–	3000	2	–

Table 5. Individual rankings.

Alternatives	A1	A2	A3	A4	A5	A6	A7	A8	A9	A10	A11	A12	A13
DM 1	4	8	1	11	7	5	9	2	12	13	3	10	6
DM 2	2	13	3	8	9	7	5	4	11	6	1	10	12
DM 3	6	13	9	1	12	11	5	8	4	2	3	7	10

As can be observed in Table 5, each DM has a different perspective to analyze the problem, prioritizing the cities in a different way. Then, the next step is to choose a voting procedure to aggregate individual rankings and to obtain a collective result.

4.3 Choosing a Voting Procedure Phase

Firtsly, it should be considered which VPs were suitable for this problem. In this way a VP that results in a ranking of alternatives can be a potential action. Therefore, the pre-selected VPs were Amendment, Copeland, Dodgson, Maxmin, Borda, Nanson and Hare.

The VP properties (criteria) considered to assess this problem were [13]: Condorcet Winner, Condorcet loser, Strong Concordet, Monotonicity, Pareto, Consistency, and Chernoff. Note that, the Independence of irrelevant alternatives was not considered because none of the VPs pre-selected satisfied this property. The Invulnerability to the no-show paradox is another property that we did not consider because we assumed that the use of the abstention strategy to gain an advantage in the evaluated problem did not contribute to the decision context.

The construction of the consequence matrix is in accordance with the binary outcome, where the number 1 means that the VP attends the property and the number 0 the otherwise. The Usual preference function was considered for all criteria because we considered binary outcome in the decision matrix. In this case, all DMs agree that DM 2 (university institution) should assume the Supra- Decision-Maker position to evaluate the weights over the VPs proprieties. They admit DM 2 had technical knowledge about VP properties, and it is a better candidate to evaluate the relative importance of criteria. In order to facilitate the evaluation of weights, the supra DM uses the ROC order to represent the importance of criteria. Thus, PROMETHEE-ROC was used to preference aggregation and obtain a VP ranking. Table 6 shows the decision matrix for choosing the VP.

Table 6. Decision matrix for choosing a voting procedure.

Voting system	Criteria						
	Condercet Winner	Condorcet Loser	Strong Concordet	Monotonicity	Pareto	Concistency	Chernoff
Amendment	1	1	1	1	0	0	0
Copeland	1	1	1	1	1	0	0
Dodgson	1	0	1	0	1	0	0
Maxmin,	1	0	1	1	1	0	0
Kemeny	1	1	1	1	1	0	0
Plurality	0	0	1	1	1	1	0
Borda	0	1	0	1	1	1	0
Approval Voting	0	0	0	1	0	1	1
Black	1	1	1	1	1	0	0
Plurality runoff	0	1	1	0	1	0	0
Nanson	1	1	1	0	1	0	0
Hare	0	1	1	0	1	0	0
ROC-weight	0.1085	0.0442	0.2276	0.1561	0.0204	0.0728	0.3704

Applying PROMETHEE-ROC, the result shown in Fig. 2 indicates that the VP chosen to evaluate the problem under study is Copeland. Therefore, this VP was indicated to aggregate the individual preferences of DMs in the process of choosing the city with the best sustainable profile in the Salgado basin region.

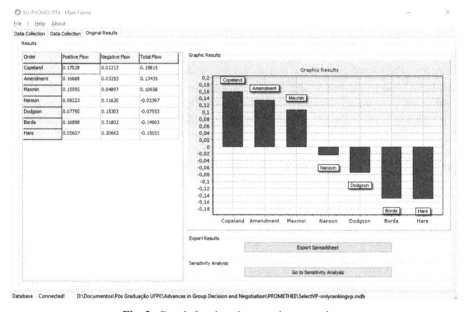

Fig. 2. Result for choosing a voting procedure.

4.4   Group Aggregation Phase

As noted in the previous section, Copeland was the VP indicated as the most appropriate to aggregate the individual preferences of the DMs involved in the problem of sustainable cities.

Copeland's method determines a score for each alternative based on pairwise comparisons. Thus, if one alternative wins one vote (+1) is given it and otherwise, is discounted one vote (−1) against it. Copeland's score is given by the difference between wins and losses. The highest score establish which alternative must be chosen [13, 14].

The result of Copeland voting procedure method to the problem of sustainable cities is described in Table 7. Alternative 11 was the winner with the highest score. This alternative represents the city of Lavras da Mangabeira, and this means that this city was the one that presented the best performance in the evaluated criteria, that is, the municipality with the greatest concern with environmental issues and sustainable development. In sequence, we can see that the cities of Aurora and Barro were in the second and third positions in the ranking of sustainable cities, respectively. The Baixio city presented the lowest performance, being in the last position of the ranking.

Table 7. Global ranking of alternatives.

Alternatives	Global ranking														
	A1	A2	A3	A4	A5	A6	A7	A8	A9	A10	A11	A12	A13	Wins	Total
A1	–	1	1	1	1	1	1	1	1	1	0	1	1	11	10
A2	0	–	0	0	0	0	0	0	0	0	0	0	0	0	−12
A3	0	1	–	1	1	1	1	1	1	1	0	1	1	10	8
A4	0	1	0	–	1	0	0	0	1	1	0	1	1	6	0
A5	0	1	0	0	–	0	0	0	1	0	0	1	0	3	−6
A6	0	1	0	1	1	–	0	0	1	0	0	1	1	6	0
A7	0	1	0	1	1	1	–	0	1	1	0	1	1	8	4
A8	0	1	0	1	1	1	1	–	1	1	0	1	1	9	6
A9	0	1	0	0	0	0	0	0	–	0	0	0	1	2	−8
A10	0	1	0	0	1	1	0	0	1	–	0	1	1	6	0
A11	1	1	1	1	1	1	1	1	1	1	–	1	1	12	12
A12	0	1	0	0	0	0	0	0	1	0	0	–	1	3	−6
A13	0	1	0	0	1	0	0	0	0	0	0	0	–	2	−8
Losses	1	12	2	6	9	6	4	3	10	6	0	9	10	–	–

5 Conclusion

A group decision model for ranking sustainable cities was proposed based on the multicriteria approach and the framework for choosing a voting procedure. In the problem modeling, the objectives and rationality of DMs were characterized, and alternatives, criteria, and parameters as intra-criteria and inter-criteria information are defined as well.

Until this point, the problem was treated with individual focus, and, thus, the objective was to analyze how each DM rank sustainable cities based on their own perspective. To aggregate the individual ranks and reach a collective ranking, the framework for choosing a VP was used to find an appropriate VP for the problem. The application of a VP resulted in a global ranking of sustainable cities.

Throughout the application of the proposed model, a set of municipalities can be evaluated according to the economic, social, and environmental objectives of sustainability. This model can be used to reward cities with the best performance as a way to encourage continuity of sustainable practices by municipalities in a region.

In the Salgado basin problem, the Lavras da Mangabeira city leads the ranking of sustainable cities.

It is important to highlight that in application it was considered nine criteria capable of representing the objectives of the study. Here, the availability of data on the institute's websites was an important factor in choosing it. Other different criteria may be included or excluded in future model applications since they provide the decision interest.

Acknowledments. The authors would like to acknowledge the financial support of Fundação de Amparo a Ciência e Tecnologia de Pernambuco (FACEPE) under grant: IBPG- 1292–3.08/19, the Coordenação de Aperfeiçoamento de Pessoal de Nível Superior (CAPES) - Financing code 001, and the Conselho Nacional de Desenvolvimento Científico e Tecnólogico (CNPq).

References

1. Zagonari, F., Rossi, C.: A negotiation support system for disputes between Iraq and Turkey over the Tigris-Euphrates basin. J. Hydrol. **514**, 65–84 (2014). https://doi.org/10.1016/j.jhydrol.2014.04.003
2. Gonçalo, T.E.E., Morais, D.C.: Group multicriteria model for allocating resources to combat drought in the Brazilian semi-arid region. Water Policy. **20**, 1145–1160 (2018). https://doi.org/10.2166/wp.2018.034
3. Du, J.-L., Liu, Y., Forrest, J.-L.: An interactive group decision model for selecting treatment schemes for mitigating air pollution. Environ. Sci. Pollut. Res. **26**(18), 18687–18707 (2019). https://doi.org/10.1007/s11356-019-05072-7
4. Urtiga, M.M., Morais, D.C., Hipel, K.W., Kilgour, D.M.: Group decision methodology to support watershed committees in choosing among combinations of alternatives. Group Decis. Negot. **26**(4), 729–752 (2016). https://doi.org/10.1007/s10726-016-9515-5
5. Schramm, V.B., Schramm, F.: An approach for supporting problem structuring in water resources management and planning. Water Resour. Manage. **32**(9), 2955–2968 (2018). https://doi.org/10.1007/s11269-018-1966-9
6. Wang, S., Ma, H., Zhao, Y.: Exploring the relationship between urbanization and the eco-environment - a case study of Beijing-Tianjin-Hebei region. Ecol. Indic. **45**, 171–183 (2014). https://doi.org/10.1016/j.ecolind.2014.04.006
7. Wei, J., Ding, Z., Meng, Y., Li, Q.: Regional sustainable assessment at city level based on CSDIS (China Sustainable Development Indicator System) Concept in the New Era, China. Chinese Geogr. Sci. **30**, 976–992 (2020). https://doi.org/10.1007/s11769-020-1158-4
8. Vučetić, A.: Importance of environmental indicators of sustainable development in the transitional selective tourism destination. Int. J. Tour. Res. **20**, 317–325 (2018). https://doi.org/10.1002/jtr.2183
9. Jeníček, V.: Sustainable development – indicators. 2013, 74–80 (2013). https://doi.org/10.17221/11/2012- AGRICECON.
10. Labella, Á., Ishizaka, A., Martínez, L.: Consensual Group-AHPSort: applying consensus to GAHPSort in sustainable development and industrial engineering. Comput. Ind. Eng. **152** (2021). https://doi.org/10.1016/j.cie.2020.107013.
11. de Almeida, A.T., Morais, D.C., Costa, A.P.C.S., Alencar, L.H., Daher, S. de F.D.: Decisão Em Grupo E Negociação - Métodos E Aplicações. Interciência, São Paulo (2019)
12. Matsatsinis, N.F., Grigoroudis, E., Samaras, A.: Aggregation and disaggregation of preferences for collective decision-making. Gr. Decis. Negot. **14**, 217–232 (2005). https://doi.org/10.1007/s10726-005-7443-x
13. Nurmi, H.: Voting procedures: a summary analysis. Br. J. Polit. Sci. **13**, 181–208 (1983). https://doi.org/10.1017/S0007123400003215
14. de Almeida, A.T., Morais, D.C., Nurmi, H.: Systems, Procedures and Voting Rules in Context: A Primer for Voting Rule Selection. Springer International Publishing (2019). https://doi.org/10.1007/978-3-030-30955-8
15. Campos, J., Souza Filho, F., Lima, H.: Risks and uncertainties in reservoir yield in highly variable intermittent rivers: case of the Castanhão Reservoir in semi-arid Brazil. (2014). https://doi.org/10.1080/02626667.2013.836277

16. do Nordeste, D.: Situation of the Salgado River may impact the reload of Castanhão - Region - Diário do Nordeste. https://diariodonordeste.verdesmares.com.br/regiao/situacao-do-rio-sal gado-pode-impactar-na-recarga-do-castanhao-1.2219925. Accessed 02 Sep 2020
17. Gonçalo, T.E.E., Morais, D.C.: Supplier selection model for a Brazilian oil company based on a multi-criteria group decision approach. South African J. Bus. Manag. **49**, 97–98 (2018). https://doi.org/10.4102/sajbm.v49i1.354
18. Felsenthal, D.S., Nurmi, H.: Voting Procedures for Electing a Single Candidate Proving Their (In)Vulnerability to Various Voting Paradoxes. Springer (2018). https://doi.org/10.1007/978-3-319-74033-1
19. Nurmi, H.: On the difficulty of making social choices. Theory Decis. **38**, 99–119 (1995). https://doi.org/10.1007/BF01083171
20. Nurmi, H.: Comparing Voting Systems. Springer Netherlands, Dordrecht (1987). https://doi.org/10.1007/978-94-009-3985-1
21. IBGE: Brazilian Institute of Geography and Statistics. https://cidades.ibge.gov.br/. Accessed 15 Sep 2020
22. Campos, J.N.B., Studart, T.M.D.C.: Drought and water policies in Northeast Brazil: backgrounds and rationale. Water Policy. **10**, 425–438 (2008). https://doi.org/10.2166/wp.200 8.058
23. Munda, G.: Social Multi-Criteria Evaluation for a Sustainable Economy. Springer, Heidelberg (2008). https://doi.org/10.1007/978-3-540-73703-2
24. Morais, D.C., de Almeida, A.T., Alencar, L.H., Clemente, T.R.N., Cavalcanti, C.Z.B.: PROMETHEE-ROC model for assessing the readiness of technology for generating energy. Math. Probl. Eng. 2015 (2015). https://doi.org/10.1155/2015/530615.
25. de Almeida Filho, A.T., Clemente, T.R.N., Morais, D.C., de Almeida, A.T.: Preference modeling experiments with surrogate weighting procedures for the PROMETHEE method. Eur. J. Oper. Res. **264**, 453–461 (2018). https://doi.org/10.1016/j.ejor.2017.08.006.
26. IPECE: Institute of Research and Economic Strategy of Ceará. http://ipecedata.ipece.ce.gov.br/ipece-data-web/module/painel-dinamico.xhtml. Accessed 15 Sep 2020
27. DENATRAN: National Traffic Department, https://www.gov.br/infraestrutura/pt-br/assuntos/denatran. Accessed 21 Sep 2020
28. SIDRA: IBGE Automatic Recovery System. https://sidra.ibge.gov.br/home/pms/brasil. Accessed 16 Sept 2020
29. ANA: National Water and Sanitation Agency. https://www.gov.br/ana/pt-br. Accessed 15 Sept 2020
30. MEC: Ministério da Educação. https://www.gov.br/mec/pt-br. Accessed 21 Sept 2020

Does Gender Differentiate in Expectations Regarding the Representation of Preferential Information in Decision Support Systems?

Ewa Roszkowska[1]([✉]) [iD] and Tomasz Wachowicz[2] [iD]

[1] University of Bialystok, Warszawska 63, 15-062 Bialystok, Poland
e.roszkowska@uwb.edu.pl
[2] University of Economics in Katowice, 1 Maja 50, 40-287 Katowice, Poland
tomasz.wachowicz@uekat.pl

Abstract. The present study reports the results of an online survey in which we examined gender-specific expectations towards the support mechanisms offered in the decision support systems. The preferred ways of declaring preferences (e.g. using numbers, words, or pictograms) and decision-makers expectations regarding the forms of representing the results by the system (e.g. rankings vs ratings) were analyzed. The relationships between gender and the declarations regarding the support mechanisms were examined using the one-tailed two proportion test and the chi-square test of independence. This study's main result is significant differences in the preferred form of representation of preference information in decision support mechanisms depending on user gender. The results show that females are more likely to use rating and more willing to declare their preferences using the non-numerical form. Consistent with this finding, females recommend more often the AHP and TOPSIS methods for solving multiple criteria problems than males, while males recommend more often SMART. These results may be used to individualize the decision-making support mechanisms to allow for more reliable preference elicitation.

Keywords: Decision support system · Preference analysis · Multiple criteria decision-making techniques · Gender

1 Introduction

The development of decision support systems started in the late 1960s when scientists began using quantitative models to assist in decision making and planning. Michael S. Scott Morton, was the first who formulated the concept of assisted decision-making. He introduced the term "Decision Support System" [9], being a pioneer of decision support research. A historical overview of the main stages in the development of Decision Support Systems (DSS) is presented in [21].

Sprague and Carlson [29] defined DSS as "a class of information system that draws on transaction processing systems and interacts with the other parts of the overall information system to support the decision-making activities of managers and other knowledge

© Springer Nature Switzerland AG 2021
D. C. Morais et al. (Eds.): GDN 2021, LNBIP 420, pp. 82–96, 2021.
https://doi.org/10.1007/978-3-030-77208-6_7

workers in organizations". Kersten and Lai [13] provide a historical overview of software used to support negotiations and aid negotiators. They notice that decision support systems help users understand the problem and its structure, formalize goals and preferences, and find solutions to the problem. They allow building the negotiation template and the negotiation offer scoring system. To build such a system, multiple criteria methods are often implemented, as is the case of Inspire [14], Negoisst [26], SmartSettle [30], Web-Hipre [19], eNego [35]. Such a negotiation scoring system allows the negotiator to evaluate offers and prepare a negotiating strategy in the prenegotiation phase [4, 35]. During the negotiation phase, it helps assess the value of the other party's offer, measure the scale of concessions, etc. Consequently, the value of the final agreement can also be measured. Therefore, errors made while building the negotiation offer scoring system may result in unreliable support for the negotiator, making them misinterpret the progress of the negotiation process and the quality of the contract negotiated [12, 22, 24, 34].

However, DSS development requires an interdisciplinary research approach involving computer science, decision analysis, statistics, psychology, and information engineering. DSS often implements models and tools of multiple criteria methods that require a specific way of interacting between the system and the user. Hence, various problems may occur with the system's proper use by the decision-makers (DMs). The analysis of the decision-makers effectiveness in DSS should be conducted in the context of the identified DMs' individual differences. They can be, among many, skills in handling the decision support methods and algorithms implemented in DSS, cognitive style, or gender. The potential misunderstanding of the mechanisms of action of support algorithms may cause incorrect analysis of preferences.

Cognitive style is a subjective process by which people perceive, organize, and use information during the decision-making process [15, 18]. It affects the way a person creates a picture of a decision-making situation to better understand it. In many cases, it determines the decision-maker preferences concerning the form of data presentation, and the way how preferences are analyzed (e.g. qualitative vs quantitative) [1]. The studies [3, 17, 31] confirm that where the decision support system considers the user's cognitive style, such a system is more effective and user-friendly. Potential problems for the system user with the interface and how information is processed may result in poor acceptance of the decision support system.

The empirical findings on gender, decision making and decision support performance have shown mixed results. Powell and Johnson [20] noted that decision support systems are designed with no gender discrimination. Still, people can make decisions in different ways and have various preferences regarding information processing. Aronson et al. [1] provided a comprehensive review of the literature, which suggests that gender differences may be related to skills and motivation, risk attitude and self-confidence, as well as decision-making style. At the same time, they stress that the results obtained are ambiguous. Therefore, it is not possible to determine whether men or women are better or worse decision-makers.

Cai et al. [5] conducted a meta-analysis of the empirical research studies (50 articles from 1997 to 2014) on gender and attitudes toward technology use. They found that "males still hold more favourable attitudes toward technology use than females, but such differences would be characterized as small effect sizes". Venkatesh and Morris [32] used the Technology Acceptance Model (TAM) and found that women's computer usage is more strongly influenced by perceived ease of use. In contrast, men's is more strongly influenced by perceived usefulness.

Handley et al. [10], Epstein [7] and Sladek et al. [28], using Rational-Experiential Inventory (REI) [8], showed that women more frequently use experiential thinking style than men. Additionally, Sladek et al. [28] reported that men more often than women used rational thinking style. Yet, other studies [2, 16] did not find gender differences in the decision-making style. The expectations towards the decision support mechanisms offered in DSS were also confronted with thinking style [23, 33], measured either by REI or the General Decision Making Style (GDMS) [27]. The experiments showed that decision-makers with high rational and low experiential modes prefer mechanisms based on the numerical scales more than other decision-makers.

In this paper, based on the decision-making experiment described in [23], an attempt is made to identify expectations regarding the representation of preferential information in decision support systems from the gender perspective. The study aims to answer the following question:

Do females and males differ in expectations regarding the representation of preferential information in decision support systems while solving the multiple criteria decision-making problems?

We categorized the expectations of decision-makers regarding the presentation of results by the system as related to rankings and ratings. The expectations regarding different ways of declaring preferences were related to the use of numbers, words or pictograms. The consistency of DMs preferences over the different support mechanisms they expect from the decision support was also examined.

The results show a high consistency regarding expectations of preference declarations with respect to options with the forms of representing results of decision analysis. Most of them chose numerical forms of preference representation. The results also indicate that the desired form of representation of preferential information may differ concerning gender. With our research, we contribute to the behavioural theory of decision-making and support. Understanding the preferred form of preference elicitation can help the analysts and software designers offer reliable decision support to DMs.

The remainder of this paper is structured as follows. Section 2 discusses the research experiment and presents the methodology applied. The results are shown in Sect. 3. The summary presents the conclusions and proposals for further research.

2 Decision-Making Experiment

To find the answer to the research question, we used the dataset from the online decision-making experiment (for details, see also [23]). In this experiment, the problem of choosing a flat to rent was considered by students. It consisted of five alternatives, each describing the resolution levels for five evaluation criteria (Table 1).

The decision support offered to the participants by the online DSS used in the experiment consisted of five main steps, which included: (1) completing the pre-decision questionnaire; (2) reading the decision-making problem; (3) setting up the criteria weights using two approaches: sliders with accompanied linguistic scale and AHP-like pairwise comparisons; (4) analyzing alternatives' performances using three multiple criteria methods AHP (Analytic Hierarchy Process) [25], SMART/DR (Simple Multi-Attribute Rating Technique/Direct Rating) [6], and TOPSIS (The Technique for Order of Preference by Similarity to Ideal Solution) [11]; and (4) completing a post-decision questionnaire.

Table 1. Decision matrix

Alternative	Rental costs	No. of rooms	Size	Equipment	Travel time to university
A	950 PLN	2 rooms (including 1 room with a kitchenette)	35 m^2	Fridge, washing machine, microwave	10–12 min
B	1200 PLN	3 rooms (including a living room with a kitchenette)	54 m^2	Fridge, washing machine, dishwasher, wireless internet	30–35 min
C	900 PLN	2 rooms+kitchen (separate)	35 m^2	Fridge, washing machine, cable internet	20–25 min
D	700 PLN	1 room+kitchen	25 m^2	Fridge, washing machine, TV, cable TV, cable internet	30–35 min
E	950 PLN	1 room+kitchen	54 m^2	Fridge, washing machine, cable internet	20–25 min

Source: Own

The methods used at stage 4 are characterized by a different way of analyzing preferences and the interface offered in this process. The AHP uses a linguistic evaluation mechanism of pairs of criteria and options for each criterion, implemented graphically based on sliders. In SMART/DR, the decision-maker assessed each option's attractiveness assigning a number from the interval [0, 100]. In TOPSIS, preferences for qualitative options were defined using a pictogram interface (so-called quality stars), associated with a seven-point Likert scale (Fig. 1).

The participants used all three methods at stage 4 to get familiar with different preference elicitation approaches and use different support mechanism. An order of the methods was fixed and the same for all participants. Yet, the other experimental setups with the same example used in the online DSS do not confirm an order effect (e.g. a fatigue effect).

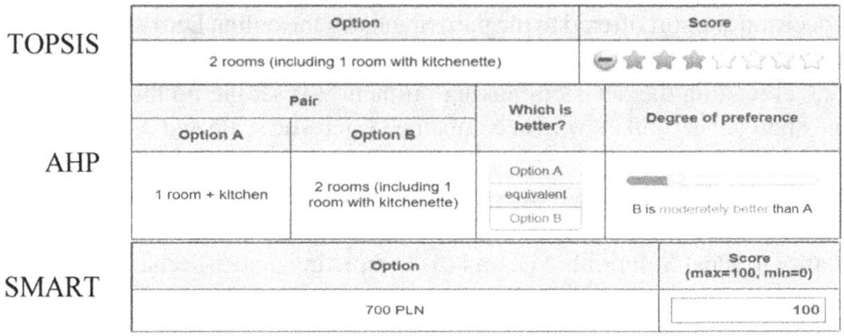

Fig. 1. Examples of the interfaces for MCDA techniques used in experiment

After completing their decision-making, the participants were asked to answer the questions from series of questionnaires. From the point of view of our research goal, the following questions from the post-decision questionnaire are considered:

Q1: *What is the sufficient effect of analyzing and comparing alternatives (rating, ranking, other information) in multiple criteria problems?*

Q2: *What is the preferred form of declaring the preferences for options within decision criteria (numerically, pictorially, verbally, in another way) in multiple criteria problems?*

Q3: *What is the preferred form of representing the performance of alternatives in the final ranking (numerically, verbally, pictorially, in another way) by DSS in multiple criteria problems?*

Q4: *What method (AHP, SMART, TOPSIS, or none of them) can you recommended for solving multiple criteria problems?*

The study was conducted in several experimental series between 2014 and 2018. Participants in the study were students of a few Polish universities. In the end, 1909 complete surveys were analyzed. The average age of respondents was 21 years, and 62% of the study participants were female. Respondents declared an intermediate knowledge of decision-making support methods equal to 2.67 on a 7-point Likert scale. No statistically significant differences between males and females were observed in declared knowledge of decision-making methods (2.69 vs 2.66; U-Mann Whitney test, $p = 0.553$).

3   Results

In the first step, the responses to Q1, Q2 and Q3 were studied. Next, the relationship between them was investigated. Hence, it was required to eliminate those respondents whose answers to Q1 were "I need other information" or to Q2, Q3 – "In another way", i.e. 75 records. Finally, the answers to question Q4 were discussed.

3.1 Expectation Towards the Representation of the Final Results of the Decision

The number of users choosing ratings (cardinal) versus rating (ordinal) or other types of representation of the final result is presented in Table 2 and visualized in Fig. 2.

Table 2. Forms of representing the final results of decision analysis

Forms of representing the final results of decision analysis	Male	Female	Total
The rating of each alternative	316	441	757
Ordering (ranking) alternatives	385	716	1101
I need other information	25	26	51
Sum	726	1183	1909

There is a significant association between gender and forms of representing the final results of decision analysis (chi-square test; $\chi^2(2) = 11.423$, p = 0.003). For more than half of the respondents (57.67%), a satisfactory result of the final analysis and comparison of alternatives is ranking. For 39.65% – it is a rating, i.e. they need to have scores for each alternative (Fig. 2). The gender analysis shows that 37.28% of females and 43.5% of males chose the rating, while 60.52% of females and 53.03% of males chose the rating (Fig. 2). The gender differences in the choice of rating (two-proportion test; p = 0.003) or ranking (two-proportion test; p < 0.001) are statistically significant.

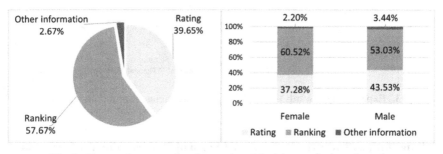

Fig. 2. Forms of representing the results of decision analysis and gender

3.2 Expectations Towards the Declaration of Preferences for Options

The respondent's choices regarding the most preferred way of declaration of preferences for options (the resolution levels of alternatives) are shown in Table 3 and visualized in Fig. 3.

There is a significant association between gender and declaration of preferences for options (chi-square test; $\chi^2(3) = 9.915$, p = 0.019). More than half of respondents (55.89%) indicated a numerical form, almost 32% of respondents identified a pictorial form, and 10.5% verbal form. It is worth noting that the numerical form allows for an

Table 3. Was for declaration of preferences for options

The way of declaration of preferences for options	Male	Female	Total
Numerical	422	645	1067
Pictorial	202	404	606
Verbal	85	116	201
In other way	17	18	35
Sum	726	1183	1909

accurate representation of preferences of options. In contrast, other forms are associated with less precision in evaluation.

Statistically significant differences were observed between females and males in the choice of preference representation for options. Women chose a pictorial representation of options preferences more often than men (34.15% vs 27.82%; two-proportion test; p = 0.001). Also, females were less likely than males to choose a numerical (54.52% vs 58.13%; two-proportion test; p = 0.062) and verbal representation of option preferences than males (9.81% vs 11.71%; two-proportion test; p = 0.095). These differences are, however, statistically insignificant.

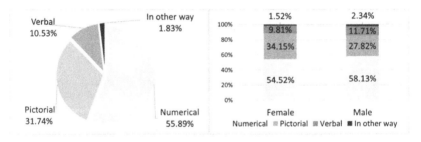

Fig. 3. Expectations towards the declarations of preferences for options and gender

3.3   Expectations Towards the Preferred Form of Representing the Performance of Alternatives in the Final Ranking by DSS

Finally, the most preferred form of representing the performance of alternatives in the final ranking by DSS was analyzed. Several answers could be given by respondents to question Q3 (e.g. numerically, verbally, pictorially). The most common responses are set into three categories: only numerical, non-numerical (verbal or pictorial) and mixed. The answers are presented in Table 4, and the results are visualized in Fig. 4.

There is a significant association between gender and the description of alternatives in the final ranking (chi-square test; $\chi^2(3) = 7.976$, p = 0.047). The vast majority of respondents (73.23%) chose the numerical form as the preferred form for presenting the alternatives' quality. The purely numerical form was indicated by 45.05% of respondents, while several forms, including numerical (mixed, including numerical) – by 28.18% of

Table 4. Description of alternatives in the final ranking

Description of alternatives in the final ranking	Male	Female	Total
Only numerical	354	506	860
Mixed	194	344	538
Non-numerical	167	320	487
In other way	11	13	24
Sum	726	1183	1909

respondents. More than a quarter of respondents (25.5%) chose non-numerical form, i.e. pictorial or verbal. Note that these results are relatively consistent with those presented in Sect. 3.2. We can confirm the previous declaration of the majority of the group as to the desire to describe the preferences for options quantitatively.

Statistically significant differences were observed for females and males (Fig. 4). Females were less likely than males to choose only a numerical description of alternatives (42.77% vs 48.76%; two-proportion test; p = 0.005). However, more often than males they chose a non-numerical description of alternatives (27.05% vs 23.00%; two-proportion test; p = 0.024). Females were also more likely to select the mixed representation of alternatives than males, but the differences here are statistically insignificant (29.08% vs 26.72%; two-proportion test; p = 0.133).

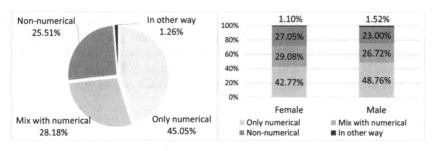

Fig. 4. Expectations towards the description of alternatives in the final ranking and gender

3.4 Expectations Towards the Forms of Representing Results of Decision Analysis vs Declaration of Preferences for Options

The relationships between the declaration of preferences for options and the representation of results of decision analysis are shown in Table 5. There is no significant association between them neither for female (chi-square test; $\chi^2(2) = 0.619, p = 0.734$) nor for male respondents (chi-square test for male; $\chi^2(2) = 5.812, p = 0.055$).

We identified three groups of respondents in Table 5 that describe the balance between the respondents' efforts at the preference elicitation stage and the informativeness of the results they expect from DSS. They may be described in the following way:

Table 5. Forms of representing the results of decision analysis, ways of declaring preferences for options, and gender

The way of declaration for options	Forms of representing the results of decision analysis				Total
	Rating		Ranking		
	Male	Female	Male	Female	
Numerical	196	249	215	387	1027
Pictorial	74	145	122	250	591
Verbal	39	44	41	72	196
Sum	309	438	378	709	1834

Effort-balanced class	Effort wasting class	Overdemanding class

- **Group 1** (Effort-balanced class) consists of respondents whose cognitive engagement at the preference elicitation stage was coherent with the expectations towards representing the results. In this group, we encounter the respondents who declared their preferences numerically and expected the offers' rating to be produced as the result, as well as those who described their preferences verbally (graphically) and accept no high precision of final evaluation of alternatives (i.e. by rank order only).
- **Group 2** (Effort-wasting class) consists of respondents who engaged in preference elicitation more (by declaring preferences numerically) but accepted ranking as the final product of such an analysis.
- **Group 3** (Overdemanding class) was represented by respondents that revealed low cognitive effort at the preference elicitation stage (declaring preferences verbally or pictorially only), but expecting the results of high-precision, i.e. in forms of the rating.

The differences for those groups concerning gender are shown in Fig. 5. There is no significant association between defined classes and gender (chi-square test; $\chi^2(2) = 1.301$, p = 0.522). The most numerous class occurred to be the effort balanced one for both females and males. No significant statistical differences between genders were identified in fractions with respect of the each type of group (p > 0.05).

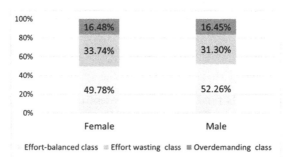

Fig. 5. Rating, ranking, declarations of preferences for options, and gender

3.5 Expectations Towards the Declaration of Preferences for Options and the Representation of Alternatives

The relationships between the way of declaration of preferences for options and a description of alternatives in the final ranking are shown in Table 6. There is a significant association between them for both female (chi-square test; $\chi^2(4) = 258.978$, p < 0.001) and male respondents (chi-square test for male; $\chi^2(4) = 193.117$, p < 0.001).

Table 6. Preferences for option and description alternatives in final ranking and gender

Description of alternatives in final ranking	Declaration of preferences for options						Total
	Numerical		Pictorial		Verbal		
	Male	Female	Male	Female	Male	Female	
Only numerical	278	384	39	81	25	32	839
Mixed	106	190	58	119	20	28	521
Non-numerical	27	62	99	195	35	56	474
Sum	411	636	196	395	80	116	1834

Consistent	Quasi-Consistent	Non-Consistent

Moving on to the strategies characteristic of explicit inductive learning, listed together with their mean scores and standard deviations in Table 18.3, it can be observed that the subjects reported using five of the GLS at a high rate of frequency. This was the case for statements 1, 6, 8, 9 and 10, with the last of these ('I listen carefully for any feedback the teacher gives me about the structures I use') being by far the most popular and generating the average of 4.45. There was just one strategic behavior which was used at a low rate of frequency by the third year students as well as the whole sample (2.00 and 2.38, respectively) and it had to do with keeping a notebook with examples of a structure for which a rule was being discovered (4). On the whole, such findings are not surprising because using different clues to figure out the rule, checking with more proficient peers whether a generalization is correct, trying to apply a newly discovered rule in a meaningful context or carefully listening for teacher feedback all represent actions which advanced learners of English are likely to engage in. On the other hand, the popularity of keeping a special notebook to facilitate rule discovery is not something that many students are likely to find particularly appealing, regardless of the educational level. What is quite baffling, though, is the high rate of reported use (3.65) of the strategy in which a learner notices that he or she has been led into an overgeneralization error and thinks about what has gone wrong (6), which would be employed in reaction to the *garden path technique* (cf. Herron and Tomasello 1992). Since this instructional option is not often used in practical grammar classes or in language teaching in general, one might wonder why this statement was given so much recognition. One viable explanation could be that it was simply misunderstood by the students or perhaps entirely alien to them, which, as was the case with the previous category, could have made them opt for what they saw as a safe option.

Three groups of respondents were identified again, based on consistency of declarations regarding preferences representtions while answering question Q2 and Q3. They may be described in the following way:

- **Group 1** (Consistent declarations) consists of respondents with complete consistency in the declarations regarding the representation of options and alternatives. These participants chose a numerical representation of options and alternatives or both non-numerical representation of options and alternatives.
- **Group 2** (Quasi-Consistent declarations) consists of respondents who chose the mixed description of alternatives in the final ranking, while the preferred declaration of preferences for options was numerical or non-numerical.
- **Group 3** (Non-Consistent declarations) is represented by respondents with a lack of consistency between the declaration of preferences for options and a description of alternatives in the final ranking. These participants chose a non-numerical representation of preferences for options and a numerical representation of alternatives, or conversely, a numerical representation of options and a pictorial or verbal representation of alternatives.

The results obtained in the Table 6 showed that there is some systematic discordance between effort and expectations toward the effects of this effort for some of the respondents in the survey. Already the previous section demonstrated the existence of groups of respondents with expectations for the representation of the final decision support results not in line with the declarations of the performance of the options. From the above results, we additionally know how inconsistent these expectations could be. For instance, we can distinguish DMs who want to declare preferential information vaguely and imprecisely but receive an information-rich (quantitative) description of the alternatives (enrichment of the scale). However, this is a relatively small percentage of respondents.

The representation of a group from the gender perspective is shown in Fig. 6. There is no a significant association between classes and gender (chi-square test; $\chi^2(2) = 3.818$, $p = 0.148$). There is no significant statistical gender difference between respondents concerning the type of consistency class ($p < 0.05$).

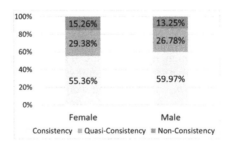

Fig. 6. Expectations towards the declaration of preferences for options, the representation of alternatives and gender

3.6 Recommendation of Multiple Criteria Methods

In Table 7, the numbers of respondents who recommended a particular multiple criteria method (AHP, SMART, TOPSIS) are provided, and the results are visualized in Fig. 7.

Table 7. Recommendation multiple criteria methods

Recommended method	Male	Female	Total
AHP	197	367	564
SMART	190	200	390
TOPSIS	311	574	885
None of them	28	42	70
Sum	726	1183	1909

There is a significant association between gender and the recommended method (chi-square test; $\chi^2(3) = 24.454$, $p < 0.001$). What is interesting, the differences in fraction of choices made by female and male DMs are significant for all methods: AHP (31.02% vs 27.13%; two-proportion test; $p = 0.035$), SMART (48.52% vs 42.84%; two-proportion test; $p < 0.001$) and TOPSIS (16.91% vs 26.17%; two-population test; $p = 0.009$).

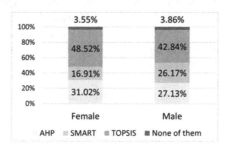

Fig. 7. Recommendation multiple criteria methods and gender

The females are more likely to recommend AHP and TOPSIS than the males, while males more likely recommended SMART. The results are consistent with the previous finding because SMART needs more numerical calculation and direct use and assignment of numbers than AHP or TOPSIS.

4 Summary

In this study, we tried to answer the question regarding the differences between males and females in the preferred types of preference information during the process of decision analysis conducted in the decision support system. We based our analyses on the dataset of the decision-making experiment we had organized in an online DSS. The two-proportion test and chi-square test were used to verify the statistical significance of the potential differences.

The groups of males and females were homogeneous in declared knowledge of decision making support methods, which prevents the effects of skills on the results obtained. We found that females were more likely than males to choose the ranking; pictorial declaration of preferences for options and non-numerical description of alternatives in the final ranking. Simultaneously, males were more likely than females to select the rating and only a numerical description of alternatives in the final ranking. In short, this synthesis provided evidence that females prefer ranking and non-numerical declaration of preferences, oppositely to males. Consistent with this finding, we also found that females recommended more often AHP and TOPSIS than males, while males – SMART.

The results obtained in the experiment confirm some gender-specific differences in schemas of DMs activities focused on solving the decision-making problems presented in the literature. The findings are consistent with Venkatesh and Morris [32] studies where females are more strongly influenced by perceived ease of use, whereas males are more strongly influenced by perceived usefulness while support decisions. The general preferences towards using numbers vs words and pictograms are related to decision style analytical vs experimental [8]. Therefore, the results are consistent with Handley et al. [7] and Sladek et al. [28] studies, where they reported that women preferred experiential information processing style more than men.

Looking at the DMs differences in behavioural characteristics and their impact on preference declarations, it may be interesting to design more detailed research that would identify the preferences towards particular decision support algorithms accompanied by some additional visualization techniques and measure how efficiently the DMs use these tools. It might occur that in such a new and advanced experimental setup gender could play a mediating or moderating role in some of the causal relationships between decision-making styles and DMs choices.

Acknowledgments. This research was supported with the grants from Polish National Science Centre (2016/21/B/HS4/01583).

References

1. Aronson, J.E., Liang, T.-P., MacCarthy, R.V.: Decision Support Systems and Intelligent Systems. Pearson Prentice-Hall, New Jersey (2005)
2. Baiocco, R., Laghi, F., D'Alessio, M.: Decision-making style among adolescents: relationship with sensation seeking and locus of control. J. Adolesc. **32**, 963–976 (2009)
3. Benbasat, I., Dexter, A.S.: Individual differences in the use of decision support aids. J. Acc. Res. **20**(1), 1–11 (1982)
4. Brzostowski, J., Roszkowska, E., Wachowicz, T.: Supporting negotiation by multi-criteria decision-making methods. Optimum-Studia Ekonomiczne **5**, 59 (2012)
5. Cai, Z., Fan, X., Du, J.: Gender and attitudes toward technology use: a meta-analysis. Comput. Educ. **105**, 1–13 (2017)
6. Edwards, W., Barron, F.H.: SMARTS and SMARTER: improved simple methods for multiattribute utility measurement. Organ. Behav. Hum. Decis. Process. **60**(3), 306–325 (1994)

7. Epstein, S.: Cognitive-experiential self-theory of personality. In: Millon, T., Lerner, M.J. (eds.) Handbook of psychology, pp. 159–184. John Wiley & Sons Inc, New Jersey (2003)
8. Epstein, S., Pacini, R., Denes-Raj, V., Heier, H.: Individual differences in intuitive–experiential and analytical–rational thinking styles. J. Pers. Soc. Psychol. **71**(2), 390 (1996)
9. Gorry, G.A., Scott Morton, M.S.: A framework for management information systems (1971)
10. Handley, S.J., Newstead, S.E., Wright, H.: Rational and experiential thinking: a study of the REI. In: Riding, R.J., Rayner, S.G. (eds.) International Perspectives on Individual Differences, pp. 97–113. Ablex Stamford, New York (2000)
11. Hwang, C.-L., Yoon, K.: Methods for Multiple Attribute Decision Making. Springer, Heidelberg (1981)
12. Kersten, G., Roszkowska, E., Wachowicz, T.: The heuristics and biases in using the negotiation support systems. In: Schoop, M., Kilgour, D.M. (eds.) GDN 2017. LNBIP, vol. 293, pp. 215–228. Springer, Cham (2017). https://doi.org/10.1007/978-3-319-63546-0_16
13. Kersten, G.E., Lai, H.: Negotiation support and e-negotiation systems: an overview. Group Decis. Negot. **16**(6), 553–586 (2007). https://doi.org/10.1007/s10726-007-9095-5
14. Kersten, G.E., Noronha, S.J.: WWW-based negotiation support: design, implementation, and use. Decis. Support Syst. **25**(2), 135–154 (1999)
15. Kozhevnikov, M.: Cognitive styles in the context of modern psychology: Toward an integrated framework of cognitive style. Psychol. Bull. **133**(3), 464 (2007)
16. Loo, R.: A psychometric evaluation of the general decision-making style inventory. Personality Individ. Differ. **29**(5), 895–905 (2000). https://doi.org/10.1016/S0191-8869(99)00241-X
17. Lu, H.-P., Yu, H-J., Lu, K.S.: The effects of cognitive style and model type on DSS acceptance: an empirical study. Eur. J. Oper. Res. **131**(3), 649–663 (2001)
18. Messick, S.: Personality consistencies in cognition and creativity. In: Messick, S. (ed.) Individuality in Learning, pp. 4–23. Jossey-Bass, San Francisco (1976)
19. Mustajoki, J., Hämäläinen, R.P.: Web-HIPRE: global decision support by value tree and AHP analysis. INFOR Inf. Syst. Oper. Res. **38**(3), 208–220 (2000)
20. Powell, P.L., Johnson, J.E.V.: Gender and DSS design: the research implications. Decis. Support Syst. **14**(1), 27–58 (1995). https://doi.org/10.1016/0167-9236(94)00014-J
21. Power, D.J.: Decision support systems: a historical overview. In: Burstein, F.W., Holsapple, C. (eds.) Handbook on Decision Support Systems 1: Basic Themes, pp. 121–140. Springer, Heidelberg (2008). https://doi.org/10.1007/978-3-540-48713-5_7
22. Roszkowska, E., Wachowicz, T., Kersten, G.: Can the holistic preference elicitation be used to determine an accurate negotiation offer scoring system? A comparison of direct rating and UTASTAR techniques. In: Schoop, M., Kilgour, D.M. (eds.) GDN 2017. LNBIP, vol. 293, pp. 202–214. Springer, Cham (2017). https://doi.org/10.1007/978-3-319-63546-0_15
23. Roszkowska, E., Wachowicz, T.: Cognitive style and the expectations towards the preference representation in decision support systems. In: Morais, D.C., Carreras, A., de Almeida, A.T., Vetschera, R. (eds.) GDN 2019. LNBIP, vol. 351, pp. 163–177. Springer, Cham (2019). https://doi.org/10.1007/978-3-030-21711-2_13
24. Roszkowska, E., Wachowicz, T.: Inaccuracy in defining preferences by the electronic negotiation system users. In: Kamiński, B., Kersten, G.E., Szapiro, T. (eds.) GDN 2015. LNBIP, vol. 218, pp. 131–143. Springer, Cham (2015). https://doi.org/10.1007/978-3-319-19515-5_11
25. Saaty, T.L.: Decision making with the analytic hierarchy process. Int. J. Serv. Sci. **1**(1), 83–98 (2008)
26. Schoop, M., Jertila, A., List, T.: Negoisst: a negotiation support system for electronic business-to-business negotiations in e-commerce. Data Knowl. Eng. **47**(3), 371–401 (2003)
27. Scott, S.G., Bruce, R.A.: Decision-making style: the development and assessment of a new measure. Educ. Psychol. Meas. **55**(5), 818–831 (1995)

28. Sladek, R.M., Bond, M.J., Phillips, P.A.: Age and gender differences in preferences for rational and experiential thinking. Personality Individ. Differ. **49**(8), 907–911 (2010)
29. Sprague Jr, R.H., Carlson, E.D.: Building effective decision support systems. Prentice Hall Professional Technical Reference (1982)
30. Thiessen, E.M., Soberg, A.: Smartsettle described with the montreal taxonomy. Group Decis. Negot. **12**(2), 165 (2003)
31. Van Bruggen, G., Wierenga, B.: Matching management support systems and managerial problem-solving modes: the key to effective decision support. Eur. Manag. J. **19**(3), 228–238 (2001)
32. Venkatesh, V., Morris, M.G.: Why don't men ever stop to ask for directions? Gender, social influence, and their role in technology acceptance and usage behavior. MIS Q. **24**(1), 115–139 (2000)
33. Wachowicz, T., Roszkowska, E., Filipowicz-Chomko, M.: Decision making profile and the choices of preference elicitation mode – A case of using GDMS inventory. In: Zadnik Strim, L., et al. (eds.) Proceedings of the 15th International Symposium on Operational Research SOR 2019, Slovenian Society INFORMATIKA (SDI), Slovenia, pp. 72–78(2019)
34. Wachowicz, T., Kersten, G.E., Roszkowska, E.: How do i tell you what i want? Agent's interpretation of principal's preferences and its impact on understanding the negotiation process and outcomes. Oper. Res. Int. J. **19**(4), 993–1032 (2019). https://doi.org/10.1007/s12351-018-00448-y
35. Wachowicz, T., Roszkowska, E.: Holistic preferences and prenegotiation preparation. In: Kilgour, D.M., Eden, C. (eds.) Handbook of Group Decision and Negotiation, pp. 255–290. Springer, Cham (2021)

Conflict Resolution

Stable Agreements with Fixed Payments on Transboundary Flood Prone Rivers

Anand Abraham[✉] and Parthasarathy Ramachandran

Department of Management Studies, Indian Institute of Science, Bangalore 560012, India
{anandj,parthar}@iisc.ac.in

Abstract. This study contributes to the existing literature on the river sharing problem. We extend the traditional river sharing model to incorporate variability in endowments and the externality of flooding. In this work, we construct a theoretical model of a successive flood prone river shared between two riparian states. We investigate the stability of agreements which allocate water as well as flood damages among riparian states. Cooperation is ensured by means of fixed annual side-payments, and responsibilities over flood damages are assumed to be assigned using the Sequential Upstream Proportional Allocation rule. If variability in water availability is taken into account, then a stable agreement must sustain cooperative behaviour for any realization of endowments, and must be resilient to scarcity or floods which occur as a consequence of variability. In order to frame such agreements, we utilise the theory of infinitely repeated discounted games. We derive a threshold limit on the discount factor, below which stability cannot be ensured.

Keywords: River sharing problem · Flood · Variability · Repeated game

1 Introduction

A flood is said to occur when a river flows over its usual confines and temporarily covers some area which it usually does not cover, thus causing damage. The scale of damage associated with a flood depends on the level of economic activity, flood prevention infrastructure, and population associated with areas prone to flood [1]. A transboundary flood is a flood which occurs on a river shared between multiple sovereign states. Transboundary floods are more threatening than normal floods, since ownership rights on transboundary rivers are not well defined, and so allocation of water as well as externality costs are causes for dispute on such rivers. Transboundary floods may be regarded as an externality on transboundary rivers since the flood damage in a downstream state may be caused due to excess water which originates from an upstream state. This raises the question regarding how such flood damages affects the cooperation between agents in the basin. In this study, we attempt to answer this question.

Some of the recent studies have shown that presence of externalities like pollution and dams may have adverse effects on water allocation and cooperation. For example, it has been shown in the context of pollution, that the overall social surplus may be reduced because of externalities [2]. Similarly, recent research has revealed that ability

© Springer Nature Switzerland AG 2021
D. C. Morais et al. (Eds.): GDN 2021, LNBIP 420, pp. 99–112, 2021.
https://doi.org/10.1007/978-3-030-77208-6_8

to construct dams across transboundary rivers can incentivize upstream states to engage in strategic storage and thus cause downstream welfare loss and social welfare degradation [3]. Compared to these externalities, flooding is more dire. The inherent variability associated with floods makes the occurance of, and the damage due to floods stochastic in nature. Further, the damage due to floods are much larger in magnitude in comparison with other externalities like pollution and dams.

In this paper, we shall refer to sovereign states as *agents*. For simplicity in nomenclature, we shall refer to transboundary successive rivers as simply a *river* and a transboundary flood as *flood*. We use a repeated game formalism to model cooperation along a two agent river, where cooperation is achieved in each period by means of constant side-payments (i.e., a fixed payment rule). We hope to investigate the conditions for the existence of stable agreements on a river which is under risk from both scarcity and flood because of variability in endowments.

1.1 Literature

The literature on river sharing problem has largely been focussed on pollution as an externality [2,4–6]. Floods are also externalities that occur on transboundary rivers. The literature on transboundary floods mostly deal with assessment of vulnerability of societies to floods [7], and identifying river basins with adequate institutional capability to handle transboundary floods effectively [8]. In a recent study, factors such as hydrological changes, population changes, and institutional mechanisms were used to identify river basins which are most vulnerable to floods [9]. It may be noted that there are very few studies which investigate transboundary floods from a game theoretic standpoint so as to address the underlying property rights issues. A notable analysis is the one carried out by Janmaat and Ruijs [10] in their two season model. In their work, they investigate the conditions under which a downstream agent would contribute towards construction of a dam in the upstream agent's territory. Dams in the upstream agent's territory can bring down the flood risk for the downstream agent. However, their model, like most works in the river sharing literature, does not adequately capture the aspect of variability. Since variability is an important characteristic of river flow [11], a study that ignores this aspect might not aptly capture some of the important dimensions of the problem [11].

The literature on variable flows in river sharing literature is very sparse. The first notable work is that of Kilgour and Dinar [12] who tackle variability by using Contingent Water Sharing Agreements (CWSA) or flexible sharing rules. Depending upon the realised flow, the quantity of water to be transferred is decided by using Pareto efficient allocation. The associated side-payments are dictated by the outcome of a bargaining problem. Use of CWSA is slightly impractical as yearly negotiations might not be feasible for river water conflicts associated with developing or under developed economies [13]. Commonly used alternatives to the contingent water sharing agreement is the fixed water sharing agreement and proportional water sharing agreement. The fixed upstream sharing rule, fixed downstream sharing rule, and proportional allocation sharing rule are compared in the context of stochastic flows [11]. They show that stability of the water allocation agreement is higher for fixed upstream sharing rule than for proportional allocation rule and is the lowest for fixed downstream allocation rule. Further they show that fixed upstream allocation agreements supported by monetary transfers are stable for any level of river flow. They also study the effect of climate change on the stability of river sharing agreements. A decrease in the mean flow decreases the stability of river sharing agreements, while an increase in variance of the river flow may have a positive or a negative effect. If non-water transfers are monetary, upstream bargaining power increases the stability, whereas non-monetary (in-kind) transfers have the opposite effect.

The single period formalism of Janmaat and Ruijs [10] does not capture the behaviour of agents when endowment values are different from the expected values. The main criticism towards this approach is the use of expected utility values which treat the dynamic situation as a static problem. A similar approach is used by Ambec et al. [14]. To analyse the stability in such a context, an infinitely repeated game model is quite apt [11,13]. The particular appeal of this approach is centered on its ability to tackle possible deviation from cooperation because of the occurrence of flood and scarcity. From this short survey of literature, one may note that the effects of floods and variable flows are not adequately studied in literature. In this paper, we wish to address this gap by proposing a repeated game theoretic model to investigate the conditions required for agreement stability in a setting with stochastic endowments and downstream flood risk.

2   A Two Agent Infinitely Repeated Discounted Game Model

Consider a successive river shared by two agents 1 and 2, where 1 is upstream of 2. We use the theory of infinitely repeated discounted games to characterize side-payments which make allocation of rights and responsibilities self enforcing. In this framework, the agents 1 and 2 may be thought of as being able to repeat their strategic interaction every year. Let t be the index for years. Let the endowment of agent $j \in \{1,2\}$ at period t be denoted by e_{jt}. These years or time periods occur sequentially and hence the repeated game may be thought of as a sequential game with perfect information. For characterizing the equilibria of these games, we make use of the Folk theorem for discounted games. In this set up, each time period (year) is termed as a stage game. During the course of each stage game, the agents interact strategically and decide on the consumption and payments during that stage. An infinitely repeated game structure makes it possible for the decisions in a stage game to be influenced by the payoffs from future time periods. Thus, an infinitely repeated game framework can make the agents cooperate in an arbitrary time period in the fear of future punishment.

A river sharing agreement made in this context has four essential parts.

1. A scheme of allocating water between riparian states: The efficient allocation (Social welfare maximizer).
2. A scheme for assigning costs during flood: ρ fraction of the downstream flood damage is assigned to the upstream agent
3. A side-payment scheme: A fixed side-payment rule
4. Punishment strategy in case of deviation from cooperation: Trigger strategy

The above four aspects completely describes how rights and responsibilities should be allocated and how the agreement can be sustained. In order to allocate water, we use an efficient consumption profile. The side payment scheme is assumed to be a fixed payment scheme since it is simpler to implement. A grim trigger strategy is taken in this case since it is the most severe punishment conceivable. The grim trigger strategy punishes deviation in one year with non-cooperation in all future years. The trigger strategy is the harshest punishment conceivable. If the trigger strategy cannot sustain cooperation, then we cannot expect any other strategy to sustain cooperation. We shall make use of the Sequential Upstream Proportional Allocation scheme to allocate damages among the agents.

Facilitating cooperation between two agents on a flood prone river requires both allocation of water and allocation of flood damages among riparian states. An appealing way to allocate water among such riparian states is as per the Pareto efficient water allocation which maximizes social welfare [15, 16]. Allocation of damages is a much more difficult task. Though there are many schemes for allocating damages along a river, they are all focussed on allocating pollution damages [4, 17–20]. The information regarding individual pollutant effluent releases are often uncertain or private, whereas water releases by individual agent that result in a flood are measurable. This is a key difference between flooding and pollution externalities. Therefore, a scheme for sharing flood damages among riparian states should take this factor of water releases into account. This means that an upstream agent which has access and control over some additional amount of water which originates in its territory should be held accountable for its consequences downstream along the river. The extra rights which the upstream agent enjoys as a result of its geographical position can also be translated into responsibilities of the upstream agent. Suppose $w_1 = max(e_1 - \hat{x}_1, 0)$ and $w_2 = max(e_2 - \hat{x}_2, 0)$ are water releases or water contributions of agents 1 and 2 located along a river shared by two agents, then an appealing way to allocate damages to agents would be such that agent 1 bears ρ fraction of any flood cost in the downstream agent 2's territory. Where,

$$\rho = \frac{w_1}{w_1 + w_2}.$$

This allocation of damages is termed as the Sequential Upstream Proportional Allocation (SUPA) [21]. The allocation may be observed to be dependent on the water releases, which are stochastic in this problem setting. It may be observed that, this allocation is not self enforcing on its own. This is due to the fact that the upstream agent does not possess any incentive to pay for damages at a downstream territory. However, by making use of side-payments in a repeated game set up, we can make the agents cooperate in terms of both water allocation and damage allocations. This cooperation occurs as a result of the agents being threatened by future punishment (continuous non-cooperation) if they deviate from the ratified agreement in the current period.

Let $e_1 \in [e_1^l, e_1^h]$ and $e_2 \in [e_2^l, e_2^h]$ be continuous random variables with CDF's G_1 and G_2. Bounded nature of random endowments is also assumed in a recent study by Ansink and Houba [13]. We shall also stick to this practice in our endeavour to characterize efficient and stable agreements.

We assume that the strategic situation has the following structure. At the beginning of a time period t, nature chooses an endowment pair (e_{1t}, e_{2t}) which is a realization in $\left[e_1^l, e_1^h\right] \times \left[e_2^l, e_2^h\right]$. Based on the endowments, the agents make their consumption choice x_{1t} and x_{2t}[1] respectively. This consumption in turn yields benefit for the agents. This benefit is captured through a benefit function that is described in the following Assumption 1.

Assumption 1. (Benefit function) *For $j \in N$, the benefit function $b_j(\cdot) : \mathbb{R}_+ \rightarrow \mathbb{R}$. Also $b_j(0) = 0$ and we also assume the function to have a satiation point at $\hat{x}_j$ with $b_j''(x_{jt}) < 0 \quad \forall x_{jt} \geq 0$ which makes the function strictly concave [16].*

We further assume that the consumption of both agents are restricted to $\hat{x}_1$ and $\hat{x}_2$ respectively. That is, even if more water was available in a particular time period, the infrastructure available for storage and distribution would allow the agent to consume no more than her satiation level.

We assume that the river in the downstream territory has a *channel safe limit* denoted by l. We assume that the channel safe limit l is large enough so that flow from agent 1 or agent 2 cannot alone cause a flood (i. e., $e_1^h - \hat{x}_1 < l$ and $e_2^h - \hat{x}_2 < l$). The assumption implies that the flood occurs due to combined actions of agents 1 and 2. The concept of the safe limit is synonymous to channel capacity in the Janmaat and Ruijs [10] model. If the flow value exceeds this channel capacity, a flood is said to occur. The damage incurred in the flood satisfies the following Assumption 2. With a slight abuse of notation, we represent $(e_1 + e_2 - x_1 - x_2 - l)^+ = max(e_1 + e_2 - x_1 - x_2 - l, 0)$. Similarly, $(e_j - \hat{x}_j)^+$ denotes $max(e_j - \hat{x}_j, 0)$ for $j \in \{1, 2\}$.

Assumption 2. (Damage function) *The damage function $d\left((e_1 + e_2 - x_1 - x_2 - l)^+\right) : \mathbb{R}_+ \rightarrow \mathbb{R}_+$ is assumed to be a strictly convex increasing function (i. e., d' and $d'' < 0$). It is assumed that $d(0) = 0$.*

Definition 1. *(Nash allocation) For a realization of endowments given by (e_{1t}, e_{2t}) in the tth stage game, the Nash allocation profile is the Subgame Perfect Equilibrium allocation for the tth stage game of the infinitely repeated game.*

The Nash allocation profile denoted as (x_1^N, x_2^N) can be obtained by applying backward induction on the utility maximization problems of agent 1 and 2 respectively. As in many of the literature in this field, we assume that the status quo allocation of property rights is as per the Absolute Territorial Sovereignty (ATS) doctrine. The ATS principle suggests that every state has rights over the utilization of resources, and responsibility over externalities within its territorial boundary. Under this property rights allocation, the utility maximization problems of individual agents and that of the two-agent system are described below. The non-cooperative water allocation is as per ATS rule. Therefore, the non-cooperative strategic interaction is sequential. That is, agent 1 moves first, followed by agent 2.

---

[1] Note that (x_1, x_2) denote a general consumption profile, which is a random variable, and (x_{it}, x_{2t}) is a specific realization of this random variable.

2.1   Agent 1's Utility Maximization Problem

$$\text{Maximize } b_1(x_1) \tag{1}$$
$$\text{Subject to,}$$
$$x_1 \leq e_1 \tag{2}$$

The optimal non-cooperative consumption is given by $x_1^N = min(\hat{x}_1, e_1)$. This consumption profile is the constrained maximizer for the above convex optimization problem. Similarly, for agent 2, its welfare maximization problem is described below.

2.2   Agent 2's Utility Maximization Problem

$$\text{Maximize } b_2(x_2) \tag{3}$$
$$\text{Subject to,}$$
$$x_1^N + x_2 \leq e_1 + e_2 \tag{4}$$

The optimal solution to this problem is $x_2^N = min(\hat{x}_2, e_2 + e_1 - x_1^N)$.

2.3   The Social Welfare Maximization Problem

If the agents were to act together, they would be concerned with maximizing their collective welfare for a random endowment pair (e_1, e_2). The following is the social welfare maximization problem for this setting.

$$\text{Maximize } b_1(x_1) + b_2(x_2) - d\left((e_1 + e_2 - x_1 - x_2 - l)^+\right) \tag{5}$$
$$\text{Subject to,}$$
$$x_1 \leq e_1$$
$$x_1 + x_2 \leq e_1 + e_2$$
$$x_j \leq \hat{x}_j \forall \ j \in \{1, 2\}$$

The social welfare comprises of benefits derived by the agents and the flood damage (if any). Based on the above welfare maximization problem, we put forth the following definition.

Definition 2. *(Efficient allocation) At an endowment realization given by* (e_{1t}, e_{2t})*, the efficient allocation* (x_{1t}^*, x_{2t}^*) *is the social welfare maximizer.*

During cooperation, the profile (x_1^*, x_2^*) is the most desirable way of allocating water. Note that $x_1^N \geq x_1^*$ and $x_2^N \leq x_2^*$. Also during cooperation, agent 1 takes up ρ fraction of flood damages.

3 Cooperation in the tth Stage Game

Cooperation refers to both agents complying with the agreement. This compliance depends on the amount of side-payment. In this section, we characterise the bounds on the annual fixed payment for a given realization of endowment, so that cooperation is assured.

3.1 Condition for Compliance of Agent 1

The proposed river sharing agreement suggests that for any endowment realization, the agents are allocated with (x_1^*, x_2^*) amount of water respectively. The most optimal deviation from this agreement for agent 1 would be to refuse transferring water to the downstream agent. This would impose a restriction on the transferable utility required so as to make the transfer of water a better option for agent 1 than consuming at the Nash allocation level. Let δ denote the discount factor and τ denote the transferable utility. For some time period t, if x_{jt}^* represents the efficient allocation and x_{jt}^N represents the Nash allocation for $j \in \{1, 2\}$. For agent 1, deviation from cooperation can happen in two ways. (1) In the event of scarcity, agent 1 does not transfer the required quantity of water, and (2) In the event of a flood, agent 1 does not bear the required share of flooding damages. Let (e_{1t}, e_{2t}) be the endowment realization during a scarce period. Scarcity in period t is characterized by $e_{1t} + e_{2t} - x_{1t}^* - x_{2t}^* \leq l$. During such a scarce period, flood does not occur, and therefore agent 1 is not required to bear any externality costs. Here the possible deviation for the upstream agent is to consume at a higher level x_{1t}^N than the required efficient consumption level. Using Folk's theorem for infinitely repeated discounted games, we write the following condition for cooperation during scarcity.

$$b_1(x_{it}^N) + \frac{\delta}{(1-\delta)}(E[b_1(x_1^N)]) \leq b_1(x_{it}^*) + \tau + \frac{\delta}{(1-\delta)}(E[b_1(x_1^*) - \rho d((e_1 + e_2 - x_1^* - x_2^* - l)^+)] + \tau)$$

$$b_1(x_{it}^N) - b_1(x_{it}^*) + \frac{\delta}{(1-\delta)}E[b_1(x_1^N) - b_1(x_1^*) + \rho d((e_1 + e_2 - x_1^* - x_2^* - l)^+)] \leq \frac{\tau}{(1-\delta)} \quad (6)$$

The above expression suggests that the transferable utility which agent 1 receives, should be larger than extra utility agent 1 derives by deviating from the cooperative path. This extra utility is constituted by extra benefit the agent 1 would obtain by consuming at the Nash allocation and expected gains agent 1 would receive by not bearing the expected ρ portion of the flood damage. The discounted total transferable utility should thus exceed the cumulative gain attained by deviating from the cooperative path. This cumulative gain includes additional benefit obtained in current year by resorting to non-cooperative consumption, and the expected gains from future periods.

If a flood occurs in the downstream territory, and if agent 1's flow contribution is positive (i. e., $e_1 - \hat{x}_1 > 0$), then agent 1 has to bear ρ fraction of this damage. The optimal deviation for agent 1 in this case would be to not pay her stipulated part of the flood damage. This translates into the following requirement on the transferable utility.

$$b_1(\hat{x}_{1t}) + \frac{\delta}{(1-\delta)}(E[b_1(x_1^N)]) \leq b_1(\hat{x}_{1t}) - \rho d(e_{1t} + e_{2t} - x_{1t}^* - x_{2t}^* - l) + \tau$$

$$+ \frac{\delta}{(1-\delta)}(E[b_1(x_1^*) - \rho d((e_1 + e_2 - x_1^* - x_2^* - l)^+)] + \tau) \quad (7)$$

$$\rho d(e_{1t} + e_{2t} - x^*_{1t} - x^*_{2t} - l) + \frac{\delta}{(1-\delta)} E\left[b_1(x_1^N) - b_1(x_1^*) + \rho d((e_1 + e_2 - x_1^* - x_2^* - l)^+)\right] \leq \frac{\tau}{(1-\delta)}$$
(8)

3.2   Condition for Compliance of Agent 2

For agent 2, the optimal deviation from the cooperative path would be to refrain from making the side-payment of τ to agent 1 after receiving water transfer or after the upstream agent bearing part of the downstream flood damage. Suppose there is no flood, then the agent 2 would cooperate in a period t only if the stream of payoffs agent 2 gets though cooperation exceeds its payoff through deviation. This translates into the following requirement.

$$b_2(x^*_{2t}) + \frac{\delta}{(1-\delta)} E\left[b_2(x_2^N) - d\left((e_1 + e_2 - x_1^N - x_2^N - l)^+\right)\right] \leq$$
$$b_2(x^*_{2t}) - \tau + \frac{\delta}{(1-\delta)} E\left[b_2(x_2^*) - \tau - (1-\rho)d\left((e_1 + e_2 - x_1^* - x_2^* - l)^+\right)\right]$$
(9)

Note that $d\left((e_1 + e_2 - x_1^N - x_2^N - l)^+\right) = d\left((e_1 + e_2 - x_1^* - x_2^* - l)^+\right)$ since $\hat{x}_1 + \hat{x}_2 = x_1^* + x_2^*$. The condition on the transferable utility simplifies into

$$\frac{\delta}{(1-\delta)} E\left[b_2(x_2^*) - b_2(x_2^N) + \rho d\left((e_1 + e_2 - x_1^* - x_2^* - l)^+\right)\right] \geq \frac{\tau}{(1-\delta)}$$
(10)

In case a flood occurs, the optimal deviation for agent 2 is not to make the side payment. This scenario also results in inequality 10. Therefore, we do not elaborate the flood scenario explicitly.

In order for the water sharing agreement to be stable. The transferable utility must satisfy the conditions 6, 8, and 10 for all realizations of river flow. The condition for stability is investigated in the next section.

4   Stable Agreements on Flood Prone Rivers

In the context of river sharing problem with variability, such as the one discussed in this setting, a stable agreement must also account for the variation in endowments and its consequences. Therefore, a stable agreement should account for scarcity of water which occurs due to variability and also the flood damages which occur when the stochastic flow exceeds the channel safe limit l. We formally define such a stable agreement as follows.

Definition 3. *(Stable agreement) A stable agreement is an agreement which comprises of water allocation, side payment allocation, punishment strategy, and damage allocation scheme that is not breached for any realization of endowment pair (e_1, e_2).*

We attempt to derive a necessary condition for the existence of stable bilateral agreements in this problem setting for sharing flood prone rivers. Before formally describing this condition in Proposition 1, we make some observations regarding the damage share $\rho d((e_1 + e_2 - \hat{x}_1 - \hat{x}_2 - l)^+)$. As stated earlier, the fraction of flood damage allocated to agent 1 is $\rho = \frac{(e_1 - \hat{x}_1)^+}{(e_1 - \hat{x}_1)^+ + (e_2 - \hat{x}_2)^+}$. In order to keep the mathematical expressions shorter, we shall use ρd as a shorthand for this damage share $\rho d((e_1 + e_2 - \hat{x}_1 - \hat{x}_2 - l)^+)$ and w_j to represent $(e_j - \hat{x}_j)^+$.

Lemma 1. *During a period where flood occurs, the flood damage share of agent 1 is maximum when endowment pair is (e_1^h, e_2^h). i.e.,*

$$\underset{e_1, e_2}{argmax}\ \rho d = (e_1^h, e_2^h)$$

Proof. Proof of Lemma 1 is given in appendix.   □

Now we shall proceed to characterize a stable agreement for the river sharing problem with flood. The rationale behind this characterization follows from the idea that a stable agreement should be one in which agents don't have sufficient incentive to deviate regardless of the realization of the endowments. A stable agreement is possible in river sharing setting only if there exist at least one transferable utility scheme which satisfies the conditions 6, 8, and 10. This result in a condition on the discount factor which may be interpreted as a necessary condition for the existence of a stable agreement among riparian states . This condition is discussed in Proposition 1.

Proposition 1. *A stable bilateral sharing agreement exists for a flood prone river flowing through two agents only if the discount factor is at least the threshold value $\delta_{th} = max(\delta_1, \delta_2)$. Where,*

$$\delta_1 = \frac{[\rho d]_{e_1^h, e_2^h}}{[\rho d]_{e_1^h, e_2^h} + E\left[b_1(x_1^*) + b_2(x_2^*) - b_1(x_1^N) - b_2(x_2^N)\right]} \tag{11}$$

$$\delta_2 = \frac{b_1(\hat{x}_1)}{b_1(\hat{x}_1) + E\left[b_1(x_1^*) + b_2(x_2^*) - b_1(x_1^N) - b_2(x_2^N)\right]} \tag{12}$$

Proof. A stable agreement exist with fixed payment scheme only if there exist one nonnegative τ which satisfies 6, 8, and 10 for all realizations of (e_1, e_2). This suggests compliance with the following inequalities 13 and 14. Inequality 13 is obtained from Eq. 8 and Eq. 10.

$$\underset{e_1, e_2}{max}\ (\rho d) + \frac{\delta}{(1-\delta)} E\left[b_1(\hat{x}_1) - b_1(x_1^*) + \rho d((e_1 + e_2 - x_1^* - x_2^* - l)^+)\right]$$

$$\leq \frac{\delta}{(1-\delta)} E\left[b_2(x_2^*) - b_2(x_2^N) + \rho d\left((e_1 + e_2 - \hat{x}_1 - \hat{x}_2 - l)^+\right)\right] \tag{13}$$

The condition 13 suggests that during any case of flood, neither of the agents should have sufficient incentive to deviate from the agreement. The condition for agent 2 (i.e., the RHS of Eq. 13) is static and is independent of the realization of endowment. But the condition for agent 1 (i.e., the LHS of Eq. 13) depends on the realization of endowment and the flood cost share borne by agent 1 due to this realization of endowments. For the agreement to remain stable during any scenario of flood, it is sufficient to show that there exist at least one side payment scheme, which satisfies the conditions 8 and 10 for the worst case flood (which corresponds to the realization which maximizes the flood cost share). The condition 14 represents a similar condition during a "normal"(no flood) year. This condition is derived from the compliance conditions 6 and 10. During such a year, scarcity could motivate the upstream agent to deviate from the agreement. This requires that a stable agreement should be robust even during the worst case scarcity where $(b_1(x_{1t}^N) - b_1(x_{1t}^*))$ is maximized. The maximized value of $(b_1(x_{1t}^N) - b_1(x_{1t}^*))$ is $b_1(\hat{x}_1)$. This requirement is mathematically represented in inequality 14.

$$\max_{e_1,e_2} (b_1(x_{1t}^N) - b_1(x_{1t}^*)) + \frac{\delta}{(1-\delta)} E\left[b_1(\hat{x}_1) - b_1(x_1^*) + \rho d((e_1 + e_2 - x_1^* - x_2^* - l)^+)\right]$$

$$\leq \frac{\delta}{(1-\delta)} E\left[b_2(x_2^*) - b_2(x_2^N) + \rho d\left((e_1 + e_2 - \hat{x}_1 - \hat{x}_2 - l)^+\right)\right] \quad (14)$$

The maximum value of (ρd) is $(\rho d)_{e_1^h,e_2^h}$. On substituting this in inequality 13 and simplifying, we get the following condition.

$$(\rho d)_{e_1^h,e_2^h} \leq \delta \left((\rho d)_{e_1^h,e_2^h} + E\left[b_1(x_1^*) + b_2(x_2^*) - b_1(x_1^N) - b_2(x_2^N)\right]\right) \quad (15)$$

$$\implies \delta \geq \frac{[\rho d]_{e_1^h,e_2^h}}{[\rho d]_{e_1^h,e_2^h} + E\left[b_1(x_1^*) + b_2(x_2^*) - b_1(x_1^N) - b_2(x_2^N)\right]} \quad (16)$$

i. e., $\delta \geq \delta_1$

Similarly, we can examine the agreement sustainability condition during short-age period which is given by inequality 14. The maximum value of $\max_{e_1,e_2}$ $(b_1(x_{1t}^N) - b_1(x_{1t}^*))$ is $b_1(\hat{x}_1)$. Upon substituting this in condition 14 and simplifying, we get the following inequality.

$$b_1(\hat{x}_1) \leq \delta \left(b_1(\hat{x}_1) + E\left[b_1(x_1^*) + b_2(x_2^*) - b_1(x_1^N) - b_2(x_2^N)\right]\right)$$

$$\implies \delta \geq \frac{b_1(\hat{x}_1)}{b_1(\hat{x}_1) + E\left[b_1(x_1^*) + b_2(x_2^*) - b_1(x_1^N) - b_2(x_2^N)\right]} \quad (17)$$

i. e., $\delta \geq \delta_2$

A stable agreement should sustain cooperation during all time periods (years). This means that the value of discount factor should simultaneously satisfy conditions 16 and 17. This means that, $\delta \geq max(\delta_1, \delta_2)$. □

It can be observed that $\delta_1, \delta_2 \in [0,1]$. Therefore, we may argue that stable agreements are possible on flood prone rivers if discount factor is sufficiently large. We refer to $max(\delta_1, \delta_2)$ as the threshold discount factor denoted by δ_{th}. Compliance with the inequality $\delta \geq \delta_{th}$ is a necessary condition for the stability of the agreement with fixed payments. This threshold discount factor brings out the preference of the players with regard to future expected payoff and current period payoff. The infinitely repeated game setup fosters cooperation by threatening inferior payoffs in future as a punishment for deviation from the agreement. The agents would sustain cooperative play when the payoffs from future cooperation is valued at least at a level described by δ_{th}. Perfectly patient players ($\delta = 1$) would place as much value on future payoffs as they place on current period payoff. The trigger punishment strategy is thus more effective for such players. For such players, the sustenance of cooperation is guaranteed so long as we pick an appropriate payment rule. In contrast, perfectly impatient players ($\delta = 0$) can never sustain cooperation. This is because these players place no value on punishments in future. Proposition 1 asserts that the players should be at least as patient as δ_{th} so that we can expect trigger strategy to work as a means of inducing cooperation.

The threshold discount factor can also be viewed as a measure of instability. Suppose $\delta_{th}^{(1)}, \delta_{th}^{(2)}$ be threshold discount factors of two agreements such that $\delta_{th}^{(1)} > \delta_{th}^{(2)}$. The agreement 1, with threshold discount factor $\delta_{th}^{(1)}$, may be argued to be more unstable than agreement 2 with discount factor $\delta_{th}^{(2)}$. A larger value of threshold discount factor means that only a smaller range of values of discount factor can ensure stability. Based on this insight, we may state the following corollary.

Corollary 1. *An agreement which sustains cooperation on a flood prone river is at least as unstable as an agreement on a river without flood*

Proof. As a consequence of Proposition 1, we may see $\delta_{th} \geq \delta_2$. Here δ_2 denotes the minimum threshold discount factor required to sustain cooperation in a year without flood. It is also equivalent to the threshold discount factor for stable agreements on a transboundary river basin without flood risk. Since the threshold discount factor for stable agreements on flood prone rivers is at least as large as δ_2, agreements on flood prone rivers are at most as stable as its counterpart on transboundary rivers without floods. □

The threshold discount factor may be seen to be independent of the choice of the fixed payment scheme and dependent on maximum flood responsibility borne by upstream agent and the maximum benefit derived by agent 1. The threshold discount factor depends inversely on the expected surplus from cooperation. This expected surplus is assumed to be positive since the agents would not have any reason to negotiate an agreement otherwise. Equation 19 reveals that a higher expected surplus makes the requirement for sustaining cooperation less stringent (i. e., the interval $[\delta_{th}, 1]$ is larger). If the upper limits on endowments are small, then flood damages will not influence the threshold discount factor. In this case, $\delta_{th} = \delta_2$. However, when the river is flood prone and the endowment distributions are such that the flood damage share is larger than δ_2, then the value of $\delta_{th} = \delta_1$.

5 Conclusion

Conventional game theoretic models which handle variability in river sharing problems use expected utility based formulations. Such models might fail to capture some of the dynamic aspects of the individual agent's behaviour. Such types of behavioural characteristics motivate us to look at actual realizations rather than expectations. The repeated game formalism used in this study allows us to do this. Some recent studies in literature [11, 13] use repeated game models in the context of scarcity. We extend the scope of these models so as to accommodate flooding externality. We use a repeated game framework to study the conditions under which the water can be shared efficiently, and flood costs can be allocated as per the SUPA rule. The analysis lets us derive a lower bound on discount factor for the cooperative agreement to be sustained as a Subgame Perfect Equilibrium with fixed side-payments in every period. The analysis reveals that agreements framed on flood prone rivers are at least as unstable as those framed on rivers without flood risk.

Appendix: Proof of Lemma 1

Proof. In order to prove this result, we find the first order partial derivatives of ρd with respect to both e_1 and e_2 and show that they are positive for all values of e_1 and e_2. Let us assume that damage fraction is non-zero thus making the problem of finding maximizers non-trivial. Formally, this means that $\rho > 0$ and thus $e_1 > \hat{x}_1$.

$$\frac{\partial[\rho d]}{\partial e_1} = \frac{\partial[\rho d]}{\partial w_1} \frac{\partial w_1}{\partial e_1}$$

$$= \frac{\partial[\rho d]}{\partial w_1}$$

$$= d\frac{\partial \rho}{\partial w_1} + \rho \frac{\partial d}{\partial w_1}$$

$$= \frac{dw_2}{(w_1 + w_2)^2} + \rho d'$$

Since the water releases $w_1, w_2 > 0$, and the damage function is strictly increasing,

$$\implies \frac{\partial[\rho d]}{\partial e_1} > 0 \tag{18}$$

The first order partial derivative of ρd is strictly positive with respect to e_1. This means that as e_1 increases, the value of damage fraction goes up. The damage fraction is maximum at e_1^h.

Similarly, if we consider $e_2 > \hat{x}_2{}^2$, then the partial derivative with respect to e_2 takes the following form.

$$\frac{\partial[\rho d]}{\partial e_2} = d\frac{\partial \rho}{\partial w_2} + \rho \frac{\partial d}{\partial w_2}$$

$$= \frac{-w_1}{(w_1 + w_2)^2} \times d + \frac{w_1}{(w_1 + w_2)}d'$$

$$= \rho \times \left[d'(w_1 + w_2 - l) - \frac{d(w_1 + w_2 - l)}{w_1 + w_2} \right] \tag{19}$$

For any convex function $g(\cdot) : \mathbb{R} \to \mathbb{R}$, the following inequality holds true.

$$\frac{g(b) - g(a)}{b - a} < g'(b)$$

---

[2] We may also inspect $e_2 \leq \hat{x}_2$ as a possible case. However, this would give us a trivial solution with partial derivative being zero and damage share of zero.

For the function d, we have

$$d'(w_1 + w_2 - l) - \frac{d(w_1 + w_2 - l)}{w_1 + w_2} > 0$$

$$\implies \frac{\partial [\rho d]}{\partial e_2} > 0$$

This means that the damage share ρd is positive for all $e_2 > \hat{x}_2$ and strictly increases. For all values of $e_2 \leq \hat{x}_2$, the damage is zero since flow from agent 1 alone is insufficient to cause a flood. This means that the damage share is maximum at e_2^h.   □

References

1. Álvarez, X., Gómez-Rúa, M., Vidal-Puga, J.: River flooding risk prevention: a cooperative game theory approach. J. Environ. Manage. **248**, 109284 (2019). http://www.sciencedirect. com/science/article/pii/S0301479719309867
2. Abraham, A., Ramachandran, P.: Effect of pollution on transboundary river water trade. In: Morais, D.C., Carreras, A., de Almeida, A.T., Vetschera, R. (eds.) GDN 2019. LNBIP, vol. 351, pp. 146–159. Springer, Cham (2019). https://doi.org/10.1007/978-3-030-21711-2_12
3. Abraham, A., Ramachandran, P.: The welfare implications of transboundary storage and dam ownership on river water trade. Math. Soc. Sci. **109**, 18–27 (2020). http://www.sciencedirect. com/science/article/pii/S0165489620300949
4. Ni, D., Wang, Y.: Sharing a polluted river. Games Econ. Behav. **60**(1), 176–186 (2007). http:// www.sciencedirect.com/science/article/pii/S0899825606001412
5. van der Laan, G., Moes, N.: Collective decision making in an international river pollution model. Natural Resour. Model. **29**, 374–399 (2016)
6. Steinmann, S., Winkler, R.: Sharing a river with downstream externalities. Games **10**(2), 23 (2019). https://www.mdpi.com/2073-4336/10/2/23
7. Bakker, M.H.: Transboundary river floods: examining countries, international river basins and continents. Water Policy **11**(3), 269–288 (2009). http://dx.doi.org/10.2166/wp.2009.041
8. Bakker, M.H.: Transboundary river floods and institutional capacity1. JAWRA J. Am. Water Resour. Assoc. **45**(3), 553–566 (2009). https://onlinelibrary.wiley.com/doi/abs/10.1111/j. 1752-1688.2009.00325.x
9. Bakker, M.H., Duncan, J.A.: Future bottlenecks in international river basins: where transboundary institutions, population growth and hydrological variability intersect. Water Int. **42**(4), 400–424 (2017). https://doi.org/10.1080/02508060.2017.1331412
10. Janmaat, J., Ruijs, A.: Sharing the load? floods, droughts, and managing international rivers. Environ. Dev. Econ. **12**(4), 573–592 (2007)
11. Ansink, E., Ruijs, A.: Climate change and the stability of water allocation agreements. Environ. Resour. Econ. **41**(2), 249–266 (2008). https://doi.org/10.1007/s10640-008-9190-3
12. Kilgour, D.M., Dinar, A.: Flexible water sharing within an international river basin. Environ. Resour. Econ. **18**(1), 43–60 (2001). http://dx.doi.org/10.1023/A:1011100130736
13. Ansink, E., Houba, H.: Sustainable agreements on stochastic river flow. Resour. Energy Econ. **44**, 92–117 (2016). http://www.sciencedirect.com/science/article/pii/ S0928765516000221
14. Ambec, S., Dinar, A., McKinney, D.: Water sharing agreements sustainable to reduced flows. J. Environ. Econ. Manage. **66**(3), 639–655 (2013). http://www.sciencedirect.com/science/ article/pii/S0095069613000429

15. Ambec, S., Sprumont, Y.: Sharing a river. J. Econ. Theor. **107**(2), 453–462 (2002). http://www.sciencedirect.com/science/article/pii/S0022053101929497
16. Ambec, S., Ehlers, L.: Sharing a river among satiable agents. Games Econ. Behav. **64**(1), 35–50 (2008). http://www.sciencedirect.com/science/article/pii/S0899825607001674
17. Dong, B., Ni, D., Wang, Y.: Sharing a polluted river network. Environ. Resour. Econ. **53**(3), 367–387 (2012). https://doi.org/10.1007/s10640-012-9566-2
18. Gomez-Rua, M.: Sharing a polluted river through environmental taxes. SERIEs **4**(2), 137–153 (2013)
19. Alcalde-Unzu, J., Gómez-Rúa, M., Molis, E.: Sharing the costs of cleaning a river: the upstream responsibility rule. Games Econ. Behav. **90**, 134–150 (2015). http://www.sciencedirect.com/science/article/pii/S0899825615000305
20. Sun, P., Hou, D., Sun, H.: Responsibility and sharing the cost of cleaning a polluted river. Math. Methods Oper. Res. **89**(1), 143–156 (2019). https://doi.org/10.1007/s00186-019-00658-w
21. Abraham, A., Ramachandran, P.: A solution for the flood cost sharing problem. Econ. Lett. **189**, 109030 (2020). http://www.sciencedirect.com/science/article/pii/S0165176520300495

Study of Water-Environmental Conflicts as a Dynamic and Complex Human-Natural System: A New Perspective

Mohsen Shahbaznezhadfard[1], Saied Yousefi[2,3(✉)], and Keith W. Hipel[3]

[1] College of Engineering, University of Tehran, Tehran, Iran
M.shahbaznezhad@ut.ac.ir
[2] Department of Architecture, University of Tehran, Tehran, Iran
sdyousefi@ut.ac.ir, s2yousef@uwaterloo.ca
[3] Department of Systems Design Engineering, University of Waterloo, Waterloo, ON, Canada
kwhipel@uwaterloo.ca

Abstract. In many parts of the world, water scarcity, climate change phenomenon, and simultaneously, increasing water demand from various stakeholders have led to serious conflicts over water and related environmental issues. These serious conflicts are lengthy in time, dynamic in nature, and very complex in essence. A key feature of this type of conflict, which is often ignored, is that in addition to the interaction among humans, the interaction between human and nature plays a significant role. In other words, such conflicts involve both human and natural systems as well as the interactions between them. Thus, they are considered as a Coupled Human and Natural System (CHANS) for which, its concepts and framework can be used to evaluate such complex conflicts. This research effort aims at presenting the CHANS approach and its core concepts for better study of the water and environmental conflicts that are both dynamic in nature and complex in essence. The use of CHANS to the conflict scrutiny provides valuable insights that help in achieving a broader understanding of water-environmental conflicts. The case study of the Urmia Lake conflict as a real-world controversy is used to show the CHANS' capabilities in dealing with the dynamics and complexities of water and environmental conflicts and highlighting their main features. The resulting outcomes of the proposed approach clearly indicate that for achieving a more comprehensive understanding as well as more sustainable management of growing water-environmental conflicts, both human and natural dimensions and their interactions must be simultaneously considered.

Keywords: Water and environmental conflicts · Coupled human-natural systems · CHANS · Complex systems · Dynamic systems · Systems analysis

1 Introduction

Limited water resources and related environmental problems, as well as the effects of climate change, have led to serious social conflicts in different parts of the world. [1, 2].

© Springer Nature Switzerland AG 2021
D. C. Morais et al. (Eds.): GDN 2021, LNBIP 420, pp. 113–127, 2021.
https://doi.org/10.1007/978-3-030-77208-6_9

If these conflicts are not managed using a sustainable and comprehensive solution, they will have destructive effects on both society and the environment [1]. The publication of numerous articles on water-environmental conflicts in recent years shows its growing importance [3]. These scientific attempts and positive steps can attract the attention of decision-makers in this domain. However, many of these studies often examine water and environmental conflicts solely in the form of a human system. In other words, the main focus of most of these studies is to examine how stakeholders interact [4], and interactions between humans and nature are less considered. Whereas, in the current era, interactions and feedback between human systems and natural systems play a significant role in creating the complexities and dynamics of water-environmental controversies [5]. Therefore, these conflicts should be studied as an integrated system in which, in addition to human interactions, interactions and feedback between humans and nature are also scrutinized. This integrated system, which includes both human and natural systems, provides a more comprehensive understanding of the dynamics and complexities of such conflicts which will lead to more insightful outcomes and of course more sustainable resolutions for the conflict at hand. To this extend, it can be said that the coupled human and natural systems (CHANS) is a suitable framework for studying water-environmental conflicts [6].

CHANS characterizes the dynamical two-way interactions between human and natural systems [6, 7]. It seeks to express that human and natural systems do not evolve in separate frameworks and in fact, they have many interconnections that play a decisive role in the overall behavior of the system over time [8]. The subject of CHANS was initially presented in a paper by Liu et al. in 2007 [6]. Of course, the basic concept of interaction between human systems and natural systems has been discussed before this research effort. The book "Panarchy: understanding transformations in human and natural systems" by Gunderson and Holling in 2001 [9] is one example in this regard. From the perspective of Liu et al. [6], the subject of CHANS aims at understanding how a human system and a natural system interact to form a whole, a unique complex system. The research effort emphasizes that it is not enough to study each of these systems separately and they should be considered as a whole. Based on CHANS frameworks, modeling and analysis of interactions between human systems and natural systems over time manifest the co-evolution of these systems [5].

After explaining the need for a systematic view, and specifically a CHANS-based view in water-environmental conflict modeling and analysis, it is necessary to show the importance of this framework for a real-world case study. In order to fulfill this need, the complex and dynamic conflict of the Urmia Lake (the largest lake in Iran), which has been modeled and analyzed in details by Shahbaznezhadfard et al. [10], is examined as a real-world problem from the perspective of CHANS in this research effort.

2   Water and Environmental Conflicts

Water-environmental conflict is defined as a human/social conflict related to water and the environment [11, 12]. Water conflicts, which can be classified as one of the most important types of environmental conflicts, occur at different levels, from local and national to international and global. The root causes of this type of conflict are divided into three main categories including socio-economic, institutional/political, and environmental factors [13]. Therefore, if a water-environmental conflict is considered as a single system, it includes two subsystems as well as the interactions, feedback, and dynamics between them. The human subsystem includes social, economic, political, institutional, etc. factors and the natural subsystem that contains water and environmental parameters. The key issue of studying this type of conflict is that in most studies related to this type of conflict, when modeling and analyzing options, strategies, and preferences of stakeholders and decision-makers, only human interactions are considered and interactions and dynamics between humans and nature are less taken into account [4].

Water-environmental conflicts will be exacerbated if they are not properly studied, managed, and resolved through comprehensive and interdisciplinary approaches [14]. Intensification of these conflicts leads to significant negative effects on both the society and the environment. However, optimal decisions in this type of conflict are challenging due to the presence of multiple stakeholders with different goals, interests, and attitudes within a complex human system [15, 16] and this can be even more challenging with the uncertainties and complexities due to the dynamics within a complex natural system and feedback between these two systems. Therefore, in the study of problems and conflicts related to water and the environment, it is necessary to consider both human and natural systems in an integrated framework in order to provide more desirable and sustainable solutions by a better and deeper understanding of their various dimensions [5].

3   Coupled Human and Natural Systems (CHANS)

Today, human and nature are intertwined in an unprecedented way, and there are complex interactions and feedback between them. A coupled human and natural system (CHANS) (known also as a coupled human-environment system) characterizes the dynamical two-way interactions between human (e.g., social, political, economic, cultural, psychological) systems and natural (e.g., hydrologic, atmospheric, biological, geological) systems [6, 7]. The concept of CHANS states that in the study of an environmental phenomenon and problem, both the relevant human and natural systems must be considered and examined as an integrated unit [5, 17]. In other words, it is not sufficient to separately study the human and natural dimensions of complex environmental problems. CHANS emphasizes that in order to better understand the dynamics and complexity of the problems, which is a prerequisite for achieving a sustainable solution, both human and natural systems must be studied as a single system [5, 6]. In this framework, methods such as System Dynamics, Game Theory, and Agent-Based models are used to model and analyze the integrated systems [18]. The subject of CHANS is studied in different sub-fields [5] that are briefly discussed below.

CHANS models based on the shape and essence of the systems they study are divided into categories such as social-ecological models, hydro-economic models, socio-hydrologic models, and integrated environmental models [5]. A review of socio-ecological systems models is provided by Schlüter et al. [19]. It can be said that socio-ecological systems models are equivalent to the CHANS models and seek to study the ecological and human dimensions of related problems. These models try to provide the best picture of the problems that arise in this field by examining the two-way interactions between human and ecological systems, which include feedback, nonlinear dynamics, self-organization, and cross-scale interactions. Hydro-economic and socio-hydrologic models are more special applications of CHANS which are often used to study water resources systems [5]. Sivapalan et al. [20] present a definition of the concept of socio-hydrology. They define Socio-hydrology as the study of the self-organization of people and their co-evolution in the landscape with respect to water availability. It focuses on long-term feedback between society and water. Harou et al. [21] provide an overview of hydro-economic models. They describe these models as frameworks that can model and analyze water resources systems by integrating the hydrological and economic aspects of the problems and can be an appropriate tool for integrated water resources management (IWRM). Integrated environmental modeling (IEM) is scrutinized by Laniak et al. [17]. This field is described as "a discipline inspired by the need to solve increasingly complex real-world problems involving the environment and its relationship to human systems and activities (social and economic)".

4   The Urmia Lake and Its Related Water and Environmental Conflict

Urmia Lake is the largest lake in Iran and located in the northwest of the country. This saltwater lake, with an area of 6000 square kilometers [22], is the twentieth largest lake in the world [23]. The Urmia Lake Basin is one of the agricultural hubs of the country due to its geographical conditions [24]. Figure 1 displays a general plan of the lake.

In the mid-1990s, the Urmia Lake was at its best in terms of water level in recent years [22, 25, 26]. At the same time, the executive branch of the Iranian government designed a lot of projects in the Urmia Lake basin with the aim of economic development and promoting food self-sufficiency [27, 28]. These development-oriented projects, which mainly included the construction and operation of numerous dams, the increase of wells and groundwater pumping stations, and the increase of cultivated area [22, 29], were often designed and implemented without much regard for the environmental aspects and its consequences [24]. These measures were taken while the environmentalists were warning about the social and environmental consequences of those programs and called on the government to take measures to protect the environment of the region. However the executive apparatus, regardless of the warnings, gradually designed and implemented the plans and projects, relying on the power and potential of the institutions under its control [24]. It should be clarified that economic development of the country, by constructing dams and renewable energy generation, is necessary and is essential part of the country development only if environmental issues are seriously taken into account.

This trend continued until the negative effects of the projects gradually showed themselves in the ecosystem of the basin, especially the Urmia Lake [30, 31]. The most obvious manifestation of these effects was the annual decrease in the water level of the Lake [30]. A diagram of the mean annual water level in the Lake over the years is shown in Fig. 2. As shown, the water level of the Urmia Lake has decreased year by year. Of course, it should be noted that according to historical hydrological data, the changes in the amount of precipitation and evaporation in the basin during those years were insignificant and did not have much effect on the changes in the lake's water level [22, 32]. The environmental conditions of the basin, especially the lake, deteriorated to such an extent that in the early 2010s the lake water level reached its lowest level in recent

Fig. 1. General map of Urmia Lake basin

years and more than 90% of the lake water dried up [22, 25, 26]. This was while the protests by the environmentalists had reached their peak. Their repeated warnings and protests, as well as the tangible negative effects on the environment in the region, have caused local communities to become involved in this conflicting issue as well. They felt more and more the serious dangers and consequences of the lake's drought, such as dust storms, rising salinity, and the loss of agricultural lands [22, 33, 34]. The combination of these factors led to social protests by the people.

It was under these circumstances that the position of the environmentalists to request the protection of the basin environment and the restoration of the Urmia Lake was strengthened. Because these expert positions were accompanied by social protests caused by the perceived dangers of the current situation, and in other words, they could moot their requests with the support of the people [33, 34]. The government, which found itself in the middle of a socio-environmental crisis, finally in 2013, decided to establish an institution called the "Urmia Lake Restoration Program (ULRP)" and tried to improve the conditions of the basin by adopting a series of environmental approaches and measures [35, 36]. At that time, this institution defined programs for the stabilization and then revitalization of Urmia Lake [35, 36].

5   The Urmia Lake Conflict from the Perspective of CHANS

As stated in Sect. 4, it can be said that the Urmia Lake conflict has been the scene of a dynamic conflict between the government executive branch and the environmentalists. At the beginning of this conflict in the mid-1990s, the executive body designed and implemented its development-oriented projects in this basin regardless of the warnings of the environmentalists and their requests to take measures to protect the environment of the basin and lake. Subsequently, the environmentalists strengthened their position by attracting the attention of local stakeholders. After about 20 years of growing and intensified controversies among the decision makers, the executive apparatus, as one of

Fig. 2. Mean annual water level in the Urmia lake (data Source: Iran Water Resources management company)

the main decision makers in this conflict, finally decided to change their position and of course their preferences. As a result, they decided to take serious measures to restore the environment of the Urmia Lake by establishing a formal institution. This dynamic conflict has been studied in full details by Shahbaznezhadfard et al. [10]. However, because this conflict is the real-life case study of this research effort, a summary is presented below.

5.1 Systematic Modeling and Analysis of the Conflict

In this study, the conflict is investigated by a Game Theory-based method called the Graph Model for Conflict Resolution (GMCR) [37, 38] in two time phases (the first phase is related to the mid-1990s and the second phase is related to the early 2010s). GMCR is a method in which conflicts are studied in two consecutive stages: 1) Modeling and 2) Analysis [39]. In the modeling stage, the decision-makers of the conflict, their options, the feasible states of the conflict based on the options, and the preferences of the decision-makers are determined to obtain the general model of the conflict. After that, the conflict analysis starts based on the constructed model. At this stage, all feasible states are evaluated from the perspective of each decision-maker based on the stability definitions, which represent and reflect a range of human behaviors in a conflict [39]. Each of these stability definitions (such as the definitions of Nash, GMR (General Metarationality), SMR (Symmetric Metarationality), SEQ (Sequential Stability), etc.) describes different degrees of human behavioral elements in a conflict, such as foresight, knowledge of preference, strategic risk, and dis-improvement [40]. Any feasible state that, according to a certain stability definition, is in a stable situation from the perspective of all decision-makers, is an equilibrium that is considered as a possible outcome and solution to the conflict [39].

To advance this process, modeling and analysis steps have been performed, respectively. In the modeling stage, the decision-makers, their options, and the feasible states of the conflict are identified. These are listed in Tables 1 and 2, respectively.

Table 1. Decision makers and their options in the conflict

DM	Option	Description
Executive apparatus	1) Only focus on development efforts	Carry out development actions without seriously considering environmental dimensions and consequences
	2) Serious consideration of environmental efforts	Adopt policies and take measures to protect the environment against development actions
Environmentalists	3) Request for serious environmental efforts	Request for adopting policies and measures seriously protect the environment against development actions

Table 2. Feasible states in the conflict

DM	Option	Feasible States				
Executive apparatus	1) Only focus on development efforts	Y	Y	Y	Y	N
	2) Serious consideration of environmental efforts	Y	N	Y	N	N
Environmentalists	3) Request for serious environmental efforts	Y	Y	N	N	N
Label		1	2	3	4	5

As can be seen, the two decision-makers of this conflict are the executive apparatus and the environmentalists. The options of these decision-makers and the feasible states of the conflict are also shown. Conflict states are indicated by the Y (yes) and N (no) symbols, which indicate the selection and non-selection of the option, respectively. Some of the generated states are illogical and impossible in reality, and therefore, are eliminated and only feasible states are taken into account. Then, the decision-makers' preferences over feasible states are determined. This step is done using the method of option prioritization and based on information and opinions collected from relevant experts as well as studying the root causes of the conflict. Preference prioritization information and state ranking from the perspective of the decision-makers are given in Tables 3 and 4, respectively.

As shown in these tables, the only differing element in the model of the conflict between the first and second phases, is the preferences of the executive apparatus. By changing their preferences in the second phase compared to the first phase, the executive body pays more attention to the protest requests of the environmentalists and from their point of view, the issue related to the protest requests of the environmentalists is raised from rank 3 to rank 2. Their preference to consider the environmental policies at the

Table 3. Preference prioritization information in the first and second phase of the conflict

	a) First Phase			b) Second Phase
Decision Makers	#P	Preference Information (From Most to Least Important)		#P
Executive apparatus	1	Executive apparatus prefers to do development		1
	2	Executive apparatus does not prefer to be limited to the constraints and costs of environmental policies		2
	3	Executive apparatus does not prefer protest requests from environmentalists		3
	4	Executive apparatus prefers to consider environmental policies if environmentalists request it		4
Environmentalists	1	Environmentalists prefer that the executive apparatus always consider environmental protection		1
	2	Environmentalists prefer to always request for environmental protection		2

Table 4. State ranking for the decision makers in the first and second phases

Decision-Makers	a) First Phase					b) Second Phase				
	States					States				
	Most Preferred				Least Preferred	Most Preferred				Least Preferred
Executive apparatus	4	2	3	1	5	4	3	1	2	5
Environmentalists	1	3	2	4	5	1	3	2	4	5

request of the environmentalists is also increased from the fourth to the third. Meanwhile, the decision-maker's preference for the limitations related to the costs and constraints for environmental policies, is decreased from rank 2 to rank 4, as shown in the above table.

When modeling both phases, they should be analyzed using the stability definitions. In this stage, the available feasible states are examined one by one based on the four stability definitions: Nash, SEQ, GMR, and SMR, each of which reflects a specific behavioral pattern of the decision-makers. To do this, instead of manual analysis, GMCR + software program [41] is used to achieve the resulting outcomes of the analysis faster and in more accurate manner, as the results are displayed in Table 5. As shown, state 2 in the first phase and state 1 in the second phase are resulted as strong equilibriums based on all four stability definitions. These results correspond exactly to the historical conditions that emerged in those two time phases.

So far, the systematic modeling and analysis of the human behavior of decision-makers in the two time phases of the conflict have been discussed. In other words, the

Table 5. Resulting outcomes of the conflict analysis in the first and second phases

a) First Phase

Stability Definitions	States				
	1	2	3	4	5
Nash		✓			
SEQ		✓			
GMR		✓			
SMR		✓			

b) Second Phase

Stability Definitions	States				
	1	2	3	4	5
Nash	✓				
SEQ	✓				
GMR	✓		✓		
SMR	✓		✓		

human interactions have been examined in two separate phases. As noted above, the changes in the executive apparatus's preferences in the second phase of the conflict altered the conditions, and while the conflict was in equilibrium in state 2 in the first phase, it went to state 1 in the second phase and reached equilibrium there. At this stage, the fundamental question is that what happened between these two phases during this period of about 20 years, and basically, what process took place to change the overall conditions of the conflict? In order to answer this key question, the concept of System Dynamics is used and explained below [10].

System Dynamics (SD) is an approach to understand the behaviors of complex and dynamic systems over time. In this method, with a comprehensive view, the relationships between system components over time are evaluated using causal feedback loop structures and the dynamics of systems are examined by the method's various quantitative and qualitative tools [42–45]. SD shows the interior structure of a system and evaluates the changes that occur by applying different decisions within the system [46]. This approach is based on the assumption that the structure of any complex system has a cause and effect connection network between its components that determines its behaviors. In causal relations between two variables, which are shown in SD models by an arrow, two types of positive and negative relations can be dominant [42]. The positive causal link between two variables indicates that their changes are in the same direction and the negative causal link indicates that their changes are in opposite directions. Combining positive and negative causal links creates feedback loops, and the set of these loops forms the overall structure of SD models [42].

The process that leads to the changes in the executive apparatus' preferences between the two phases of the conflict is analyzed using SD concepts. The water level of Urmia Lake can be considered as a function of precipitation, evaporation, solely development projects, and environmental protection efforts in the basin. In such a way that the water level of the lake has positive causal links (in the same direction) with the rate of precipitation and environmental protection efforts and negative causal links (in opposite directions) with the rate of evaporation and solely development projects in the basin [22, 32, 47]. However, as mentioned in Sect. 4, based on historical hydrological data, changes in precipitation and evaporation over the period of 20 years have not had a major impact on the lake's water level [22, 32]. Therefore, it can be said that in the case of the water level of Urmia Lake, during this period, only development measures and environmental considerations have been effective. In the mid-1990s, the executive apparatus began a downward trend in the water level of the Urmia Lake by implementing development projects regardless of their environmental aspects. On the other hand, it can be said that as the water level of each lake decreases, the environmental problems increase (negative causal link) and the increase in environmental problems in an area will increase social protests [48]. In other words, the extent of environmental problems and the severity of social protests have a positive causal link. Increasing social protests also put pressure on the government to increase attention to the issue, which in turn augments efforts to protect the environment [48, 49]. Accordingly, with the beginning of the downward trend of the water level of the Urmia Lake and its intensification, environmental problems gradually increased in the basin and area of Urmia Lake. As environmental problems intensified, social protests gradually increased. The intensification of social protests strengthened the position of the environmentalists in the conflict with the government's executive apparatus [22, 33], and this eventually, led the apparatus to change its preferences and establish an official institution to take measures to revitalize and protect the Urmia Lake [35, 36]. The feedback loop related to the transition period of the conflict is shown in Fig. 3.

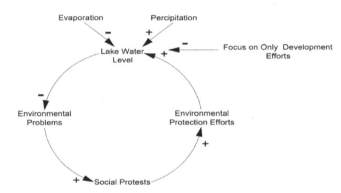

Fig. 3. The Feedback loop related to the transitional period of the conflict

As shown and explained above, within the transition period between the two phases of the conflict, the SD concepts were used to incorporate the relationship that had been established between the environmental dimensions of the Urmia Lake conflict, and its social dimensions. In other words, a system was presented in this stage that reflects the environmental and social dimensions simultaneously and also, their interaction during the transition from the first to the second phase of the conflict was elaborated.

5.2 Incorporation of the Two Subsystems

As explained above, a systematic study of the conflict was carried out using the two approaches of GMCR and SD. In this section, the overall conflict system is introduced which has been derived from the incorporation of the two subsystems of the human and the natural. Their incorporation and interaction describe the overall behavior of the system over time and as such, the dynamic of the conflict is described. In other words, the aim is to emphasize and highlight this fact that with respect to water and environmental conflicts, the interactions are not only among humans, but also, the interaction among humans and nature plays a significant role. The overall system of this conflict and its subsystems are shown in Fig. 4.

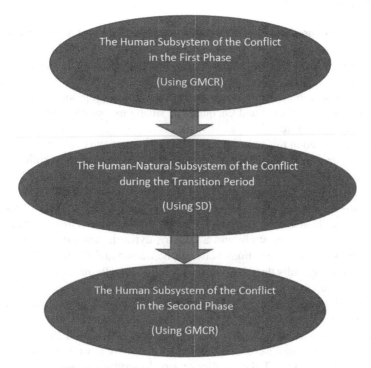

Fig. 4. The overall system of the Urmia lake conflict

The study reviewed in Subsect. 5.1 can be divided into two general parts. In the first part, the conflict was examined in two separate time phases using GMCR, from the perspective of a human system that considers only human interactions. In the second part, the transition period from the first phase to the second phase of the conflict was examined using the SD, from the perspective of a human-natural system, which reflects the interactions between humans and nature (Fig. 4). It is important to note that in addition to the human interactions in water-environmental conflicts, the human-natural interactions also play an important role in their dynamic nature. With respect to the conflict related to the Urmia Lake, it was highlighted that along with the interactions of the executive apparatus with the environmentalists (as the human interactions) in the first and second phases, the interactions, taken place between humans and the nature during the transition period, can significantly change the initial resulting outcomes of the GMCR approach. During this transition period, the decrease in the water level of the Urmia Lake and the resulting environmental problems created social protests, and these protests eventually changed the overall conditions of the conflict by affecting the preferences of the executive apparatus. These are human-natural interactions that change in different time periods and they have to be never ignored within the dynamic nature of complex water and environmental conflicts.

6 Conclusions

This research effort presented CHANS, a novel approach to better understand and manage complex and dynamic water and environmental conflicts that are seriously growing around the globe. Water scarcity and water demand increase have caused controversies about the usage of this valuable natural resource as well as conflicts over environmental issues. If water-environmental conflicts are not managed appropriately and sustainably then, they turn to exacerbated and uncontrolled situations that have irreparable effects on both society and nature.

It was emphasized in this research effort that, the water and environmental conflicts as a coupled human-natural system require the simultaneous study of both human and natural aspects. To achieve this objective, an effective framework within the CHANS approach was presented and the features of the framework, needed for examining the human and the natural dimensions and their interactions, were explained. To show the robustness of the CHANS approach, a real-life case study of water/environmental conflict in Iran was used. The case study was a lengthy, dynamic, and complex controversy that clearly presents the interactions between the human and the natural aspects. The CHANS could successfully demonstrate that the human and the natural aspects represent two subsystems, and their interactions lead to an integrated system. In other words, both human and natural aspects must be simultaneously considered if studying complex water and environmental conflicts otherwise, sustainable conflict resolution may not be achieved when only human aspect of a conflict is considered. In this regard, the CHANS approach provides a comprehensive understanding as well as more sustainable management for the Urmia Lake conflict as a real-world dynamic controversy in the Middle East, studied in this research effort.

Finally, the results of this research effort provide an insightful understanding that every complex water and environmental conflicts include the natural side as a fact and ignoring this aspect would lead to short-sighted resolutions that even may turn to more serious conflicts in the future. The proposed CHANS approach conveniently fits itself within a new and emerging perspective of water-environmental conflict management territory where innovative approaches are used to achieve sustainable resolutions for complex conflicts resulting in saving tremendous amounts of time, money, and efforts.

References

1. Wolf, A.T., Kramer, A., Carius, A., Dabelko, G.D.: Managing water conflict and cooperation. State World 2005 redefining Global Security, pp. 80–95 (2005)
2. Nordås, R., Gleditsch, N.P.: Climate change and conflict. Polit. Geogr. **26**(6), 627–638 (2007)
3. Le Billon, P., Duffy, R.V.: Conflict ecologies: connecting political ecology and peace and conflict studies. J. Polit. Ecol. **25**(1), 239–260 (2018)
4. Hipel, K.W., Fang, L., Cullmann, J., Bristow, M.: Conflict resolution in water resources and environmental management. Springer (2015). https://doi.org/10.1007/978-3-319-14215-9.pdf

5. Noel, P.H.C.: Studying coupled human and natural systems from a decentralized perspective: the case of agent-based and decentralized modeling. University of Illinois at Urbana-Champaign (2015)
6. Liu, J., et al.: Complexity of coupled human and natural systems. Science (80-) **317**(5844), pp. 1513–1516 (2007)
7. Alberti, M., et al.: Research on coupled human and natural systems (CHANS): approach, challenges, and strategies. Bull. Ecol. Soc. Am. **92**(2), 218–228 (2011)
8. Werner, B.T., Mcnamara, D.E.: Dynamics of coupled human-landscape systems. Geomorphology **91**(3–4), 393–407 (2007)
9. Gunderson, L.H., Holling, C.S.: Panarchy: understanding transformations in human and natural systems. Island press, Washington, D.C. (2001)
10. Shahbaznezhadfard, M., Yousefi, S., Majouni, E.: Study of the Urmia Lake dispute using incorporation of system dynamics and graph model for conflict resolution approaches. J. Leg. Aff. Disput. Resolut. Eng. Constr. **13**(3) (2021)
11. D.A.C. OECD: Water and violent conflict, Issues Brief, Mainstreaming Confl. Prev. www. oecd.org (2005)
12. Scheidel, A., et al.: Environmental conflicts and defenders: a global overview. Glob. Environ. Chang. **63**, 102104 (2020)
13. Gehrig, J., Rogers, M.M.: Water and conflict: incorporating peacebuilding into water development. Catholic Relief Services (2009)
14. Bob, U., Bronkhorst, S.: Environmental conflicts: Key issues and management implications. African J. Confl. Resolut. **10**(2) (2010)
15. Mirchi, A., Watkins, D., Jr., Madani, K.: Modeling for Watershed Planning, Management, and Decision Making, Watersheds: Management, Restoration and Environmental Impact. Nova Science Publishers, New York (2010)
16. Shahbaznezhadfard, M., Yousefi, S., Hipel, K.W., Hegazy, T.: Dynamic-based graph model for conflict resolution: systems thinking adaptation to solve real-world conflicts. In: 20th International Conference on Group Decision and Negotiation (2020)
17. Laniak, G.F., et al.: Integrated environmental modeling: a vision and roadmap for the future. Environ. Model. Softw. **39**, 3–23 (2013)
18. Madani, K., Shafiee-Jood, M.: Socio-hydrology: a new understanding to unite or a new science to divide? Water **12**(7), 1941 (2020)
19. Schlueter, M., et al.: New horizons for managing the environment: a review of coupled social-ecological systems modeling. Nat. Resour. Model. **25**(1), 219–272 (2012)
20. Sivapalan, M., Savenije, H.H.G., Blöschl, G.: Socio-hydrology: a new science of people and water. Hydrol. Process **26**(8), 1270–1276 (2012)
21. Harou, J.J., Pulido-Velazquez, M., Rosenberg, D.E., Medellín-Azuara, J., Lund, J.R., Howitt, R.E.: Hydro-economic models: concepts, design, applications, and future prospects. J. Hydrol. **375**(3–4), 627–643 (2009)
22. Hassanzadeh, E., Zarghami, M., Hassanzadeh, Y.: Determining the main factors in declining the Urmia lake level by using system dynamics modeling. Water Resour. Manage. **26**(1), 129–145 (2012)
23. Alesheikh, A.A., Ghorbanali, A., Nouri, N.: Coastline change detection using remote sensing. Int. J. Environ. Sci. Technol. **4**(1), 61–66 (2007). https://doi.org/10.1007/BF03325962
24. Azizi, G., Nazif, S., Abbasi, F.: Assessment of performance of Urmia basin dams using system dynamic approach. Arid Reg. Geogr. Stud. **7**(25), 16–19 (2016)
25. Zarghami, M.: Effective watershed management; case study of Urmia Lake, Iran. Lake Reserv. Manage. **27**(1), 87–94 (2011)
26. Alipour, H., Olya, H.G.T.: Sustainable planning model toward reviving Lake Urmia. Int. J. Water Resour. Dev. **31**(4), 519–539 (2015)

27. Bashiri, F.: Water governance , taking its biggest victim in the Middle East ; Tragic case of Urmia lake, Lund University (2019)
28. Peace, R., Change, G., Dalby, S., Moussavi, Z.: Environmental security , geopolitics and the case of Lake Urmia's disappearance. Glob. Chang. Peace Secur. 1–17 (2016)
29. Garousi, V., Najafi, A., Samadi, A., Rasouli, K., Khanaliloo, B.: Environmental crisis in Lake Urmia, Iran: a systematic review of causes, negative consequences and possible solutions. In: Proceedings 6th International Perspectives Water Resources Environment, Izmir, Turkey, no. February, pp. 1–10 (2013)
30. Karbassi, A., Bidhendi, G.N., Pejman, A., Bidhendi, M.E.: Environmental impacts of desalination on the ecology of Lake Urmia. J. Great Lakes Res. **36**(3), 419–424 (2010)
31. Khatami, S., Berndtsson, R.: Urmia Lake watershed restoration in Iran: short- and long-term perspectives. In: 6th International Perspective on Water Resources and the Environment (2013 IPWE) (2013)
32. Khazaei, B., et al.: Climatic or regionally induced by humans? Tracing hydro-climatic and land-use changes to better understand the Lake Urmia tragedy. J. Hydrol. **569**, 203–217 (2019)
33. Shadkam, S.: Preserving Urmia Lake in a changing world: reconciling anthropogenic and climate drivers by hydrological modelling and policy assessment (2017)
34. Madani, K.: Game theory and water resources. J. Hydrol. **381**, 225–238 (2010)
35. Hamidi-Razi, H., Mazaheri, M., Carvajalino-Fernández, M., Vali-Samani, J.: Investigating the restoration of Lake Urmia using a numerical modelling approach. J. Great Lakes Res. **45**(1), 87–97 (2019)
36. Sarabi, S.E.: Impacts of Institutional arrangements on the adaptive capacity of the Urmia Lake basin (2018)
37. Kilgour, D.M., Hipel, K.W., Fang, L.: The graph model for conflicts. Automatica **23**(1), 41–55 (1987)
38. Fang, L., Hipel, K.W., Kilgour, D.M.: Interactive Decision Making: the Graph Model for Conflict Resolution, vol. 11. John Wiley & Sons, Hoboken (1993)
39. Xu, H., Hipel, K.W., Kilgour, D.M., Fang, L.: Conflict Resolution Using the Graph Model: Strategic Interactions in Competition and Cooperation, vol. 153. Springer (2018). https://doi.org/10.1007/978-3-319-77670-5.pdf
40. Madani, K., Hipel, K.W.: Non-cooperative stability definitions for strategic analysis of generic water resources conflicts. Water Resour. Manage. **25**(8), 1949–1977 (2011)
41. Kinsara, R.A., Petersons, O., Hipel, K.W., Kilgour, D.M.: Advanced decision support for the graph model for conflict resolution. J. Decis. Syst. **24**(2), 117–145 (2015)
42. Sterman, J.D.: System dynamics: systems thinking and modeling for a complex world. MIT Sloan Sch. Manage. **147**(3), 248–249 (2002)
43. Richmond, B.: Systems thinking: critical thinking skills for the 1990s and beyond. Syst. Dyn. Rev. **9**(2), 113–133 (1993)
44. Madani, K., Mariño, M.A.: System dynamics analysis for managing Iran's Zayandeh-rud river basin. Water Resour. Manag. **23**(11), 2163–2187 (2009)
45. Mirchi, A., Madani, K., Watkins, D., Ahmad, S.: Synthesis of system dynamics tools for holistic conceptualization of water resources problems. Water Resour. Manage. **26**(9), 2421–2442 (2012)
46. Ahmad, S., Simonovic, S.P.: Spatial system dynamics: new approach for simulation of water resources systems. J. Comput. Civ. Eng. **18**(4), 331–340 (2004)
47. Teferi, E., Uhlenbrook, S., Bewket, W., Wenninger, J., Simane, B.: The use of remote sensing to quantify wetland loss in the Choke mountain range, Upper Blue Nile basin, Ethiopia. Hydrol. Earth Syst. Sci. Discuss. **7**(4), 6243–6284 (2010)

48. Agnone, J.: Amplifying Public Opinion : The Policy Impact of the U.S. Environmental Movement Dramatic Events : Social Movement Protest, vol. 85, no. 4 (2007)
49. Amenta, E., Young, M.P.: Making an impact: Conceptual and methodological implications of the collective goods criterion, How Soc. movements matter, pp. 22–41 (1999)

Collaborative Decision Making Processes

Analysis on the Temporal Transition of Social Issues Related to Disaster Prevention Using Text Data

Madoka Chosokabe[(⊠)], Keishi Tanimoto, and Satoshi Tsuchiya

Faculty of Engineering, Tottori University, Tottori, Japan
mchoso@tottori-u.ac.jp

Abstract. In recent years, text analysis has been applied to newspaper articles in order to analysis social issues. However, it is difficult to identify a specific theme and to show trend using text analysis alone. This study applies deep machine learning to the huge amount of text data available and clarifies social issues and their temporal change by focusing on the social issues of disaster prevention in Japan. We extracted words of the text of newspaper article data about disaster prevention, and applied the skip-gram approach of word2vec to calculate the similarity with a specific keyword that was specified in advance. Next, by applying Nonnegative Matrix Factorization (NMF), we performed clustering of words based on the degree of similarity of them and estimated the characteristics of the transition of each cluster. The characteristic result comparing evacuation with volunteers is the content of the agendas in the middle stage (2006–2010) and the final stage (2011–2014). In the middle stage, evacuation was characterized by education, whereas volunteers were characterized by disaster experience. In the final stage, evacuation was characterized by system issues, while volunteers were characterized by education and operation.

Keywords: Social issues · Disaster prevention · Newspaper · Word2vec

1 Introduction

In the planning process and decision-making process of the government, officials need to address a high-priority agenda as reflecting the social conditions and needs of the times. As identifying the high-priority agenda in the society, it is necessary to assess situations from a broader perspective. A text analysis for mass media and social media is one of practicable approach to grasp the social situation and needs. For example, analyzing newspaper articles can help easily and visually identify social issues when they were written. It has been difficult to sort out social issues and their changes from a long-term perspective. One of the reasons for this difficulty was that the techniques and analysis methods for quantifying an ordering of priority of social issues had not yet been fully developed. However, in recent years, text analysis methods have improved. In addition, regarding data analysis, text data has become easy to obtain with the creation of databases and the development of data business.

© Springer Nature Switzerland AG 2021
D. C. Morais et al. (Eds.): GDN 2021, LNBIP 420, pp. 131–142, 2021.
https://doi.org/10.1007/978-3-030-77208-6_10

Mass media is an effective method of identifying a major issue regarding certain social phenomena [1–3]. If the event has a large social impact, the mass media will report on it every day. On the other hand, if the issue has a small impact on society, the media will not cover it for a long time after the initial coverage. There are several areas of content reported by mass media including politics, the economy, and sports. Furthermore, each area addresses problems and conflict. Here, in this paper, we make the key assumption that mass media and social interest influence each other. That is, it is possible to extract the topics recognized as problems by the general population using the content of mass media coverage. Newspaper articles are especially useful for keeping track of social issues that are perceived by public. In our previous study [4], we assumed that there was a strong relationship between our daily wording and the wording in newspaper articles. We referred to the discussion that it has been discussed that newspaper articles reflect community's recognition on social issues, in the field of political science [5, 6].

The process of disaster prevention planning and reconstruction planning requires reflecting social interest and issues as rapidly as possible. Disasters not only adversely affect our lives, but depending on the scale of the disaster, they can have long-term effects on society. Therefore, it is necessary to take prompt recovery measures. For example, in the 2011 Great East Japan Earthquake, it was reported, surprisingly, that the estimated economic impact of the supply chain disruption was at least 0.35% of GDP [7]. It was also reported that due to the disruption of the supply chain caused by the earthquake, the number of employees leaving jobs in areas that were not directly damaged increased [8]. In order to prevent such losses, giving priority to addressing the issues related to disaster-prevention and recovery is required.

In preparation for future disasters, it is necessary to clarify the areas where social issues related to disaster have not yet been resolved and to prioritize solutions. However, in the long run, it is unclear which problem of disaster prevention or reconstruction have been solved and which have not. Since many natural disasters such as earthquakes and typhoons occur in Japan, several governmental measures have been taken throughout the years. Nevertheless, every time a disaster occurs, past failures are repeating. For example, during an evacuation, some residents often do not take safety actions because of insufficient information transmission. Therefore, it is difficult to say that the situation has improved. In some cases, however, governmental measures have worked effectively. We need to identify social issues and prioritize them to be discussed for solution.

In this research, we develop a method for linguistically classifying social issues about a specific theme in the field of disaster prevention using newspaper articles covering 20 years of disaster prevention. Then, we clarify what kinds of the people's interests of social issues are changing and how.

2 Approach

Newspapers are useful tools to help grasp long-term public opinion and social situation. The advantage of newspaper articles over Social Networking Service (SNS) is that articles of the same quality have been accumulated for many years. Garg et al. show historical trends and social change using 100 years of text data consisting of books and newspaper articles [9]. In this research, we identify topics that are still recognized as issues by the public and topics that are not recognized as issues. We reported that newspaper articles may be useful in assessing public small group discussion and that it is possible to capture changing perspectives on social issues from newspaper articles [6, 10]. Furthermore, we evaluated the discussion of disaster recovery using newspaper articles [11]. In the above example, if topic A was reported the same amount in the past as it is today, then social interest about topic A continues to exist. In other words, the priority of topic A has not changed. On the other hand, if topic B was reported in the past but is no longer reported in the present, then this means that the priority of topic B has changed lower.

There are two technical issues here. The first is how to identify topics from newspaper articles and the second is how to define change. A topic model [12], a method for unsupervised classification of documents, is very useful as a solution to these issues. However, when trying to extract a topic from a large amount of text data, selection may be difficult due to the huge number of word combinations. Therefore, it is necessary to determine a meaningful keyword in advance.

Research on extracting meaningful content from huge texts is progressing. In particular, a tool called word2vec was developed by Thomas Mikolov during his employment at Google, bringing great technological progress to natural language processing [13]. Many subsequent studies have applied word2vec to newspaper articles. Szymanski used the New York Times corpus to reveal temporal word similarities [14]. He stated that temporal analysis of word embedding can capture social change. Sasaki applied word2vec

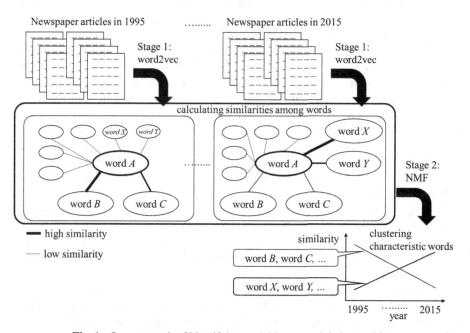

Fig. 1. Our approach of identifying social issues and their transition

to local news after the Great East Japan Earthquake and clarified reconstruction trends [15].

In this research, we use word2vec for the large-scale newspaper corpus in the field of disaster prevention. The word2vec method is very effective at calculating the relationship between multiple words. On the other hand, co-occurrence analysis can calculate only two words at a time. For example, the connection between word A and word B is known. However, it takes an enormous amount of time to see all the word connections. Calculation is possible by applying skip-gram and vectorizing words. Next, the degree of similarity between a specific keyword determined in advance and other words is calculated for each year. By performing Non-negative Matrix Factorization (NMF) based on the degree of similarity, we quantitatively clarify what kind of social issues by the public in disaster prevention has changed over time. Figure 1 shows our approach of identifying social issues and their transition.

3   Methodologies

3.1   Analysis Procedure

Assuming that social issues will be revealed from newspaper reports, we will find topics related to disaster prevention issues and clarify their transition over time. This analysis has two stages. In the first stage, we find words used at the same time such as "disaster prevention" and "agenda" in newspaper articles. Here, we use word2vec to calculate the distributed representation of keywords for newspaper articles from each year. Then, the synonyms for multiple keywords are calculated for newspaper articles of each year and the keywords are fixed. The second stage uses NMF to estimate topics from the words used at the same time such as "disaster prevention" and "agenda" for a 20-year period.

First, we use the word2vec tool to acquire the distributed representation of each word for the extracted word group, and then words similar to the three specified keywords are calculated for each year. The keywords are "disaster prevention," "agenda," and "evacuation," followed by "disaster prevention," "agenda," and "volunteer." That is, words similar to multiple keywords are extracted using word2vec. By extracting a group of words with a high degree of similarity to the two keywords "disaster prevention" and "agenda," we can infer the words that are often used when a disaster prevention agenda is written about in a newspaper article. This is calculated for each year's articles. However, at this point, it is not a topic.

We apply NMF to the row vector of estimated word value of each year to clarify the topic, and further cluster the words that were used with the words "disaster prevention" and "agenda." At this time, the transition of the word group (topic) for each year is clarified quantitatively (i.e., we infer topics from words belonging to a cluster). We then clarify the transition of topics.

In other words, the patterns of words that appear around the disaster prevention agenda are divided into several groups. We will clarify how they change and then determine whether the public interest in the social issues have increased or decreased.

3.2 Word2Vec

Word2vec is a name of tool that calculate distributed representation of words by using neural networks of two layers. After entering the text corpus, distributed representation of words is output. Word2vec has two models: continuous bag-of-words model (CBOW) and skip-gram [13]. The CBOW model maximizes the conditional probability of the target word appearing from the words in context. The skip-gram model is the opposite of CBOW, and predicts multiple words before and after from the central word. By calculating the distributed representation of words, it is possible to perform addition and subtraction operations between words [14–16].

3.3 Non-negative Matrix Factorization

A method of approximating a matrix as a product of two non-negative matrices was proposed as Positive Matrix Factorization [17]. After that, Lee and Seung [18, 19] proposed a multiplicative algorithm that can solve problems efficiently while guaranteeing non-negativity. The similarity of the words calculated by word2vec is used as the element of the matrix. The matrix with the words from each year are represented in rows and the columns of years are created as follows.

Here, x_{ij} represents the similarity of words i in year j. The number of words m is the words for which the similarity can be calculated with both "disaster prevention" and "issue."

$$X = \begin{pmatrix} x_{11} & \cdots & x_{1n} \\ \vdots & \ddots & \vdots \\ x_{m1} & \cdots & x_{mn} \end{pmatrix} \tag{1}$$

A matrix consisting only of non-negative elements is given as $X_{M \times N}$. NMF uses two matrices: $W \in \Re^{M \times K}$ and $H \in \Re^{K \times N}$. The inner product of approximate is as follows:

$$X_{M \times N} \approx W_{M \times K} H_{K \times N} = \begin{pmatrix} w_{11} & \cdots & w_{1k} \\ w_{21} & \cdots & w_{2k} \\ \vdots & \vdots & \vdots \\ w_{m1} & \cdots & w_{mk} \end{pmatrix} \begin{pmatrix} h_{11} & \cdots & h_{1n} \\ \vdots & \vdots & \vdots \\ h_{k1} & \cdots & h_{kn} \end{pmatrix} \tag{2}$$

Here, K is the number of bases as $K \leq \min(M, N)$ and is given in advance. All matrix elements are non-negative: $x_{ij} \geq 0$, $w_{ik} \geq 0$, and $h_{kj} \geq 0$. The general solution is to find H and W so that $\|X\text{-}WH\|^2$ is the minimum.

4 Results and Discussions

We collected newspaper articles containing specific keywords on disasters. Fourteen keywords are specified in Article 2 of the Disaster Countermeasures Basic Act in Japan: disaster, storm, tornado, heavy rain, flood, landslide, debris flow, storm surge, earthquake, wave, eruption, landslide, large-scale fire, and large-scale explosion.

We collected newspaper articles from the CD Mainichi Newspaper Series. We performed a morphological analysis on the collected texts using MeCab. Parts of speech were limited to nouns. Figure 2 shows the number of documents and words in newspaper articles by year. The number of newspaper articles in 1995 and 2011 are particularly high due to the occurrence of the Great Hanshin-Awaji Earthquake in 1995 and the Great East Japan Earthquake in 2011.

We obtained a distributed representation of words in the skip-gram of word2vec. We analyzed the newspaper articles through 20 years for each year. We used a Genism package for the calculation of Word2vec. The maximum distance between the current and predicted word within a sentence was 10, and the dimensionality of the word vectors was 100. All words with a total frequency lower than five were ignored.

After acquiring the distributed expression of all words, we calculated the similarity of the words that co-occur with both words in the following two patterns:

I.   Three words such as "disaster prevention," "issue," and "evacuation," hereinafter we call "evacuation."
II. Three words such as "disaster prevention," "issue," and "volunteer," hereinafter we call "volunteer."

In addition, we extracted vocabulary that appeared in all years for 20 years. The number of vocabularies in pattern I was 2245, and the number of vocabularies in pattern II was 2247. We applied NMF to patterns I and II to perform clustering. We determined K using the cophenetic correlation coefficient. As for the results, $K = 5$ in the case of evacuation and $K = 6$ in the case of volunteers. We call groups divided based on the number of K as topics.

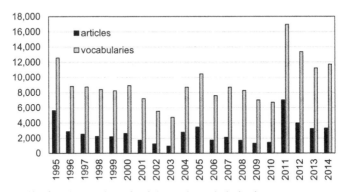

Fig. 2. The number of articles and vocabularies in a newspaper

4.1   Issues of Evacuation

Table 1 summarizes the top 20 nouns in Japanese for each topic about evacuation. In Fig. 3, the y axis shows the H element and the x axis shows the year. If the element of H

is large in a certain year, it is a characteristic topic for that year. For example, in 2014, Topic 3 is the most characteristic topic. The contents of each topic are inferred as the following:

- Topic 1: "minister," "guideline," and some personal names. These nouns suggest the content is politics, but there are many words that are difficult to interpret.
- Topic 2: "large cities," "city center," "nuclear power," and "lifeline." Additionally, "strengthening," "system," "expansion," and "establishment." These nouns suggest the key issues are disaster countermeasures for large cities. This topic is most characteristic between 1995 and 2001.
- Topic 3: "manual," "map," "communication," "reflection," "lessons learned," "training," "thorough," and "proposal." These nouns suggest the key issue is a review of evacuation methods. It is the most characteristic topic since 2011.
- Topic 4: "independence," "town," "distribution," and "usually." These nouns suggest daily activities for disaster prevention in a small community. The value increases regularly. It is the most distinctive topic in 2002.
- Topic 5: "game," "production" "course," and "program." These nouns suggest the key issue for disaster prevention education for residents. It is the most characteristic topic from 2006 to 2010.

Table 1. Top 20 nouns in Japanese for each topic about "evacuation"

Topic 1	*Tamura*, The Ministry, *Umeda*, violation, soft, calm, route, *Ichiro*, guideline, reflection, *Taro*, *Fujita*, inn, defense, group, *Watanabe*, speed, *Okada*, review, policy
Topic 2	Strengthening, metropolis, desolating, atomic energy, aggregation, system, lifeline, city center, security, integration, situation, convert, operation, expansion, establishment, advance, prefectural office, destruction, urgent, average
Topic 3	Manual, map, transmission, hard, stock, proposal, explanation, efforts, drill, lesson, reflection, nursing, item, thoroughness, inadequacy, effectiveness, behavior, wireless, perfection, smoothness
Topic 4	Last fall, autonomy, town, *Abe*, self-reliance, money, student, every day, organization, mission, induction, distribution, care, school year, tragedy, map, goods, half, worry, prevention
Topic 5	Two years ago, festival, following year, course, game, reproduction, making, course, list, spread, flood disaster, work, cooking, Great Kanto Earthquake, welfare, know-how, person himself, admission, volunteer, program

Note: These words are the top 20 nouns in Japanese. An italicized word is a person's or town name

4.2 Issues of Volunteer

Table 2 shows 20 nouns in Japanese with large elements of W. In Fig. 4, the y axis is the H element and the x axis shows the year. If the element of H is large in a certain

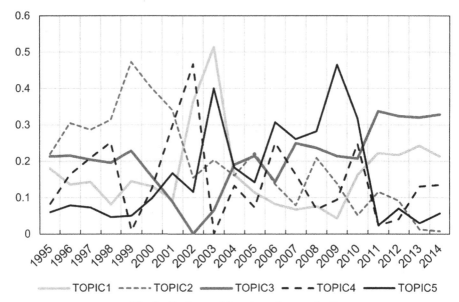

Fig. 3. Topic transition about "evacuation"

year, it is a characteristic topic in that year. The contents of each topic are inferred as the following:

- Topic 1: "university," "this spring," "elementary school student," "admission," and "grade." These nouns suggest that the key issue is education, but it is difficult to interpret clearly.
- Topic 2: "living experience," "tragedy," "experience," and "lessons learned." These nouns suggest that the key issue is disaster experience. It has a high value from 2006 to 2009.
- Topic 3: "administration," "government," and personal names. This is difficult to interpret.
- Topic 4: "opportunity," "explanation," "approach," "education," and "practice." These nouns suggest that the key issues concern on-site educational training. It has a high value from 2013 to 2014.
- Topic 5: "division," "advancement," "policy," "private," and "thorough." These nouns suggest the key issue concerns operation. It has a high value from 2011 to 2012.
- Topic 6: "verification," "discussion," "public office," "official residence," and "framework," These nouns suggest political content, but it is again difficult to interpret.

4.3   Discussions

Table 3 shows the disaster chronology in Japan. In this section, we consider the relationship between the topic transition and social situation with reference to the disaster history in Table 3. Regarding the key issue of evacuation, Topic 2 is characteristic at the

Table 2. Top 20 nouns in Japanese for each topic about "volunteer"

Topic 1	Game, two years ago, university, inn, festival, program, *Fuji* mountain, this spring, lawyer, elementary school students, indoor, cooking, prayer, admission, chorus, student, grade, foodstuff, cultivation, calm
Topic 2	Living experience, tragedy, disastrous scene, best, expansion, firefighting, every day, residents, recent years, experience, individual, community, nerve, lesson, autonomy, proposal, flood disaster, map, stock, operation
Topic 3	Net, uniqueness, last fall, theory, government office, *Abe*, administration, autonomy, literature, forum, impression, *Otsu*, *Ishihara*, commentary, high grade, organization, feature, disastrous scene, reliance, foundation
Topic 4	Opportunity, explanation, efforts, education, flood disaster, allowance, map, know-how, program, point, seriousness, practice, smoothness, hard, actual situation, examined, feeling, wide area, wisdom, middle school students
Topic 5	Sharing, advance, developing, policy, private company, orbit, soft, arrangement, thoroughness, next fiscal year, way, pharmaceuticals, electron, acceleration, at night, closure, formation, guideline, aggregation, volcano
Topic 6	Verification, debate, major powers, chief cabinet, official residence, metropolis, framework, space, *Fujita*, review, atomic energy, federal, way, foreign ministry, emphasis, prudence, reflection, industry, cabinet ministers, system

Note: These words are the top 20 nouns in Japanese. An italicized word is a person's or town name

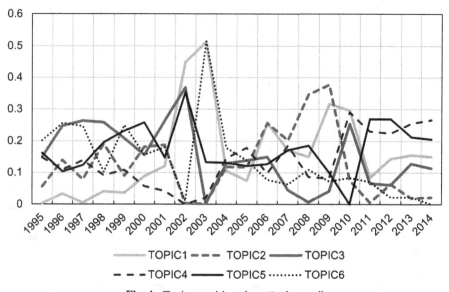

Fig. 4. Topic transition about "volunteer"

beginning as shown in Fig. 3. In Japan, the Great Hanshin-Awaji Earthquake occurred in 1995 and the Tokai Village JCO critical accident occurred in 1999, causing a large-scale disaster and a critical accident in a large city. The Tokai Village JCO critical accident was the first fatality in Japan due to accidental exposure. As a result, the Act on Special Measures for Nuclear Disaster Countermeasures was enacted in 2000. Topic 2 has been decreasing since 2001. Topic 5 is characteristic during the middle stage. This is about disaster prevention education. This is probably because in 2005, the contents of the national disaster prevention plan regarding the development of national movements to practice disaster preparedness and the promotion of corporate disaster prevention were added. Topic 3 is characteristic in the final stage. This is largely due to the Great East Japan Earthquake that occurred in 2011. Many people were delayed for the evacuation from the tsunami, so that it becomes necessary that the evacuation transmission method and behavior should be updated.

Table 3. Disaster chronology in Japan

Year	Disaster Name
1995	Great Hanshin-Awaji Earthquake
1999	Tokai Village JCO Critical Accident
2000	Eruption of Mt. Usu Eruption of Miyakejima and Niijima-Kozushima inland earthquake
2004	Typhoon No. 23 Niigata prefecture Chuetsu earthquake
2005	2006 heavy snowfall
2007	Niigata Chuetsu-Oki earthquake
2008	Iwate-Miyagi inland earthquake
2010	Heavy snowfall from November 2010
2011	Tohoku region Pacific Ocean Earthquake (Great East Japan Earthquake) Typhoon No. 12 The 2011 heavy snow storm
2012	The 2012 heavy snow storm
2013	The 2013 heavy snow storm
2014	The 2014 August heavy rain storm (Hiroshima landslide) Mt. Ontake Eruption

Notes: Regarding dead and missing persons, and storm and flood damage, this impacted more than 500 people. Snow damage affected more than 100 people, and earthquakes, tsunamis, and volcanic eruptions affected more than 10 people. An emergency disaster countermeasures headquarters based on the "Countermeasures Basic Act" was established

Regarding the key issue for volunteers, Topics 3 and 6 are characteristic at the beginning as illustrated in Fig. 4. These topics are about politics and institutions. In the middle stage, Topic 2 increased rapidly from 2006 to 2009. The content here is about disaster experience. At the end stage, Topics 4 and 5 are characteristic.

The characteristic result comparing evacuation with volunteers is the content of the agendas in the middle stage (2006–2010) and the final stage (2011–2014). In the middle stage, evacuation was characterized by education (Topic 5), whereas volunteers were characterized by disaster experience (Topic 2). In the final stage, evacuation was characterized by system issues (Topic 3), while volunteers were characterized by education (Topic 4) and operation (Topic 5). In this way, we were able to distinguish the issues related to disaster prevention from the perspective of evacuation and the perspective of volunteers.

5   Conclusion

In this research, we developed a method to clarify the transition of social issues by focusing on specific words in newspaper article data in the field of disaster prevention. Specifically, we extracted only the nouns of the text of newspaper article data that expresses social issues, and applied the skip-gram approach of word2vec to calculate the similarity with a specific keyword that was specified in advance. By specifying multiple keywords, it is now possible to perform a more specific analysis to find topics, such as for "volunteer" or "evacuation" in the field of disaster prevention. Next, we performed clustering of words based on the degree of similarity of them and estimated the characteristics of the transition of each cluster by applying NMF. Based on the analysis, social issues became clear by looking at the characteristics of words in each cluster. In addition, by observing the transition of the cluster, we estimated how social issues changed. The results distinguished the social issues related to disaster prevention from the perspective of evacuation and the perspective of volunteers.

In this study we preliminarily selected three specific three words as keywords, such as "disaster prevention," "agendas," and "volunteers," and calculated the degree of similarity with other words using them. We think this affected the analysis results. Therefore, it is necessary to examine the selection and number of words as keywords at next research.

Acknowledgment. This study was funded by JSPS KAKENHI Grant Number JP18K13851.

References

1. Thompson-Saud, G., Gelcich, S., Barraza, J.: Marine environmental issues in the mass media: Insights from television, newspaper and internet searches in Chile. Ocean Coastal Manage. **165**, 154–160 (2018). https://doi.org/10.1016/j.ocecoaman.2018.08.015
2. Ho, G.W.K., Chan, A.C.Y.: Media portrayal of a hidden problem: an analysis of Hong Kong newspaper coverage of child maltreatment in. Child Abuse Negl. **83**, 62–73 (2016). https://doi.org/10.1016/j.chiabu.2018.07.002(2018)
3. Du, Q., Han, Z.: The framing of nuclear energy in Chinese media discourse: A comparison between national and local newspapers. J. Cleaner Prod. **245** (2020). https://doi.org/10.1016/j.jclepro.2019.118695
4. Chosokabe, M., Takeyoshi, H., Sakakibara, H.: Study on temporal change of social context. In: The case of Bicycle Riding Issue in Japan, Proceedings of the 2014 Group Decision and Negotiation, pp. 315–322 (2014)
5. Prince, V.: Social identification and public opinion: effects of communicating group conflict. Am. Assoc. Public Opinion Res. **53**(2), 197–224 (1989)

6. Brains, L.C., Wattenberg, P.M.: Campaign issue knowledge and salience: comparing reception from TV commercials. TV News Newspapers **40**(1), 172–193 (1996)

7. Tokui, J., Kawasaki, K., Miyagawa, T.: The economic impact of supply chain disruptions from the Great East-Japan earthquake. Japan World Econ. **41**, 59–70 (2017). https://doi.org/10.1016/j.japwor.2016.12.005

8. Kondo, A.: The effects of supply chain disruptions caused by the Great East Japan earthquake on workers. Japan World Econ. **47**, 40–50 (2018). https://doi.org/10.1016/j.japwor.2018.03.007

9. Garg, N., Schiebinger, L., Jurafsky, D., Zou, J.: Word embeddings quantify 100 years of gender and ethnic stereotypes. PNAS, **115**(16), E3635–E3644 (2018). https://doi.org/10.1073/pnas.1720347115

10. Chosokabe, M., Umeda, H., Sakakibara, H.: The contribution of social context to participatory planning processes within a Japanese community. Group Decis. Negot. **25**(5), 923–940 (2015). https://doi.org/10.1007/s10726-015-9466-2

11. Chosokabe, M., Sakamoto, M., Tanimoto, K.: Comparative study of local and national newspapers: a case study of the reconstruction in response to the great East Japan Earthquake. In: Proceedings of the 2018 Group Decision and Negotiation, pp. 91–98 (2018)

12. Silge, J., Robinson, D.: Text Mining with R: Tidy Approach, 6 Topic modeling (2021). https://www.tidytextmining.com/topicmodeling.html

13. Mikolov, T., Chen, K., Corrado, G., Dean, J.: Efficient estimation of word representations in vector space. In: Proceedings of Workshop at International Conference on Learning Representations (ICLR). arXiv:1301.3781 (2013)

14. Szymanski, T.: Temporal word analogies: identifying lexical replacement with diachronic word embeddings. In: Proceedings of the 55th Annual Meeting of the Association for Computational Linguistics (Short Papers), pp. 448–453 (2017). https://doi.org/10.18653/v1/P17-2071

15. Sasaki, D.: The basic trend of media reports on residents' return in Fukushima: in the realms of text mining analysis. J. Asian Dev. **3**(1), 65–72 (2017). https://doi.org/10.5296/jad.v3i1.10572

16. Goldberg, Y., Levy, O.: word2vec Explained: deriving Mikolov et al.'s negative-sampling word-embedding method. arXiv:1402.3722 (2014)

17. Paatero, P., Tapper, U.: Positive matrix factorization: a non-negative factor model with optimal utilization of error estimates of data values. Environmetrics **5**(2), 111–126 (1994)

18. Lee, D.D., Seung, H.S.: Learning the parts of objects by non-negative matrix factorization. Nature **401**, 788–791 (1999)

19. Lee, D.D., Seung, H.S.: Algorithms for non-negative matrix factorization. Adv. Neural Inf. Process. Syst. **13**(1) (2001)

Diplomat: A Conversational Agent Framework for Goal-Oriented Group Discussion

Kevin Hogan$^{(\boxtimes)}$, Annabelle Baer, and James Purtilo

Department of Computer Science, University of Maryland,
College Park, MD 20742, USA
khogan@umd.edu

Abstract. Recent work in human-computer interaction has explored the use of conversational agents as facilitators for group goal-oriented discussions. Inspired by this work and by the apparent lack of tooling available to support it, we created Diplomat, a Python-based framework for building conversational agent facilitators. Diplomat is designed to support simple specification of agent functionality as well as customizable integration with online chat services. We document a preliminary user study we conducted to help inform the design of Diplomat. We also describe the architecture, capabilities, and limitations of our tool, which we have shared on GitHub.

Keywords: Conversational agent · Goal-oriented discussion · Online chat

1 Introduction

Group discussion is a cornerstone of human collaboration. Unlike a lecture or dictation, it is a medium of information exchange which allows *all* group members to freely and candidly express their ideas and opinions. Unfortunately, the same characteristic of group discussion that promotes this ideal, namely its organic and unstructured nature, renders it entirely vulnerable to misaligned behavior. We suspect most readers have been a party to a discussion gone haywire, perhaps due to an emotional disagreement or a particularly charismatic discussion participant.

It comes as no surprise, therefore, that the annals of scientific research have, for the past century, been littered with contributions to the understanding and improvement of group discussion. Echoing Thorndike's assessment [27], we identify Münsterberg as perhaps *the* pioneer in this research area with his early work on jury deliberations [20]. Selected works between then and now have

This work was supported by the United States Office of Naval Research under Contract N000141812767 and partially funded by an NSF REU grant, REU-CAAR, CNS-1952352.

© Springer Nature Switzerland AG 2021
D. C. Morais et al. (Eds.): GDN 2021, LNBIP 420, pp. 143–154, 2021.
https://doi.org/10.1007/978-3-030-77208-6_11

explored the comparison of individual and group performance on problem-solving [16,18,25], formal modeling of group decision-making [3,7], and group creativity [15,19,32].

As computer scientists, we're primarily interested in the application of computers towards the improvement of group discussion, a more modern research area that blossomed alongside personal computing in the late 1980 s. Nunamaker et al. were the first to introduce the term "Electronic Meeting System" (perhaps a descendant or variant of the "Group Communication Support System" [23]), which categorizes technologies "designed to directly impact and change the behavior of groups" [21]. Over the past few decades, researchers have produced a plethora of systems [2,4,26,28] that fit this categorization (though usage of the term itself seems to have waned over the years).

Our work fits in this broad category as well, but can more specifically be classified as research seeking to automate the role of the facilitator in group goal-oriented discussion. We've long known of the benefits that facilitators add to group conversations [29], but the advent of advanced natural language interfaces to computation has spurred the development of conversational agents (CAs) to assist or replace these facilitators [14,17,22,24]. Beyond the obvious benefit of scale and reproducibility, a CA can also provide the unique benefit of being consistently unbiased in its facilitation (assuming it is programmed without bias, of course).

In our investigation of this area, we noticed an absence of software frameworks to develop CAs for group goal-oriented conversation. This stands in contrast to variety of frameworks available to develop CAs for dyadic conversations (i.e., virtual assistants and chatbots) [6,13]. In this work, we seek to fill this gap, designing for Internet-based text communication due to the popularity of this medium and the frequency of CAs built around it. We make the following contributions:

1. A preliminary user study exploring participant perceptions of conversational agents and reactions to specific features.
2. Diplomat, an open-source Python-based framework for the development and deployment of CA discussion facilitators[1].

The rest of the paper proceeds as follows: Sect. 2 describes prior research related to each of the contributions listed above. Section 3 describes the preliminary user study mentioned in our first listed contribution. Section 4 describes the architecture, implementation, and limitations of Diplomat. Section 5 discusses possible future research directions inspired by this work, and we conclude in Sect. 6.

2   Related Work

We highlight related work in two areas (corresponding to each of our main contributions listed in the Introduction): that which examines the effect of a conversational agent in discussion and that which simplifies the development of

---

[1] https://github.com/kevin-hogan/diplomat.

conversational agents. Within the former area, we see an abundance of work in the context of dyadic, or one-on-one, conversation. XiaoIce, one of the world's most popular chatbots, has been studied for its ability to emotionally connect with users [31]. Ciechanowski et al. study the differences between user reactions to text-based and avatar-based versions of an agent [5]. Zhao et al. study the mechanism for rapport building in dyadic interactions with a CA [30]. We also see efforts in the context of group discussion, which pertains to our work more directly. CAs have been studied for their ability to aid facilitators [17], replace facilitators [14], increase critical thinking [9], prime conversations [12], create arguments [11], and improve conversation flow [8]. Our preliminary user study described in Sect. 3 helps to validate a general conclusion found throughout this work: that conversational agents can improve group discussions and provide value to their participants.

Work aiming to simplify the development of conversational agents is heavily focused on the dyadic discussion context. Several solutions exist for the development of commercial chatbots, such as Microsoft BotFramework, IBM Watson, and Google DialogFlow. Xatkit is a more research-oriented framework based in model-driven engineering that provides a domain-specific language for the specification of chatbot rules and allows for flexible integration with intent-recognition providers [6]. However, none of these frameworks are tailored towards group, goal-oriented discussion. The Neem Platform [1] is a research test-bed for collaborative applications which includes support for "virtual participants". However, this support appears to be a small part of a broader platform and there is no publicly-available implementation. Diplomat, in contrast, is entirely focused on supporting the development and deployment of conversational agents for group discussion. We've released the software as a tool for those who may benefit from this support in their research or other efforts.

3 Preliminary User Study

3.1 Summary

To explore the impact of a conversational agent in a goal-oriented group conversation, we set up an experiment in which five groups were instructed to chat about an opinion-oriented prompt and reach a conclusion. We used the Wizard-of-Oz method [10] so that a human researcher could participate in the discussion while masquerading as an automated agent. This method allowed us to examine the effect of an agent without the cost of its implementation. The researcher interacted in discussions according to the pre-defined ruleset described in Sect. 3.2. In Sect. 3.4 we discuss the takeaways from this study and how it motivated the design of Diplomat. This study was performed after being approved by the Institutional Review Board, University of Maryland, College Park with Ref. no. 1633038-1.

3.2   Procedure

The experiment was held remotely and coordinated using video conferencing. We did not observe any uncontrollable variables such as internet connection or other distractions that played a role in the outcome of the experiment. Participants were undergraduate volunteers randomly (with the exception of some scheduling constraints) split into five groups of four or five students each. Following from our selection of Internet-based chat as our preferred communication medium (see Sect. 1), we chose to host participant discussions on the popular chat provider, Slack. Each group discussed in a separate channel, and was unable to see the channels for other groups. At the beginning of the session, the moderator (under the identity of an autonomous agent) announced a question prompt and instructed participants to discuss this topic in their channel for 20 min (or until reaching consensus, if this happened sooner). At the end of the session, the participants filled out a survey via Google Forms answering questions about their feelings towards the conversation.

Our "agent" interacted with participants differently for each conversation. The rules for each of the five scenarios are presented in the list below. We designed the rules based on our intuitions about what would promote constructive and fair deliberations.

- **Information**: The agent will send new links and suggest new topics to the users when there is a lull (2 min silence) in conversation. These links were predetermined by taking the first 5 links from a Google search of the full text of the prompt.
- **Timing**: The conversation will be actively timed (20 min). The agent will give time warning signals when there are 10, 5, and 2 min remaining.
- **Under/Overspeaking Notification**: The agent will address users who haven't spoken in 8 messages after speaking their last message. The agent will address users who have spoken over $\frac{1}{2}$ the messages in a grouping of 8 or more messages.
- **Rules 1–3 combined**: All rules apply
- **Control**: The agent will not be a part of the control conversation

Using a post-experiment survey, we measured the users' 1) satisfaction with the outcome of the meeting and 2) reactions to the agent. Kim et al. reports inconsistent user attitudes as a result of the study, but states user testimonies that support the idea that the conversational agent removed "relational burdens" by addressing users' participation as an objective measure [14]. We wanted to understand if our intervention scenarios could similarly reduce burdens. We also measured the frequency of expected behaviors in response to agent interventions (we omit the Timing intervention because, after the experiment, we realized the difficulty in articulating and measuring an expected response from this intervention). These expected behaviors are listed below:

- **Information**
  - People respond to link with insights clearly taken from the suggested link.

- **Underspeaking Notification**
  - No direct response, but the person says a new message within the next 5 messages. 5 messages was chosen because on average, each conversation had 5 people, giving the user a small window of time to think about and message their response.
- **Overspeaking Notification**
  - No direct response, but the person stops responding for any period of time greater than 5 messages for reasons stated above.

3.3 Results

As mentioned in the previous subsection, the post-experiment survey asked for both satisfaction with the outcome of the meeting and the reactions of participants to the agent. With one exception across all participants, participants expressed satisfaction with the meeting outcome. Therefore, we don't observe any substantial differences in satisfaction across the various rule scenarios we tested. The participants had expressed mixed reactions to the agent. Roughly 50% of all participants (excluding the control group) indicated in a free-form response that they would choose to include the agent in another conversation. However, about 25% expressed a negative impression of the agent, calling it "annoying" and "not super useful". The remainder were neutral. Participants assigned an agent in the Under/Overspeaking scenario responded most positively, with 2 positive and 2 neutral reactions. Those assigned to an agent in the Information scenario were most critical of the agent.

For each of the expected behaviors, the majority of users responded as expected. There two cases across all experiments where the agent addressed a user for overspeaking. In one case, the user only sent a total of two more messages in the remaining third of the conversation. The other user initially sent less frequent messages, but eventually returned to a higher frequency by the end of the conversation. There were three cases of underspeaking. In all of the cases, the notification happened so close to the end of the conversation, we do not have sufficient data to observe how the agent impacted the users' participation in the long run. However, in each of these instances, the user sent at least one message after the notification from the agent.

3.4 Takeaways

We caution against drawing strong conclusions from the experiment presented for several reasons. First, this was a small study with only enough participants to conduct one group discussion for each of the tested scenarios. Without repeated trials in each scenario, it is impossible to discern whether variations in outcomes and perceptions across groups are caused by agent intervention rules or instead by the differences in participant opinions and tendencies. Second, intervention rule activation is infrequent by design, which, while sensible in preventing the agent from overwhelming the conversation, makes it difficult to analyze the typical effect of a given intervention type. Finally, participants were prompted to discuss a topic on which they may have had varying levels of interest and prior knowledge. We believe that additional framing and context of the conversation topic may lead to more consistent engagement across participants.

We share this experiment in spite of these concerns because we maintain that there are lessons to be gleaned from it. The results motivate a larger-scale experiment to alleviate some of the aforementioned concerns. This is precisely the driving force behind our decision to build Diplomat (described in the next section), which we see as an enabler of scale (the Wizard-of-Oz method, which requires the participation of a trained operator, is not as scalable). Also, our results indicate that even very crude intervention rules such as those we tested in this study are viewed as valuable by some participants. This motivates further research into more advanced or tunable interventions that may provide much more value to a group discussion.

4 Diplomat

4.1 System Design

As described in Sect. 3.4, we were inspired to develop a framework that would facilitate the specification, configuration, and composition of the sort of conversational agent interventions we tested. Like the human "agent" from our Wizard-of-Oz experiment, agents implemented in our tool communicate with groups via Internet-based chat discussions.

We based the design of our tool, which we've called Diplomat, on the following definitions and principles.

- Definitions
    - A *transcript* represents the entire history of a group chat conversation consisting of all messages, the authorship of those messages, and the timestamps at which those messages were received.
    - An *intervention* is any interaction in the chat interface generated by the agent (currently, a message is the only supported intervention type).
    - A *reactive intervention* is an intervention triggered by user activity (e.g., our "Overspeaking" intervention)
    - A *passive intervention* is an intervention triggered only by the passage of time (e.g., our "Timing" intervention)
    - An *agent feature* is a deterministic rule that can be expressed as a function from a transcript to a list of interventions.
    - A *feature configuration* is a set of parameters that can be modified to tweak the behavior of a chatbot feature (e.g., the "window size" for our overspeaking feature).
- Principles
    1. Agent features can be combined in a single agent, but should operate independently of one another.
    2. The framework should not be coupled with any particular chat service. It should, however, provide a straightforward method for integration with these services.

3. The programming model for features should be simple and modular

Our solution is a Python-based framework that allows for the specification of agent features in the form of a subclass. In Fig. 1 we see the base class for agent features. A feature subclass must implement a constructor which receives a feature configuration dictionary (loaded by the framework from a JSON file) and must produce an instance of the subclass parameterized by the configuration. It also must implement generate_interventions, which (consistent with the agent feature definition above) receives a transcript and returns a list of interventions. Diplomat guides its users towards the fulfillment of Principle 1 by requiring the implementation of each feature in a separate subclass. This requirement also encourages the modularity referred to by Principle 3. As Principle 1 mentions, a particular instance of an agent may consist of several features. Whether or not a feature is enabled for an agent is determined by the presence or absence of a configuration for that feature in the JSON file that specifies the full desired configuration for an agent. As an additional note regarding feature specification, we highlight the fact that the *entire* chat transcript is provided to generate_interventions. This allows for stateless feature specification even for functions depending on long-term correspondence of chat data.

```python
class FeaturePlugin(metaclass=abc.ABCMeta):
    @abc.abstractmethod
    def __init__(self, config: dict):
        pass

    @abc.abstractmethod
    def generate_interventions(
        self,
        chat_transcript: List[Message],
        author_id_for_chatbot) -> List[Message]:
        pass
```

Fig. 1. The abstract base class that users of diplomat must extend to implement new conversational agent features.

In fulfillment of Principle 2, the framework provides another base class that can be flexibly extended for integration with a variety of chat services (see Fig. 2). Users of the framework need not directly manage interactions with the rest of the framework when specifying the integration. Instead, they must only define the connection to the API from which a transcript is loaded, the conversion of that transcript to the internal representation, the conversion of interventions from the internal representation to the chat service API representation, and the post of interventions via the chat service API for writing messages. The constructor allows the user to tailor the polling interval to their liking.

Figure 3 illustrates the architecture of Diplomat and describes the lifecycle of an intervention in relation to the components of that architecture. We won't

```
class ChatServiceToBotIntegrator(metaclass=abc.ABCMeta):
    def __init__(self, path_to_config: str, seconds_per_poll: float):
        ...

    @abc.abstractmethod
    def request_transcript_and_convert_to_message_list(self) -> List[Message]:
        pass

    @abc.abstractmethod
    def post_agent_interventions(self, interventions: List[Message]) -> None:
        pass
```

Fig. 2. The abstract base class that users of diplomat must extend to integrate with an external chat service.

restate the phases of the lifecycle captured in the figure, but we will add some commentary and clarification here. The first two steps in the lifecycle surround the integration with external chat services described in the previous paragraph. The logos in the figure (for readers who may be unfamiliar) represent popular chat services. Diplomat provides an example integration to Slack, but does not provide additional integrations out-of-the-box. Another point of clarification is that Diplomat only support interventions in the form of messages from the agent. We leave the terminology general, however, as we hope to support additional forms of intervention in the future (emoji reaction, message replies, private messages, etc.) without modification to the overall architecture.

4.2   Limitations

Diplomat was designed with simplicity as a first-principle. The consequence is that the framework, especially in its nascent form, is limited in its performance, its expressiveness, and its accessibility. While the computational performance of Diplomat has not been analyzed thoroughly, some issues are apparent from its architecture. For example, Diplomat receives full conversation transcripts from chat services via polling. This means that Diplomat will redundantly load old conversation data continuously rather than keep track of a transcript locally (updating as new messages come in). To avoid potential complexities associated with state management, we opted for the simpler, polling approach for our initial release of the software. Beyond this, we note that only one Diplomat agent can be run per Python process, and that IO with the external chat service is synchronous. While introducing concurrency to the framework would allow for more efficient utilization of resources, it also introduces complexity that we chose to avoid undertaking for now. Due to these limitations, we recommend Diplomat for use in short conversations with modest numbers of participants.

Diplomat's expressiveness is limited due to the independence of agent features and the uniformity of interventions. A user may reasonably desire to develop a conversational agent in which features are dependent. The simplest example of this would be an agent that, at a given time, only produces one intervention

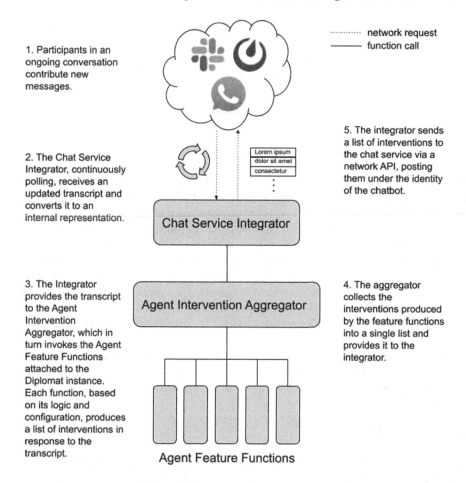

1. Participants in an ongoing conversation contribute new messages.

2. The Chat Service Integrator, continuously polling, receives an updated transcript and converts it to an internal representation.

3. The Integrator provides the transcript to the Agent Intervention Aggregator, which in turn invokes the Agent Feature Functions attached to the Diplomat instance. Each function, based on its logic and configuration, produces a list of interventions in response to the transcript.

5. The integrator sends a list of interventions to the chat service via a network API, posting them under the identity of the chatbot.

4. The aggregator collects the interventions produced by the feature functions into a single list and provides it to the integrator.

Fig. 3. Diplomat architecture diagram and intervention lifecycle

corresponding to the feature that was most directly triggered by chat activity. Unfortunately, a Diplomat user would have to combine all dependent conceptual features into a single implemented feature to create an agent with this behavior. The uniformity of interventions (i.e., the fact that the only currently supported Diplomat intervention type is a message) has been described in the previous subsection.

When we mention the "accessibility" of Diplomat, we mean its accessibility to those who wish the develop agents on top of the framework. Rather than provide an interface for agent specification that is abstracted from code, say via a domain-specific language or a drag-and-drop interface, our interface is the implementation of a Python class. This requires that users have programming skills. Also, while we provide some examples of chat service integration and agent features along with our software release, these examples are, as of this writing, not numerous. Users may have to invest significant time building agents with Diplomat.

Despite these limitations, we've released Diplomat with the optimism that it will provide value to those looking to develop conversational agents for group discussion and that it will, over time, develop into a more mature and robust framework.

5 Future Work

We propose future research in two main thrusts: 1) conversational agent research at scale, and 2) improvement of Diplomat. In the first thrust, we're interested in multiple forms of "scale". The most obvious form is scaling the participation in experiments. As described in Sect. 3.4, an abundance of data is essential to understanding the nuanced effect that a conversational agent can have on a group discussion. We also consider scaling the diversity of agent interactions. We plan to experiment with a much wider variety of intervention rules than those described in Sect. 3.2. This may include simple rules with diverse configurations (e.g., tweaked thresholds for under/overspeaking, agents with permutations of a feature set) or more complex rules rooted in advanced NLP techniques (e.g., topic modeling, sentiment analysis).

Research into improving Diplomat will be based on addressing the limitations described in 4.2. We hope to cultivate a community of researchers interested in this tool and to continue maintaining it as an open-source project.

6 Conclusion

In this paper, we introduced Diplomat, a Python-based framework for implementing conversational agents to be deployed in group, goal-oriented discussion. We also document a user study which, while preliminary and narrow, provides us with insights into how group discussion participants react to various interventions by a conversational agent. By investing in a framework like Diplomat, we hope to accelerate the development of conversational agents that can mitigate the familiar difficulties group discussion can too often present. The unprecedented collaborative capabilities with which the information age provides us will only be blessings if we have mechanisms to ensure their constructive and responsible use.

References

1. Barthelmess, P., Ellis, C.A.: The neem platform: an evolvable framework for perceptual collaborative applications. J. Intell. Inf. Syst. **25**(2), 207–240 (2005)
2. Briggs, R.O., De Vreede, G.J.: Meetings of the future: enhancing group collaboration with group support systems. Creativity Innov. Manage. **6**(2), 106–116 (1997)

3. Brodbeck, F.C., Kerschreiter, R., Mojzisch, A., Schulz-Hardt, S.: Group decision making under conditions of distributed knowledge: the information asymmetries model. Acad. Manage. Rev. **32**(2), 459–479 (2007)
4. Chandrasegaran, S., Bryan, C., Shidara, H., Chuang, T.Y., Ma, K.L.: Talktraces: real-time capture and visualization of verbal content in meetings. In: Proceedings of the 2019 CHI Conference on Human Factors in Computing Systems, pp. 1–14 (2019)
5. Ciechanowski, L., Przegalinska, A., Wegner, K.: The necessity of new paradigms in measuring human-chatbot interaction. In: Hoffman, M. (ed.) AHFE 2017. AISC, vol. 610, pp. 205–214. Springer, Cham (2018). https://doi.org/10.1007/978-3-319-60747-4_19
6. Daniel, G., Cabot, J., Deruelle, L., Derras, M.: Xatkit: a multimodal low-code chatbot development framework. IEEE Access **8**, 15332–15346 (2020)
7. Davis, J.H.: Group decision and social interaction: A theory of social decision schemes. (1973)
8. DeLoach, S.B., Greenlaw, S.A.: Effectively moderating electronic discussions. J. Econ. Educ. **38**(4), 419–434 (2007)
9. Goda, Y., Yamada, M., Matsukawa, H., Hata, K., Yasunami, S.: Conversation with a chatbot before an online EFL group discussion and the effects on critical thinking. J. Inf. Syst. Educ. **13**(1), 1–7 (2014)
10. Green, P., Wei-Haas, L.: The rapid development of user interfaces: Experience with the wizard of oz method. In: Proceedings of the Human Factors Society Annual Meeting, vol. 29, pp. 470–474. SAGE Publications Sage CA, Los Angeles, CA (1985)
11. Hamilton, L.A.C.F.L., Hunter, A., Potts, H.W.: Argument harvesting using chatbots. In: Proceedings of COMMA 2018 Computational Models of Argument, vol. 305, p. 149 (2018)
12. Isbister, K., Nakanishi, H., Ishida, T., Nass, C.: Helper agent: Designing an Assistant for human-human interaction in a virtual meeting space. In: Proceedings of the SIGCHI Conference on Human Factors in Computing Systems, pp. 57–64 (2000)
13. Janarthanam, S.: Hands-on Chatbots and Conversational UI Development: Build Chatbots and Voice User Interfaces with Chatfuel, Dialogflow. Twilio, and Alexa Skills, Microsoft Bot Framework. Packt Publishing Ltd, Birmingham (2017)
14. Kim, S., Eun, J., Oh, C., Suh, B., Lee, J.: Bot in the bunch: Facilitating group chat discussion by improving efficiency and participation with a chatbot. In: Proceedings of the 2020 CHI Conference on Human Factors in Computing Systems, pp. 1–13 (2020)
15. Lamm, H., Trommsdorff, G.: Group versus individual performance on tasks requiring ideational proficiency (brainstorming): a review. Eur. J. Soc. Psychol. **3**(4), 361–388 (1973)
16. Laughlin, P.R.: Group problem solving. Princeton University Press, New Jersey (2011)
17. Lee, S.C., Song, J., Ko, E.Y., Park, S., Kim, J., Kim, J.: Solutionchat: real-time moderator support for chat-based structured discussion. In: Proceedings of the 2020 CHI Conference on Human Factors in Computing Systems, pp. 1–12 (2020)
18. Lorge, I., Fox, D., Davitz, J., Brenner, M.: A survey of studies contrasting the quality of group performance and individual performance, 1920–1957. Psychol. Bull. **55**(6), 337 (1958)
19. McLeod, P.L., Lobel, S.A., Cox Jr., T.H.: Ethnic diversity and creativity in small groups. Small Group Res. **27**(2), 248–264 (1996)

20. Münsterberg, H.: The mind of the juryman (1914)
21. Nunamaker, J., Dennis, A., Valacich, J., Vogel, D., George, J.: Electronic meeting systems to support group work. Commun. ACM **34**, 40–61 (1991)
22. Peng, Z., Kim, T., Ma, X.: Gremobot: exploring emotion regulation in group chat. In: Conference Companion Publication of the 2019 on Computer Supported Cooperative Work and Social Computing, pp. 335–340 (2019)
23. Pinsonneault, A., Kraemer, K.L.: The impact of technological support on groups: an assessment of the empirical research. Decis. Support Syst. **5**(2), 197–216 (1989)
24. Shamekhi, A., Liao, Q.V., Wang, D., Bellamy, R.K., Erickson, T.: Face value? exploring the effects of embodiment for a group facilitation agent. In: Proceedings of the 2018 CHI Conference on Human Factors in Computing Systems, pp. 1–13 (2018)
25. Shaw, M.E.: A comparison of individuals and small groups in the rational solution of complex problems. Am. J. Psychol. **44**(3), 491–504 (1932)
26. Siemon, D., Becker, F., Eckardt, L., Robra-Bissantz, S.: One for all and all for one-towards a framework for collaboration support systems. Educ. Inf. Technol. **24**(2), 1837–1861 (2019)
27. Thorndike, R.L.: The effect of discussion upon the correctness of group decisions, when the factor of majority influence is allowed for. J. Soc. Psychol. **9**(3), 343–362 (1938)
28. Van Genuchten, M., Cornelissen, W., Van Dijk, C.: Supporting inspections with an electronic meeting system. J. Manage. Inf. Syst. **14**(3), 165–178 (1997)
29. Viller, S.: The group facilitator: a CSCW perspective. In: Bannon, L., Robinson, M., Schmidt, K. (eds.) Proceedings of the Second European Conference on Computer-Supported Cooperative Work ECSCW 1991, Springer, Dordrecht (1991) https://doi.org/10.1007/978-94-011-3506-1_6
30. Zhao, R., Papangelis, A., Cassell, J.: Towards a dyadic computational model of rapport management for human-virtual agent interaction. In: Bickmore, T., Marsella, S., Sidner, C. (eds.) IVA 2014. LNCS (LNAI), vol. 8637, pp. 514–527. Springer, Cham (2014). https://doi.org/10.1007/978-3-319-09767-1_62
31. Zhou, L., Gao, J., Li, D., Shum, H.Y.: The design and implementation of xiaoice, an empathetic social chatbot. Comput. Linguist. **46**(1), 53–93 (2020)
32. Ziller, R.C., Behringer, R.D., Goodchilds, J.D.: Group creativity under conditions of success or failure and variations in group stability. J. Appl. Psychol. **46**(1), 43 (1962)

Convergencies and Divergencies in Collaborative Decision-Making Processes

Valentina Ferretti[1,2]([✉]) [iD]

[1] Politecnico di Milano, 20133 Milan, Italy
`valentina1.ferretti@polimi.it`
[2] London School of Economics and Political Science, London WC2A 2AE, UK

Abstract. This study analyzes a collaborative multi-methodology intervention designed and deployed to support rural regeneration initiatives in a wicked problem context, i.e. that of planning and management in a World Heritage site. In particular, the intervention consisted of three stages, i.e. framing, prioritizing and designing and integrated the following methodologies: SWOT analysis with Geographic Information Systems (GIS) and Multi Criteria Decision Analysis (MCDA), then GIS, MCDA and Stakeholders analysis and in the last stage stakeholders' analysis and choice experiments. The objective of this paper is to detect and analyze opportunities for convergence and divergence in the decision-making process, among the different methods being integrated, among the different actors in the process, and among the methods' methodological requirements and the collaborative process' characteristics. As a result, this study highlights promising synergies among different methods for more effective multi-methodology interventions design, as well as specific needs for better conflict support and anticipation in collaborative decision-making processes.

Keywords: Multi-methodology · Actor Network Theory · Spatially explicit decision support system

1 Introduction

Territorial planning, which has been recognized since the 70' as belonging to the domain of inherently wicked problem situations [1] or ill-defined problems [2], has recently been characterised by an increasing use of collaborative decision making approaches [e.g. 3], to deal with the presence of multiple stakeholders with often conflicting points of view, and multi methodology interventions [e.g. 4; 5], to deal more effectively with both the soft and the hard components of the problem situation (e.g. the presence of intangible objectives, the need to frame complex societal challenges, the need to aggregate preferences and data, etc.).

This study provides an account of a collaborative multi-methodology intervention designed and deployed in a real decision-making context, i.e. to support rural regeneration initiatives in a World Heritage site. The World Heritage site under analysis is the vineyard landscape of Langhe, Roero and Monferrato (hilly area in the Piedmont Region

© Springer Nature Switzerland AG 2021
D. C. Morais et al. (Eds.): GDN 2021, LNBIP 420, pp. 155–169, 2021.
https://doi.org/10.1007/978-3-030-77208-6_12

in Italy) which became a new UNESCO Site in 2014. The whole intervention consisted of three key stages. The first stage concerned the framing of the problem/opportunity for the rural area under consideration and combined the following three techniques: Strengths, Weaknesses, Opportunities and Threats (SWOT) Analysis, Geographic Information Systems (GIS) and Multi Criteria Decision Analysis (MCDA) to develop a spatially explicit frame of the challenge to be addressed (for more details on this stage and its impacts, please, see [6]). The second stage consisted in the prioritization of the locations where it was most strategic to intervene first and combined the following three techniques: Stakeholders' analysis and classification, GIS and MCDA to develop a spatially explicit decision support tool able to rank competing hotspots in need of regeneration processes [7]. The third stage consisted in the co-design of regeneration solutions for the hotspot most in need and combined stakeholders' analysis with discrete choice experiments to develop practical recommendations for rural regeneration supported by the local community (for more details on this stage and its impacts, please, see [4]).

The research objective of this paper is twofold. The first aim is to detect and analyse opportunities for convergence and divergence in the decision-making process, among the different methods being integrated, among the different actors in the process, and among the methods' methodological requirements and the collaborative process' characteristics. In particular, convergencies among methods allow to obtain more informative results compared to what is usually obtained with just one of the proposed methods, while divergencies among methods refer to challenges to their effective integration. This first objective will be achieved by looking at the design and development of the decision-making process from a novel perspective, i.e. the Actor Network Theory [8] one which considers models and technology as mediators on our preferences, actions and decisions [e.g. 9]. The second aim of this study is to discuss (i) promising synergies among different methods for more effective multi-methodology interventions design and (ii) specific needs for better conflict support and anticipation in collaborative decision-making processes.

This work is innovative in two directions. First, it designs and tests a novel combination of methods to support collaborative decision-making in the context of rural regeneration. Indeed, while MCDA has already been coupled with several problem structuring approaches [5], the spatially explicit integrated framework proposed in this study is novel and has been designed to more effectively address three key stages of the decision-making process, i.e. framing, prioritizing and designing (see Sect. 2). The second direction of innovation concerns the observational lens used to study convergencies (e.g. synergies and agreement) and divergencies (e.g. conflict) in the different stages of the collaborative decision making process. Indeed, in this study methods and processes are considered as mediators on people's judgements and decisions [8] and very few studies exist which embrace this perspective.

The work thus contributes to the following three key disciplines: (i) group decision making, by sharing lessons learned on how to better address conflict and leverage on agreement during the different phases of the decision-making process, (ii) multi-methodology research, by contributing to the debate about the impacts of this approach in real applications and (iii) territorial planning and sustainability assessments, by developing guidelines and sharing expected impacts from a real intervention in the domain of rural regeneration processes.

The reminder of the paper will first guide the reader in the understanding of the values characterising the territorial context under analysis (Sect. 2.1) as well as of the design and development of the multi methodology intervention (Sect. 2.2). The paper will then zoom into the three stages of the intervention, i.e. framing (Sect. 2.3), prioritizing (Sect. 2.4) and designing (Sect. 2.5), by highlighting and discussing for each of them the observed convergences and divergencies. Finally, the conclusions section will discuss the lessons learned as well as potential avenues for future research.

2 Group Decision Making for Rural Regeneration: The Case of a World Heritage Site in Italy

2.1 Contextualisation

The focus of the decision-making process under analysis is the World Heritage site of Langhe, Roero and Monferrato, a vineyard landscape in the Piedmont Region (Italy) characterized by multiple exceptional values (i.e. environmental, architectural, cultural and economic, Fig. 1).

Fig. 1. Vineyards in the Langhe area (source: [10])

The area is divided into a core UNESCO area which covers 10,789 ha and includes 29 municipalities, which is surrounded by a buffer area, embracing 100 municipalities and covering 76,249 ha, whose function is to provide an additional layer of protection to the World Heritage property.

Becoming a World Heritage site means that conflicting needs coexist in the same area, i.e., conservation and protection needs as well as new development needs, from both the environmental and social points of view [4]. Moreover, the vineyard landscape of Langhe, Roero and Monferrato interests many stakeholders, including: (i) local marginalized communities who are at risk due to the recent trend towards the abandonment of villages for the big cities, (ii) tourists from all over the world who come to admire the stunning landscape modelled through centuries and to taste top quality food and wines, (iii) territorial authorities, who need to allocate resources in a sustainable way across all municipalities included in the core UNESCO area, (iv) tourism associations, who promote the exceptional value of the local landscape and cultural traditions and, finally, (v) environmental advocates, who seek to preserve biodiversity in this unique and challenging context. This area thus represents a challenging decision environment calling for a collaborative approach, which has been developed in close collaboration with the Tourism organization of Alba, Bra, Langhe and Roero, the Association for the Wine Landscapes of Langhe-Roero and Monferrato Heritage, the Technical Office of La Morra Municipality and the Higher Institute for Territorial Systems and Innovation (the leading actor involved in the UNESCO site candidacy preparation, SiTI, Turin).

2.2 The Design and Deployment of the Multi-methodology Intervention

The overall planning and decision-making process included two main stages, i.e., the divergent thinking phase and the convergent thinking phase which in turn developed through three key steps, i.e., the framing step, the prioritization step and the design step (Fig. 2).

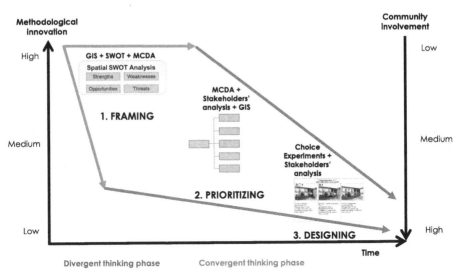

Fig. 2. The different phases of the collaborative decision-making process in the case study under analysis

The divergent thinking phase of the process consisted in framing the decision situation under consideration, by clarifying the need, purpose and urgency of a possible intervention. To address this step, the decision analyst together with the client organisations decided to develop a spatially explicit SWOT analysis and combined it with MCDA to map the strengths and weaknesses of the exceptional territory under analysis (please, see [6] for a detailed account of this first stage). Several problem structuring methods are available to address the initial stage of a complex decision problem [e.g.,

5] but combining SWOT with MCDA seems to be most aligned to the characteristics of decision problems in the territorial planning domain [e.g., 15].

The output of the framing step was the discovery that the system of abandoned historical rural buildings represented both a weakness and a future opportunity for the whole UNESCO area. After recognising the need to address the issue of the abandoned rural buildings within the core UNESCO area, it was decided to develop the subsequent convergent phase of the process in two steps. The aim of the first step of the convergent thinking phase was to obtain an agreed priority list of buildings to be regenerated for recreational purposes in the Municipality of La Morra (the municipality in the core UNESCO area with the highest concentration of abandoned buildings). This step thus aimed at the prioritization of the different locations needing rural regeneration. To achieve this aim, stakeholders' analysis was combined with GIS and MCDA (please, see [7] for a detailed account of this step). Among the many MCDA methods that have been developed to prioritize solutions, the Multi Attribute Value Theory approach has been selected for this project based on the guidelines for MCDA and GIS integration [19]. The results of prioritization step led to the identification of the most urgent and strategic abandoned rural building to be regenerated first.

The second step of the convergent thinking phase thus focused on the co-design, together with the local community, of the best requalification option for the rural building identified as the most strategic one in the prioritization step. While many methods exist to evaluate different alternatives and select the best performing one, less attention has been paid to how to creatively generate those alternatives [17]. To test the effectiveness of promising approaches, this project used discrete choice experiments coupled with stakeholders' analysis to collect the community's preferences on the characteristics of the ideal regeneration solution for the building under analysis (please, see [4] for a detailed account of this last step).

Figure 2 also shows that while the level of methodological innovation is maximum in the divergent thinking phase and the framing step (where we proposed a novel combination of methods) and then decreases in the convergent thinking phase, the opposite is true for the level of community involvement. Indeed, community participation was minimum in the initial divergent thinking phase of this project due to the employment of cognitive demanding techniques and significantly increased in the subsequent convergent thinking phase (i.e. prioritizing and designing steps), during which MCDA has been used with the input of all relevant stakeholders [7] and choice experiments have been developed by interviewing 100 respondents among residents and tourists [4].

2.3 Framing

Methods and Innovation
As it often happens in wicked problems, situations which are not acceptable to stakeholders may not yield at first glance a statement of a problem to be solved, or may yield multiple problems whose statements may be contradictory or messy [11]. Indeed, this project did not start with a clear statement of a problem to be solved but rather with a need expressed by the Tourism organization of Alba, Bra, Langhe and Roero to better know the territorial strengths and weaknesses of the region in order to properly support

the planning of the future of an area considered of universal value [4]. This can be considered as a relatively broad initial frame of the situation. Appropriately framing a decision means reaching a clear understanding of the problem/opportunity to be addressed, as well as a clear understanding of what needs to be achieved [12].

To address the framing step of the process, the author used the decision analysis framework of purpose, perspective and scope [13] and extended it to urban regeneration processes. This was achieved by making the framework spatially explicit and therefore able to address the important role of place and neighborhood in determining the spatial extent and relevance of the problem to be solved [11]. Table 1 shows which methods have been used to achieve purpose (what decision should be made, why and when), to identify the different perspectives to be involved (stakeholders and experts) and to scope the decision effort (by differentiating among decisions already make, decisions to be made now and decisions that can be made later or separately, [6]).

Table 1. The framework used to frame the decision context

The components of an appropriate frame	The methods used in this intervention to address each component
Purpose	GIS + SWOT analysis + MCDA
Perspective	Stakeholders' identification and classification techniques (semi structured interviews, power interest matrix)
Scope	GIS + SWOT analysis + MCDA, as well as the decision hierarchy (to clarify and validate the agreed scope)

The approach is innovative as it proposes a novel framework for the framing phase of urban and territorial regeneration processes by gaining inspiration from the decision science literature on the three components of an appropriate frame (i.e. purpose, perspective and scope, [13]). Moreover, to properly support and inform the above mentioned three components, the study proposes the novel use of a specific set of tools which are well aligned to the nature of spatial wicked problems.

Results and Discussion
Table 2 shows the results of the framing step. It is important to highlight that the three components (purpose, perspective and scope) should not be seen as three independent and subsequent steps but rather as an integrated unicum where the three components inform and influence each other in an iterative way with revisions and update loops [6]. The capacity to link outputs and inputs from one component to the other in a transparent way, grounds the results on a shared understanding and structuring of the problem and allows to agree on an appropriate frame, which is neither too narrow, neither too broad.

Table 2. Purpose, perspective and scope for the decision context under analysis

The components of an appropriate frame	Results
Purpose	By overlaying the geographical maps associated to the SWOT indicators and by weighting their relevance through MCDA, it became possible to identify a key weakness in the territorial system under analysis, i.e. the presence and density of abandoned buildings in the core UNESCO area [6]. This weakness was at the same time considered as a strategic opportunity for a collaborative process of inclusive territorial regeneration of a heritage asset with environmental, historical, architectural, and cultural values Summarizing statement of purpose: to decide how to regenerate the abandoned farm with the highest potential within those located in the municipality of La Morra (core UNESCO area)
Perspective	By using a combination of the focus group technique over an half a day workshop with the participation of experts from the SiTI Research Institute and the snow-ball sampling approach consisting of interviews with the project's clients, we identified the following perspectives to be involved in the process: the technical offices of the core areas municipalities (ID n. 1), the technical offices of the buffer zone municipalities (ID n. 2), local residents (ID n. 3), tourists (ID n. 4), cultural associations (ID n. 5), the Tourism organization of Alba, Bra, Langhe and Roero (ID n. 6), the Association for the Wine Landscapes of Langhe-Roero and Monferrato Heritage (ID n. 7), the Piedmont Region Authority (ID n. 8), local entrepreneurs and producers (ID n. 9), local professionals (ID n. 10), UNESCO (ID n. 11), scientific experts and advisors (from the Higher Institute for Territorial Systems and Innovation, SiTI, Turin, ID n. 12). The classification of these stakeholders allowed to understand who to involve in the following phases of the project (see Sect. 2.4 and 2.5)
Scope	The combined GIS-SWOT-MCDA approach also helped to scope the decision problem/opportunity by allowing to identify worrying concentrations of abandoned rural buildings in some municipalities within the core UNESCO area and therefore develop the awareness of the urgency to act with appropriate plans and regeneration measures in the municipality characterized by the highest density, i.e. La Morra. While the initial scope of analysis was indeed the whole UNESCO area, it then became clear that the focus of the first decision effort should have been the abandoned buildings in the Municipality of La Morra

Table 3 proposes insights from the analysis of the convergencies and divergencies observed during the framing stage of the collaborative decision-making process.

Table 3. Convergencies and divergencies in the framing step

Convergencies	Among the methods being integrated	A synergy has been observed when combining the following approaches: - GIS-SWOT-MCDA: the development of a spatially explicit SWOT analysis with appropriately weighted indicators allowed to generate clear and objective awareness about the density of some key issues (e.g. the concentration of abandoned buildings). Also, the spatially explicit approach to heterogeneously weight the indicators across the area under analysis, allowed to obtain four final maps of strengths, weaknesses, opportunities and threats more aligned to the reality - Stakeholders' analysis and MCDA: stakeholders with IDs 12, 7 and 6 (Table 2) were involved in the preference elicitation stage of MCDA in the framing step. This allowed to generate aggregated results more representative of the power dynamics existing among the key stakeholders - Decision hierarchy and Stakeholders' analysis: using the decision hierarchy to separate the decisions already made from the focus of the present decision effort and from the decisions to be made separately or later on allowed to develop clarity and confidence about who to involve in the subsequent phases of the process
	Among the different actors in the process	The following methods fostered agreement and consensus building among the participants: - Sensitivity analysis in GIS-SWOT-MCDA: showing and discussing the outcome of the sensitivity analysis performed on the aggregated results of the GIS-SWOT-MCDA approach allowed the participants to develop confidence and agreement on the most urgent issue to be addressed -Adopting a spatially explicit approach (i.e. integrating GIS with SWOT and MCDA) also allowed to foster agreement on the issue to be tackled as visualising information about density and proximity made things clearer for all the participants -Eliciting non homogenous spatial swing weights allowed participants to agree on the higher importance of certain indicators in those areas characterised by high density of the aspect under analysis

(continued)

Table 3. (*continued*)

Divergencies	Among the methods' requirements and the collaborative process' characteristics	The preference elicitation approach selected in the MCDA procedure (i.e. the swing weights elicitation protocol) to define the level of trade-offs among the considered indicators is not aligned to the characteristics of a collaborative decision-making process. Indeed, the swing weights elicitation protocol is typically performed by developing a questionnaire and asking each participant in the process to fill it in individually [14]. A collective discussion should follow the elicitation to generate a learning effect and increase agreement
	Among the different actors in the process	The elicitation of preferences and in particular of the weights representing the relative importance of the SWOT indicators under consideration constituted a moment of divergence as different stakeholders have different priorities. However, the different views were taken into account by using the swing weights elicitation protocol and aggregated by taking the average value

An important insight emerging from Table 3 concerns the advantages of using a spatially explicit approach in the decision-making process. While SWOT analysis is indeed often left at the level of just pinpointing some key factors [15], the present multi methodology approach helped to generate both awareness about the issue to be addressed as well as agreement among the participants about its relevance.

2.4 Prioritizing

Methods and Innovation

The output of the divergent thinking phase highlighted that there were 14 abandoned rural buildings in the Municipality of La Morra (geographical extension of the Municipality: $24,17 \text{ km}^2$, number of inhabitants as of August 2020: 2715). The urgent demand coming from this Municipality was twofold. Their first need was to analyse in detail the set of abandoned buildings scattered across their territory and thus identify the most strategic one to be recovered first. Once agreed on the priority of intervention, the second need was to co-design with the local community the best solution for the regeneration of the building under consideration. To develop a priority list of locations where to intervene with rural regeneration measures, we integrated the stakeholders' analysis results (see Table 2) with GIS and MCDA. In particular, MCDA was used to identify and weight the fundamental objectives to be achieved when selecting the most strategic abandoned building to be regenerated first in the Municipality of La Morra. GIS was used to provide a geographical map representing the distribution of values for each objective in the

Municipality under analysis. Finally, stakeholders' analysis was used to involve key local actors (stakeholders with IDs 12, 7, 6, 1, 5, 3, 9, 10 in Table 2) in the preference elicitation and aggregation phases of the MCDA approach [7].

The approach is innovative from the context of application point of view. Indeed, the literature has focused more on urban regeneration rather than rural renewal [e.g., 3] and this study offers a magnifying lens on the key challenges and characteristics of rural regeneration in World Heritage Sites, which are characterized by higher levels of conflict among strategic objectives and therefore require the combined use of stakeholders' analysis, MCDA and visualisation analytics [e.g. 4].

Results and Discussion

The proposed multi-methodology approach thus allowed to obtain a transparent and shared ranking of abandoned historical rural buildings located in the Municipality of La Morra from the most strategic to be recovered first to the least suitable one. Table 4 proposes insights from the analysis of the convergencies and divergencies observed during the collaborative decision-making process.

Table 4. Convergencies and divergencies in the prioritization step

| Convergencies | Among the methods being integrated | A synergy has been observed when combining the following approaches: - Stakeholders' analysis and MCDA: stakeholders with IDs 12, 7, 6, 1, 5, 3, 9, 10 (Table 2) were involved in the preference elicitation stage of MCDA for the prioritisation of the abandoned buildings where to intervene with regeneration measures. This allowed to generate aggregated results more representative of the power dynamics existing among the key stakeholders - GIS and MCDA: the development of a spatially explicit MCDA process allowed to better understand which objectives were worth to be included in the model and which ones were not (because of spatially homogeneity of values thus leading to lack of differences among the considered alternatives). The same approach also allowed to express more informed judgements about the relative weights of the considered objectives as it allowed to visualise the spatial distribution of their values for the different alternatives being analysed |

(continued)

Table 4. (*continued*)

	Among the different actors in the process	The following methods fostered agreement and consensus building among the participants: - MCDA: the approach allowed the participants to agree on the set of fundamental objectives to be considered for the selection of the most strategic building to be recovered first in the Municipality of La Morra - Sensitivity analysis in MCDA: showing and discussing the outcome of the sensitivity analysis performed on the final ranking of buildings allowed the participants to develop confidence and agreement on the most strategic building to be regenerated first
Divergencies	Among the methods' requirements and the collaborative process' characteristics	As mentioned in Sect. 2.3, the preference elicitation approach based on the swing weights elicitation protocol is not fully aligned to the characteristics of a collaborative decision-making process. Indeed, this step was performed by developing a questionnaire and asking each participant in the process to fill it in individually, while a protocol able to support the elicitation of weights in a collective way would probably generate more learning
	Among the different actors in the process	The elicitation of the weights of the different objectives under consideration for the selection of the most strategic abandoned building to be regenerated constituted again a moment of divergence as different stakeholders have different priorities. However, the different views were taken into account by using the swing weights elicitation protocol and aggregated by taking the average value [7]

An important insight emerging from Table 4 concerns the need for adaptation of some consolidated approaches for preference elicitation in Decision Analysis (e.g. the swing weights elicitation protocol) to make them more user friendly and therefore suitable for stakeholders' involvement. This could be achieved by enhancing them with visual analytics [e.g. 4] and proper facilitation.

2.5 Designing

Methods and Innovation
Once the most strategic abandoned building to be regenerated first had been identified in the prioritization phase of the process, the last need expressed by the client organisations (stakeholders with ID 1, 6 and 7 in Table 2) concerned the design of the best regeneration solution given the characteristics of the building. To support community involvement in the design phase of rural regeneration solutions, we combined stakeholders' analysis with discrete choice experiments [16] to generate feasible and inclusive solutions [4]. Choice experiments are used to study individual choices using preferences expressed about various profiles, i.e. several versions of a product or service. Respondents are asked to choose their preferred alternative among several hypothetical alternatives in a choice task, with each alternative defined in terms of their attributes and the levels these attributes can take.

This approach is innovative as it contributes to the recent debate about how to design creative but feasible alternative solutions [17], by proposing and implementing a tool for co-designing alternatives together with the local community.

Results and Discussion
We collected the preferences of 100 respondents (representatives of stakeholders with IDs 1, 3, 4, 5, 9, 10 in Table 2) and therefore were able to estimate the level of appreciation for the different combinations of attributes characterising the regeneration scenarios for the most strategic building to be renewed in the Municipality of La Morra. These results allowed us to provide specific recommendations to the Mayor of La Morra Municipality for the design of the requalification solution for the abandoned building which best meet the expectations of the local community, i.e. the creation of a bicycle renting facility [4]. Table 5 proposes insights from the analysis of the convergencies and divergencies observed during the collaborative decision-making process.

Although stakeholders' preferences have been collected individually, the visualisation of the results of the comprehensive set of interviews allowed the decision makers in the Municipality of La Morra to confidently converge towards the most desirable solution for the regeneration of the first abandoned building.

Table 5. Convergencies and divergencies in the design step

Convergencies	Among the methods being integrated	Integrating Stakeholders' analysis with discrete choice experiments helped to involve in the interviews those actors who really had an interest in the project and therefore obtain more representative results
	Among the decision makers in the process	The visualisation of the results collected from 100 respondents allowed the decision makers to develop both agreement and commitment for the final solution leading to a concrete action plan and a nudge to update the territorial management plan
Divergencies	Among the methods' requirements and the collaborative process' characteristics	Discrete choice experiments typically require to propose multiple choice tasks to the respondents in order to ensure a balanced presence of the different possible combinations of attributes and levels of the considered project. This implies a significant cognitive effort on the side of the participants to ensure consistency across answers and may therefore lead to fatigue and randomness in the final answers to the final choice tasks
	Among the different actors in the process	Participants' preferences are typically divergent for the different combinations of attributes, depending on the category to which the stakeholders belong to and on their own needs. Therefore, in discrete choice experiments preferences are collected individually through interviews

3 Conclusions

Two key lessons for group decision making have been learned from the present study. First, adopting a spatially explicit approach to decision making (e.g. through the use of maps and GIS) seems to facilitate agreement among actors and to generate synergies among different methods, thus leading to more representative and inclusive results. Second, to better address conflict in group decision making processes, visual analytics should be employed to facilitate the adaptation of some consolidated approaches for preference elicitation and make them more user friendly for stakeholders' involvement.

The multi methodology approach proposed in this paper allowed to activate a learning process within the client Municipality about the fundamental objectives and values to pursue for rural regeneration, but also to develop an agreed priority list of strategic locations where to intervene. The work thus contributes to the debate on multi methodology approaches [18] by providing evidence of the impacts of this approach from a real intervention in a challenging societal context.

The following avenues for future research are envisaged: (i) the exploration of synergies between GIS and stakeholders' analysis for collaborative decision-making processes better able to map the dynamics existing among the different stakeholders and reflect the heterogeneous distribution of impacts and (ii) the testing of other mixes of methods to discover where the synergies are strongest and approaches more effective. Though rural regeneration is a specific context of application, the author hopes that the proposed selection and combination of methods may be informative for similarly complex but different group decision support processes.

References

1. Rittel, H.W.J., Webber, M.M.: Dilemmas in a general theory of planning. Policy Sci. **4**(2), 155–169 (1973)
2. Rowe, P.G.: Design Thinking. MIT Press, London (1987)
3. Cerreta, M., Daldanise, G.: Community branding (Co-bra): A collaborative decision making process for urban regeneration. Lecture Notes in Computer Science 10406 LNCS, pp. 730–746 (2017)
4. Ferretti, V., Gandino, E.: Co-designing the solution space for rural regeneration in a new world heritage site: a choice experiments approach. Eur. J. Oper. Res. **268**(3), 1077–1091 (2018)
5. Marttunen, M., Lienert, J., Belton, V.: Structuring problems for multi-criteria decision analysis in practice: a literature review of method combinations. Eur. J. Oper. Res. **263**, 1–17 (2017)
6. Ferretti, V.: Framing territorial regeneration decisions: purpose, perspective and scope. Land Use Policy **102**, 105279 (2021)
7. Ferretti, V.: Rural regeneration and the reframing of problems: a multi actor decision analysis approach. Sustainability (2021b, under review)
8. Latour, B.: Reassembling the Social – An Introduction to Actor-Network-Theory. Oxford University Press, Oxford (2005)
9. Boerboom, L., Ferretti, V.: Actor-network-theory perspective on a forestry decision support system design. Scand. J. For. Res. **29**, 84–95 (2014)
10. SiTI: Istituto Superiore sui Sistemi Territoriali per l'Innovazione 2013. Dossier di Candidatura Unesco per il sito piemontese I Paesaggi Vitivinicoli di Langhe-Roero e Monferrato, Turin (2013)
11. Johnson, M.: Community-based operations research: introduction, theory, and applications. In: Johnson, M. (ed.) 2012. Community-Based Operations Research: Decision Modeling for Local Impact and Diverse Populations, pp. 3–36. Springer, Boston, MA (2012). https://doi.org/10.1007/978-1-4614-0806-2_1
12. Spetzler, C., Winter, H., Meyer, J. Decision Quality. Value Creation From Better Business Decisions. John Wiley and Sons, Hoboken, New Jersey (2016)
13. Tani, S.N., Parnell, G.S.: Frame the decision opportunity. In: Parnell, G., Bresnick, T., Johnson, E. (eds.) Handbook of Decision Analysis. John Wiley & Sons, Hoboken (2013)
14. Ferretti, V., Grosso, R.: Designing successful urban regeneration strategies through a behavioral decision aiding approach. Cities **95**, 102386 (2019)

15. Geneletti, D., Bagli, S., Napolitano, P., Pistocchi, A.: Spatial decision support for strategic environmental assessment of land use plans. A case study in southern Italy. Environ. Impact Assess. Rev. **27**, 408–423 (2007)
16. Lancaster, K.J.: A new approach to consumer theory. J. Polit. Econ. **2**, 132–157 (1966)
17. Colorni, A., Tsoukiàs, A.: Designing alternatives in decision problems. J. Multi-criteria Dec. Anal. **27**(3–4), 150–158 (2020)
18. Myllyviita, T., et al.: Mixing methods – assessment of potential benefits for natural resources planning. Scand. J. For. Res. **29**(1), 20–29 (2014)
19. Ferretti, V., Montibeller, G.: Key challenges and meta-choices in designing and applying multi-criteria spatial decision support systems. Decis. Support Syst. **84**, 41–52 (2016)

Author Index

Abraham, Anand   99
Ackermann, Fran   16
Al-Salaymeh, Ahmed   3

Baer, Annabelle   143

Chosokabe, Madoka   131
Correia, Marina Carvalhedo   41

da Silva, Gabriela Silva   68
Danielson, Mats   3
de Almeida, Adiel Teixeira   41, 68

Eden, Colin   16
Ekenberg, Love   3

Fasth, Tobias   3
Ferretti, Valentina   155
Frej, Eduarda Asfora   41

Hipel, Keith W.   113
Hogan, Kevin   143
Horita, Masahide   55

Komendantova, Nadejda   3

Larsson, Aron   27

Mihai, Adriana   3
Morais, Danielle Costa   68

Paulsson, Andreas   27
Purtilo, James   143

Ramachandran, Parthasarathy   99
Rêgo, Leandro Chaves   68
Roszkowska, Ewa   82

Sabino, Emerson Rodrigues   68
Shahbaznezhadfard, Mohsen   113
Suzuki, Takahiro   55

Tanimoto, Keishi   131
Tsuchiya, Satoshi   131

Vito, Vincenzo   16

Wachowicz, Tomasz   82

Yousefi, Saied   113

Printed in the United States
by Baker & Taylor Publisher Services